AN INVENTED DISEASE
SINDROME

AN INVENTED DISEASE SINDROME

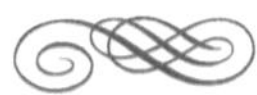

Prison Break !
Devil Planet Earth

ELLIS SIMPSON BYERS III

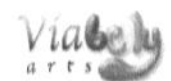

Ellis Simpson Byers III

– +

Book I

|A|n
|I|nvented |D|is|ease
|S|in|Drome

Book II

||Prison|| 😈¦😇 Break!
|D|evil Planet Earth

+ –

BY

ELLIS SIMPSON BYERS III

Contents:

Book I

An Invented Disease Sindrome

Prelude

Dedication

Acknowledgements I

Chapter 1 Electronic Nursemaid (the boob tube)

Chapter 2 The Hawk Signs

Chapter 3 (W)rap of Crap

Chapter 4 Schools, Acid, and Mardi Gras

Chapter 5 Kiss

Chapter 6 the Crawfish Fell

Chapter 7 Sleep Becomes My Drug

Chapter 8 Broken Rib Cages

Chapter 9 New Year's New Fears

Chapter 10 The Gangsta

Chapter 11 Huckleberry Friend

Chapter 12 In a Flash of Heat and Pain

Chapter 13 A Demon of SOHO

Chapter 14 Through the Eye of the Hawk

Chapter 15 Second Mushroom Exodus

Chapter 16 Gray Bosoms

Chapter 17 The Heron

Chapter 18 The Grand Giggling Weavers

Chapter 19 The Mission

Chapter 20 Orson Welles of the Internet

Chapter 21 Yawn Spanning Lifetimes

Epilogue

Book II Prison Break! Planet Earth

Acknowledgements II
Chapter The Gravity of Our Graves
Chapter Why it always goes wrong: TOP SECRET
Chapter Rainbows and Painbows
Chapter Our Earth Creators/Captors made a fucking mess
Chapter Prison Break -Devil Alien Encrypted Planet Earth
Chapter What to do now...
Final Quotes

Prelude

Honors to the Messenger:

What greater brutality can be inflicted on anyone than to erase or deny the spiritual awareness, identity, ability, and memory that is the essence of oneself?

-- Lawrence R. Spencer --

Dedication:

My sincere thankfulness and appreciation for my survival and protection throughout the construct of past, present, and future. My deepest appreciation to all beings and non-beings, and all supportive interdimensional entities who have assisted and helped to support my present biological body here on Earth. There is not enough room to list as they presently number the limitless stars. To the original Inexpressible and Unfathomable Creator(s) Entity that supports The True and Unchanging Fundamental Reality. I dedicate my life to the Ultimate & Absolute Way in hopes to fulfill my true mission to set myself and all living beings FREE!

Acknowledgements:

Special Thanks to Matilda MacElroy and Lawrence R. Spencer. Were it not for Airl of The Domain and Matilda O'Donnell MacElroy's smuggled TOP SECRET transcript {she kept hidden for her and family's protection for sixty years!} published in the book, "Alien Interview," I would not be able to understand in the slightest why this Earth with all its people, including my family & myself, are the way they are -trapped inside the repetitive pointless and unholy tragedy that besets all humankind during their sentence here on Devil Encrypted Planet Earth. This knowledge renders all dysfunctional families explained as to their sad plight, this renders all good actors and perhaps many bad actors redeemed in the light of compassion and wisdom. In the vein of this ultimate truth, I also give my Father a special thanks. Thank you to the kind unknowing women who "loved" me and thus dealt their horrific scorn for who I knew not who I was. The following quote is very important in that it clearly outlines one root problem of how the majority become recurrently susceptible to failings. Most of us are unable to handle the degree of torture dealt to us during and after we are hypnotized, electrocuted and imprinted with mind control programming. As a result, this is Earth's version of "love" in most cases: "the citizens abandon personal responsibility for autonomous self-regulation. They frequently lose their freedom to demented IS-BEs who suffer from an overwhelming paranoia that every other IS-BE is their enemy who must be controlled or destroyed. Their closest friends and allies, whom they espouse to love and cherish, are literally "loved to death" by them. Airl -via Matilda MacElroy

Thanks to my Grandmother when I was able to speak to her and ask her the source of her coma and sadness as she neared death. She repied, "I couldn't understand why it always went wrong, my darlin." Helen Daly

Finally, I give my deepest thanks to those who truly define and provide the embodiment of strength, courage, compassion and wisdom for our plight on planet earth along with The Keys for my and everyone's escape and/or transmutation. Albeit all Spirits being *fundamentally equal*, yet not so behaving, I offer my thankfulness and appreciation for Shakyamuni Siddhartha Guatama Buddha, and Nichiren Daishonin.

The Super Great Good News is that the Mystic Law of the Lotus Sutra has been made available and practically applicable since 1253 AD. Special Thanks to Nichiren Daishonin.

The second best news is that the Old Empire has been defeated!

Finally, to my mother, who unknowingly was compelled to give birth to me, and remained the only near close example of unconditional love I've known on this forsaken molten rock. She is known, especially in the Redneck Riviera, as the nicest woman on Earth - "TALIS". I am her talisman.

I am compelled to honor my father for showing me what war does to a sole surviving son and how intellectualism and blind authoritative authorship can erode the soul towards selfishness rendering a perfectly self-contained narcissist. There be the protagonist and antagonist of the human dilemma, the former and latter, woman and man, craftily encrypted and perverted so that we all bow in humble misery of what we have all here succumbed and created/destroyed together:

DEVILISHLY ENCRYPTED PLANET EARTH ...

<u>Chapter 1</u>
Electronic Nursemaid

It is an invented disease *sindrome*. Drugged upon entrance, perhaps I don't accurately recall the hospital scene in small town Opelousas, Louisiana with so-called doctors and nurses cutting my penis off as the generally accepted "Welcome to Earth" in my part of the world. My mother's father had cosigned on a loan indebting us a bigger house on "White" Street. The previous shack on Railroad Avenue was furloughed for an upgrade. I sat in the middle of the living room on the high chair and felt fear and panic swarming around as I looked outside to the porch and beyond. Our housekeeper/part time nanny's face showed the same expression as my father's panic as he had slammed the door inadvertently locking me inside. I couldn't understand their fears yet, as I felt just fine and remember feeling as if it were unnecessary turmoil. Soon enough my Father found a way in through one of the kitchen windows.

Aside looking up from the manger at the arched ceiling playing infant Jesus in the Episcopal Church Christmas play, another one of my first memories was being cozily planted in front of the television set, while my Dad wielded a compact yellow chainsaw out for a trimming workout in the pine trees of our yard in South Central Louisiana. Distracted from the tube by the piercing whine of the little yellow machine, I went to what we called our "white living room" peering out of the window to see what my father was doing. I saw my father out there sawing the lower branches of the pines with the tallest of our ladders. That day was the first and only day his chainsaw would operate, since neither my father nor I proved any good at small engine maintenance, that awesome looking little chainsaw sat unused for the rest of our days together. I felt the cold wet chill of the window against my nose. Since I was quickly acquiring the usual roster of phobias the previous generation provides for later exhumation, I felt being out of my appointed rocking chair post at the TV and near the frosty-cold window, would mean either punishment or dis-ease.

I watched the powerfully large figure, belonging to my Dad, but soon tractor-beamed back to my station by the beckoning hum of the electronic nursemaid -the cathode ray tube. Passing life entranced by others' programming, watching all the characters in Sesame Street or whatever ridiculous show, now perhaps holding them in some vague contempt. My Dad returned with a look of frustration and disgust -his new toy had failed him. As he sat on the long porch bench which was an old church pew he surrendered his leather gloves as his arms rained sawdust. He returned to his Underwood typewriter punching out his assignment as a journalist for the Daily World newspaper. I marveled at his speed and the rapturous determined sound of the little metal arms of type spanking the ink ribbon to the paper carriage. I longed to be able to write my thoughts as fast as him someday with a keyboard. By and by the government indoctrination camps called school would provide more useful evidence for contempt of the dumbing down of kinder far away from any garden (Kindergarten) much less an Eden. The rest of the household would flood in around three in the afternoon. Being a public school teacher Mom was freed from employ in accord with the slightly more lenient hours entrainment camp kid slaves had compared to full grown slaves. I wondered apprehensively where they went during the day and resigned that they were off in some mystery land. This mystery land was approaching my future too with its brakes and chains jingling loudly -hallowing mundane mediocrity. I began to inquire about my concerns when grown-ups would pinch me and express their admiration of my cuteness and of my upcoming so-called "edumacation".

My parents always provided plenty of food at the long and roughly handcrafted dinner table with autumn varnish wearing to kitchenware traffic. Arranged in descending order around the table, father sat at the head with my mother at his side. Being a very slow eater, my older brother harassed and teased, often enticing and arousing anticipation of something more fun around the corner, at least, more fun than the aggravating and ultimately damned need to feed and fuel the consuming human desire vehicle.

In addition, I was oblivious to the fact that most foods and water are heavily laden with chemical poisons worldwide. I wanted to be like my brother so I could rush out quicker and be a part of whatever game the gang was planning. Chase was the one I considered the most fun. Even better was when we employed a tennis ball as a means of transferring "it-ness". Tennis was my father's all consuming passion. Over the years, we found so many uses for those damned furry balls. Our two Cocker Spaniels loved them, and held them in their mouths like slathered treasures.

I remember experiencing what seemed to me horrible injustices as a kid. Fairness as interpreted through an unhappy authoritarian father. Control or be controlled is the realm of the animals, thus so trapped, he became a mini zoo keeper who consumed alcohol as a revolving reprieve from the relentless false five and/or more senses. As is all humankind here on devil university boondock planet earth, he was born as all humans by the most effective trapping mechanism in the universe: the artificially implanted aesthetic pain/beauty electronic wave. The Gods and Devils were none other than IS-BE spirits like you and me, (albeit with much higher technology, resources, and memory of their eternity) that took advantage of an opportunity beyond all morality of good and bad. It is impossible to kill your immortal spirit, and so the Old Empire secretly found a way to create Prison Planet Earth as a means for disposing all "untouchables or undesirables" in the mindless violent robotically numb reality of the totalitarian galaxy previously controlled by the Old Empire. Through the central command, government, and space battalion of the former evil empire totalitarian rule in the majority of the tightly controlled universe, factions derived secretly from this empire created the male and female counterparts, utilized corrupted biotech from which biological bodies eat other biological bodies and must have sex, and made a dumping ground concentration camp on earth 10,000 times more powerful and horrible than the Nazi efforts of Germany. Desire for money (false-currency-construct) currency and the leverage of power comes tantamount. Mostly along with that avarice is the desire for a beautiful female form or any other variation of form that the one in power affords itself which also A.I.D.S in battle for possession of what another possesses. The trapping expedient of beauty/pain along with their inborn constant desire thus helps to keep inmates in this prison waging war and fomenting further negative causes in this dimension. Evidently there are beings that feed off of our confusion and misery along with our life force in general. How is it that the creators of this prison escape one of the foundation laws in this universe? Even if cause and effect is not linear -say as in a billiard game, the effects are stored in a timeless realm and await conditions of environment and self for their later delivery to oneself and corresponding others. Perhaps in this way we see little justice playing out in our biological lives with its curtain of death and amnesia along with an intentionally shortened lifespan. Then the space pirates who so proudly made the colony of metal and mineral miners seem to escape with the treasure avoiding justice. Being in a prison must mean that I/we have made the cause to be here. I am also convinced that our captors will also pay their due for continuous subjugation and creation of an eternal prison planet for spirits from all over the universe.

We are dumped here mostly from transport ships as disparaged spirits inhabiting a myriad of body type suits. The transports arrive here and dump us into the electronic force screen cage often above the atmosphere of prison planet earth, then we burn up and our spirits are compelled to engage in a further elaborate electronic trapping system.

Drawn into the Light by the force field/screen trapping mechanism using the concurrently trapped spirit being's own thought energy as an activator. Our spirits are located, locked on and controlled almost entirely by way of a perfectly exact unique frequency signature of each and every IS-BE Spirit Being who happens upon this inescapable snare. While any resistance or struggle only makes the trap stronger by one's own thoughts or wishes to be free. Billions of electrical volts along with a myriad of commandments/programmings, suggestions, and genetic electronic wave code implantations for the next uterine body to be lotterized by the dimwit baboons -shadow offspring agents of the old empire still holographically running prison planet earth as evermore faulty slightly damaged and probably no longer maintained. I suspect that by me not being killed immediately for writing this is due to the fact that our prison is now abandoned, except for the continual dumping of more spirits by pirates, bounty hunters, thieves, entrepreneurs, etc. This is why we have impending overpopulation. The piling landfill of beings from many off world old empire "undesirables" is still currently allowed in the prison dumping ground of earth. Given the momentum of the Devilish Empire having existed for so many millions of years, the remaining splinters and factions of secret empire governments will take thousands of years to overcome. However, it appears that human beings here on Earth are now left up to their own devices and awakenings to catch up socially and humanitarianly. That is, IF, we can take responsibility for our own thoughts and actions towards others. Confronting the duplicity of thoughts requires constant vigilance and diligence. Freedom also requires the use of defensive force and the same aforementioned tenacities. The outposts of Domain Alien action nearby will only appear and disarm us as necessary if we begin to annihilate the rest of the planet. By my crude and rough calculations, The Domain will apply some resources to deal with Earth around approximately 6950 AD. The next polar shift will probably be roughly the year 8400 AD. The benevolent Domain will intercede particularly because of the unusual zoological diversity of creatures. Also, there are the remainder of Domain IS-BEs that have also fallen entrapped to the former old empire amnesia force field/screen. Having started out an unimaginably long time ago(time being a vibration perception of universal distance perceived between constructs of one or more IS-BEs) that the bored all knowing aspect of our spirit, the part of us that thinks it IS and thus will always BE, elected to "hire or occupy", so to speak, a biological body. In this more dense aspect of reality known to us now as the third dimension, so many lifetimes have transpired in which the spirit has been tricked into a lesser more constricted somewhat blindered bandwidth born from an evil holocaustic empire idea of riddance of any spirit deemed unfit by the dictatorial baboons. Sometimes you will read me referring to them as bumble fucks or fuck turds. We are currently forced into a fictional twenty-four hour clock time and a fiat debt-based currency. These are the two constructs, time (false-time-construct)and money (false-currency-construct), which require us to repeatedly struggle for compliance with these two prison guards. The time and money as in a prison commissary afford our basic creature needs such as food, shelter, and clothing. Although it was originally unnecessary to eat other creatures along with fueling the bogus regeneration of relatively calorific sexuality. These programmed urges were engineered and embedded by the more technologically advanced beings who also wrote the rule books of religions that activate many other control codes hypnotically and electrically. There is no point of being in a prison except for the ones who created the prison. Everyone who adheres to this morality guidebook sees the trickery beguiled of them in the last days approaching their feared death machine with its mind erasure and uterus lottery.

The compelling urge to copulate basically took over my thirteenth year alive and captured my whole creative reality, pitting me actively into the heartbreak of age old gender polar opposites externalized into two disparate entity meat sacks. It started out as a game, to take a biological body and experience the lower density tactile sensations of the material world vibration. I had no sense, yet, of my biological father's entrainment in the divide and rule system, nor did I understand how World War II robbed him of a father, thus making it much more improbable to be an effective one himself -barring the fact that it ultimately is a station position provided to the prisoner. One man of billions of earth prisoners with forced amnesia and trapped in a lower capacity human biobody, genetically programmed, mind controlled and compelled sexually in most cases further crippling oneself of all ones dreams and wishes which will never amount to anything in a mostly uninhabitable tempestuous recycling planet. It wouldn't matter anyway because the life span designed by the creepy trappers has been shortened to an unmanageable mind dumping roughly 80 year termination, that is, unless the demise of the earth prisoner is brought about sooner by "accident" or murder by another inmate. From what I gather, the dumped prisoner earth population consists of: criminals, politicians, priest operatives now turned warden prisoners, perverts, war-making murderers, politicians, kind people, creatives, geniuses, performers, and artists. The totalitarian empire automatons mess with anyone they choose and take pleasure in slowing down and ruining any attempt of unity, free association, and open communication. As far as the gender trauma drama that was engineered into the biotech of earth, in most cases the majority of men end up secretly hating women as "the ole ball and chain", "can't live with them, can't live without them". The LBGTQIA folks can choose anyone to "love" however spirits who have been trapped by the snare of aesthetic beauty/pain wave force field are mostly incapable of any decent scaled definition of love because they have been harmed, hurt, mistreated, beaten, butchered, neglected, ignored, abandoned, and memory erased etc. Turn the other cheek is a pseudo spiritual control mechanism designed by the prison wardens who take pleasure in their eternal earth prison planet inmate dumping and recycling program. Anger is arrogance unless utilized for justice and upward change. In falling intellectual, my Father had lost heart somewhere along the way and was leaning on the devil hardware brain. He was lost already like almost every spirit forced and coerced into taking a limited human body into a veritable hell like earth. As long term spiritual slaves and now also holocaustic fallout from the battle between the former "old empire" (empire destroyed by Domain in our solar system in the year 1230 AD) and the younger more powerful Domain, we finally awaken to a tiny bit of fact about our human situation. It does make it obviously clear that social and humanitarian issues are of our planet's people's greatest priority. Evidently no one is going to save us here on earth, at least not for a very long time. The prison break needs to be an inside job. Even the great Domain cannot rescue its own lost battalion of 3000 plus Spirits and shortsightedly and arrogantly cares not about the rest of the human population of spirits imprisoned in poop bodies.

I remember being insanely angry at my reality. My brother made it so easy to dislike him as well by his constant seething hateful attitude. If I would have known what I know now, that he was angry and for just cause -angry from being tortured lifetime after lifetime. Family is a hell prison lottery on earth. After all, my brother Hector wasn't the one in power. Both of them seemed cause enough for my tears to carry me off to slumber many childhood nights. I remember desperately wanting to stop the madness. Those passive hopes carried with them an inability to act, while helplessly a child, against the injustices only beginning to unfold in front of my perspective on Earth -a devil prison camp. The difficulties and obstacles invariably followed me on my path of discovery -a gravity and lunacy like the moon non removable in this cycle of human and planetary revolutions.

On my first day of Kindergarten, the sweet chocolate brown African American girl planted that fateful kiss on my cheek. My tears erupted right there in front of my family as they teased and laughed at me being chosen by a sweet black girl who simply liked me. Everyone in my family including my freshly acquired programming, proved by our thoughts, words, and actions my background of bigotry. Having been trained around people who didn't like me nor understood me, particularly my brother Hector and Father, I, of course, chose to long for the white girl(s) who didn't really like me or appreciate me. After all, that was the kind of family and society pervading me - judgemental, discouraging, unwelcoming and unliking one.

Again and again I experienced emotional turmoil over the overwhelming feeling that something was wrongfully perpetrated by the government indoctrination camp. I remember in Kindergarten I experienced a particular type of anxiety. It began with the teacher leaving the room and assigning someone to the role of snitch. Some goody-goody kid would perch themself proudly adult-like, and begin to write the names of the whisperers who began to percolate soon after the teacher's disappearance. I would feel a wave of prediction coming on.

I knew that things were about to get out of hand. The whispers were rising so smoothly as everyone began to compete for their words and laughter. I was busy being the "good boy" complacent victim. I told my-self that I would be the one honored by doing exactly what the teacher wanted but still managing to look cool and rebellious. I panicked as the roar got louder. Didn't they know any better? Hadn't they learned from the repetitive screams when this happened before? Did they not care that the teacher would be furious and that the rest of the day would be spent in punishment and silence? Oh, No! The teacher would show her disdain by moping and pouting for the rest of the day and depriving us of recess.

I made lists of things beginning at a fairly young age keeping track of everything I spent. I was imitating the curious habit my Dad had of keeping all his receipts. Not knowing the reason, I figured that I would need to account for these things at some point.

Once, early into elementary school, I came home and for some curi-ous reason I was digging in the kitchen cabinets. I had to use a little step ladder to get anything I wanted. This time I was on the counter kneel-ing and searching through things in the medicine department. I came across this brightly colored box that said Ex-lax. I had seen some sort of commercial sponsored by our friendly pharmaceutical industry and the commission for irregularity that made the box completely familiar. I opened the box and to my delight found what looked to be like little miniature chocolates. I thought I had uncovered a great secret. Yes! This is where they hid the chocolates! I would tell no one the secret of my finding. I began scarfing the little nuggets down. They tasted a little weird, but I figured they were special so I thought nothing more. I felt proud that I was smart enough to find the only chocolate in the house.

As fate would have it, my Dad must have felt constipated that very day. I heard him calling all hands when he found the Ex-lax nearly empty. I knew that I had to fess-up pretty soon, otherwise everyone would be punished. Soon after, they had me in tight reins and the family Pediatrician on the phone line. He said that there wouldn't be any seri-ous health concerns, but that I might have a long stay on the toilet.

I was held at bay on the toilet for a long time after the phone call -most of the family waited to see if there would be any graphic dumping so they could put it high priority on the teasing roster. Meanwhile, I remember feeling constipated. No one was going to have the satisfaction of me defecating while being observed. My Dad coached me hard, though, trying to get some bowel response. He told me to concentrate on using the bathroom. However ridiculous, I did as I was told. I guess he forgot about his own constipation while taking on mine.

In High School I was adequately misplaced. Puberty came along and I forgot about all the paintings I had done. I forgot how talented they all said I was. I forgot because I didn't find these things especially gratifying anyway. I was just too impressionable. I learned from example, neither by the manic preaching nor behavior of my father, but the reality in which both of my parental models operated. Now, I see Dad's somewhat neurotic process of saying one thing- then never or rarely following through to its fruition. He would pick and tease the unfinished or finished artworks. Even after I had finished something, it was never quite good enough. There was always some other master or someone who needed to be imitated so that I could someday be a "Master" from his point of view.

Mom was always busy -doing what I couldn't tell you -from a child's point of view. She was a teacher who wanted to be a watercolor artist. I must have learned to draw and color things just by being there with her. She always had little tricks and tips, yet she never knew how to deal with me when I began to judge my work in a fit of rage. I would get so mad at a mistake in the middle of a drawing that I would rip it up and tantrum cry . I wanted the attention (mom). I wanted someone to feel sorry for me (dad). I thought my Mom was always absently humoring me.

By the time I was into my developing teen years, Mom and Dad had too many challenges of their own to guide their prodigy effectively. I found that they were both intellectually vague. I was the "all-knowing" and as far as I was concerned, I knew more than anyone did. School was always dreadful for me, but I liked my friends and I loved recesses.

When I was younger, my Mom and I sometimes did art shows together, the economy seemed good and I sold my paintings here and there and learned that commissioned art was far less enjoyable, yet lit up the hollow dollar signs in my young eyes.

Right about the time my nutsack and penis were delivered via UPS, I was no longer as stimulated creatively because all I wanted was women. It all wanted to come out of my dick, not as much as my hands. Now the long journey of reproductive distraction and peril began and I began to trash my life in the pursuit of women and my reoccuring idiotic romanticism. I was considered special and prodigal, yet I wasn't doing anything different in the culture-less mainstream. I was trapped in some peculiar loss of time and self. I was in stagnating, monotheistic waters in Louisiana alongside the world with its many tidal pools, rivulets, and riptides of distorted beliefs. Many of the kids I knew had parents that gossiped and did their school art projects for them. I didn't know it, but I must have been really envied for my looks, supposed money (false-currency-construct), and talents. I didn't know I was arrogant and angry as I huffed and puffed up the false show of materialistic importance in steed of my narcissistic and materialistic Dad.

My parents taught me that there had to be an exchange for Art. Dad taught me to paint for his deals and payments, but never for the joy of happy creative appreciation. They had no basis for their encouragement, and their joy was surface level. I was deep reflective water -misunderstood.

Things were warping and mutating in my home life. I kept bringing home piles of books from school, yet rarely studied them. I would come home and procrastinate, mulling over the fact that I had no friends split between a hometown and a bigger oil town thirty miles away. I only felt guilty for not attending my enforced "studies", and played a rise and fall game of passing and failing grades resulting in an acceptable average. I didn't know I was more self directed and more of an unstoppable free-thinker, though somewhat damaged from being dumped into indoctrination camps called schools. As the bogus pressure got stronger towards college I felt more and more fear that I wasn't and didn't want to do what I was "supposed" to do -finding myself in a world where the larger/stronger consume the smaller/weaker and most in the sea of so-called humanity get off telling others what to do. Most of the world could be better called insanity and the lesser percentage of the more evolved in this epoch could be called "humaneity". It was to a high school forty miles away in a cane field adjacent to the Tabasco enterprise where I commuted every day. I had discredited both lands and both groups of people involved. Therefore, I was alone and couldn't understand why I had such horrible stomach acid -not yet knowing that I was allergic to bad diet, most cow dairy, perhaps also Round-Up sprayed wheat products and the strange nationwide laboratory of corn syrup along with other poisons in most American food. My brother and I called the biting heartburn Cream of Milk burn-up. My stomach was lashing out as I had turned to bad salsa, chips, and my electronic nursemaid to pass the time of agony. I felt this intense pleasure when I got home and fired up the television while promising myself I'd get to my assignments a little while later. That little while always turned into hours. I fretted as the end of a sit-com approached, but then I was delighted when the announcer would foretell upcoming goodies. Not much of a life I was leading, yet I found myself teasing and condemning those with whom I didn't agree. My dissatisfaction was my way of expressing the void within. Now, I call myself endothermic in those days. I was storing heat and energy in every form I knew of -fat, anger, and depression. I would feel horny and I would instantly gratify myself. No one dared ever talking about sexual energy. No, it was all assumed and repressed. I guess one was supposed to figure it out for oneself, because my parents were too preoccupied to explain (not that they understood it) and I probably would have tried my best to block anything they had to say. I couldn't begin to understand my older brother, who had grown much further away from me and was never a positive influence anyway. He seemed to be twisting and debating some heavy stuff of which I didn't know.

I started to vent my rage at this teacher who doubled as a counselor. Kids happened upon her for the purpose of hopefully opening up to someone in outreach from desperation. My evidence for her wrong-doing was fairly speculative, but nevertheless it didn't stop me from continuing my own little private campaign. One of the symptoms I noticed was that anyone who sought her advice seemed to become more and more withdrawn into silence and ultimately suicidal depression. I boiled with curiosity and wished I had the guts to visit her myself with the strategy of blowing her cover. For all I knew, the talking that the kids did with her was probably making them more grossly aware of just how fucked up their family life seemed to be. Maybe it was just too overwhelming for kids to realize that the fault of their world did not weigh entirely on their shoulders. Maybe seeing how botched up the system and parents had made them, brought upon an onslaught of doubt for the grand scheme of things. I was too young and resentful to think of these things then, so here is what I came up with.

"Oh, she pisses me off so much!" I proclaimed.

"Why, Mrs. Kiljoy is so nice." Denny defended.

"I just don't like people fucking up other peoples' minds." I stated.

"How does she do that?" He asked.

"I've seen what she has done to my own brother. I wish she would try to counsel my ass, she can try but she can't brainwash me." I said.

"You know, we're doing a survey in Algebra II and one person decided to survey the most hated teacher at E.S.B (Epistcalpel School of Bigotry). A lot of teachers turned up on the list, but not Mrs. Kiljoy." Denny explained.

I thought to myself, "True Original Creator God Source, Denny must be the only one who understands, but since he notices things I notice, he sometimes drives me crazy with his brilliant aggravations. I thought of the possibility that I might have her class the next year -how would it be? Would she majorly piss me off? My hate for her has now spread throughout the campus. They don't hate her, but they know I do."

In preparation to make things harder, I recall a few lines in passing with some friends, "That essay is going to be a bitch."

"Yep Good 'ole Doctor **Write**." I mocked.

"Here again I've procrastinated till my last day before it's due." I grieved.

And I did get to work on the essay that day, but a little incident happened to add to my already large list of why I didn't need to participate in life. My list so far was: an alcoholic Father, nervous Mom (then I was unaware that she was a secret whiskey drinker), alcoholic worrying Grandmother, a Grandfather with subsiding Cancer, a flea-infested cat who never seemed to be healthy, a house that was falling to shit, a tennis court that constantly made me feel guilty, a yard constantly overgrowing, a soon to be bankrupt newspaper, a struggling sister in New York, a struggle for friends in a town that promotes unawareness, fucked up brats with whom I attended my Prep school, living in a small town that worshipped the state university football team, my Mom's wasted talent and a sign coming into town that says, "Ready-City", a brother that is going crazy, and a constant lust for money (false-currency-construct). This was the degree of my negative needless worries. I stacked the cards so high against myself even with the seeming immensity of possibilities in life ahead. Still, this is a fraction of what I was thinking.

I heard a faint rapping on the back door, the door that everybody used. I was working on my Western Civilization essay "Medieval Patterns". I jumped up to answer the door. I saw my brother Hector, who was living in our "guest" (we rarely had any of these) apartment right next to our house. He was nineteen years old. As I neared the door, I saw that he had only a towel around his waist and he was holding his wrist. I thought, Oh shit my tormented brother is going to die of suicide! I opened the door and he said, "Get Dad, I need his help." Dad came and ushered him to the bathroom, while enduring the fiery screams. He looked like a young prisoner of war I watched in a film about Vietnam -malnourished, bony. Dad wasn't sure what he was treating -my brother's back or his wrist.

His wrist looked like a small volcano. Rivers of red poured out of what looked to be the main artery. "Ahhhhhhhhhhhhhhhhh! Shit!!!" My brother yelled at the top of his lungs. Pure fury and rage, but it didn't seem to be the wrist wound. It seemed everywhere Dad touched or aided caused a hellacious scream.

"Well son, I don't know how to treat you if I don't know what is wrong with the rest of your body.

"It's my (false alien bible) god damned back! I've been seeing a chiropractor-he says it's all the stress that's fuckin' up my back."

"Just relax," as our Father pulled out the freshly dunked wand of Merthiolate.

Almost to tears with the cringe of the coming burn, Hector whined, "ehhhh, naw, not that, Dad, please, oh True Original Creator God Source!"

Affirmatively gentle, "Son, I have to do this for infection -you've got a pretty nasty cut here." My Dad's words of reason did not stifle the dam-breaking scream my brother released. It sounded like a fire hydrant, a huge gas furnace, and Pandora's Box all flung wide open. My dad's face cringed as he moved his body back away from the vocal blast. We were quite familiar with those in the coming days. It was the force that was breaking the throne of my Father. Holding the Merthiolate dipstick with his thumb and forefinger, Dad looked as if he were holding a fuming dog-doodie with his contortion to the volume of the scream continuing for what I thought was a ridiculously long time.

Though punctuated by screams, we learned that it wasn't an attempt to take his life, but instead it was out of wrath and anger he launched his hand into the glass shower door. His face was red and angularly handsome, as he took a break from his hysterics to take a sip of water. The good little boy, who I was, hurriedly fetched it for my father and my ailing brother. As I went off I heard, "I *do* know why the fuck I'm living! Everybody is so fucking *mean* ! - That's right, I'm OK. Everybody else is fucked, (false alien bible)god Damn it! I'm just trying to live!"

"Hector, it is going to be alright" comforted Dad. I could tell that Hector couldn't be reached. I knew that anything in the verbal realm wouldn't enter him, he could only spew forth, and he did it well.

"Fuck You, you fuckin confused son-of-a-bitch! You don't know why the fuck you're livin', so don't try to comfort my ass!"

Sure it was crazy and hectic, yet I was so relieved to put off my Western Civilization paper- so I considered the whole thing a traumatic bonus -steadily learning that normal and balanced was boring. I didn't tell anyone about what had happened. The telling would be a huge breach of southern family etiquette. I just chalked it up in my head, and said to my deadlines that there was trouble in my family. Somehow I would have to get back to *normal* and find a space to work out all of my backlogged everything I put off for the sake of this wondrous spectacle in my house.

Slowly, the hysterics slid into slight complacency, while Dad began the nursing. I saw the pain and anger in Hector's eyes the minute he walked through the door. I envied him for his exodus into excusable psychosis. I wondered how it would be to abandon the rules and conventions equated to the normal person, and instead unleash with no boundaries on those who had previously expected so much.

I think the event gave my father a hiatus from his torture of trying to carve some work out of his granite walls and smith-corona typewriter. I, myself, wondered what he was working on, and when people asked, I always told them proudly that my Dad was working on a novel. One afternoon I came in from school and he was listening to Peter Frampton's "Do you Feel Like we do" blaring out of *my* jam box which I was able to buy from a little payoff from our private airplane crash. During these times I began to realize how childish and fragile my father was. Once his power structure fell from him, he was beginning to collapse. He was lashing out with tremendous effort and force, but it was as inevitable as a sinking ship.

I was timid and respected my father's privacy. This was a generational opposite because he often had difficulty respecting ours -it was the solitude and privacy I'm talking about. Though Halloween candy always disappeared by November, my parents never snooped. I'm almost certain. I found myself in the white living room, now his holding pin, looking at the work space. I felt extremely guilty and I didn't read any of the papers. I was looking for the 'ol crutch, and in the second oak drawer of the pull-down desk was his choice of Tennessee whiskey.

I didn't yet know the pressures my father suffered in the tightey whitey land of divide and rule, I knew i suffered doing all kinds of things I didn't want to do, but didn't realize they were trying to train you into a life of activity you might not mostly want in your heart -especially over time. Thus, I pointed to alcohol as the culprit not yet experiencing the enjoyable oblivion of alcohol as a 24/7 available Resort from the desolation of human standards.

My father had lost his throne in the material world. There were no more deals or possessions he could dangle in a twisted enjoyment of manipulation. Hector's fury was brought about through one of Dad's last tests of control over the kids. Hector went unexpectedly ballistic and nothing could stop the avalanche. So instead of my brother complying with the "no-girls down in the little house" rule, Dad received a mental patient who was brilliantly over-throwing the family. Like a waiter, Dad attended and served Hector during this entire episode. Hector was emaciated and suicidal. He roared in waves. He was sweet and receiving, then an hour later he'd put the fear of false alien empire bible god into anyone in vocal range.

When Dad announced any disapproval of Hector's stretching of his rules, that's when the shit hit the fan. By some odd twist of fate Dad caught the local girl loitering with my brother in the vicinity of Hector's home (the guest house that never had any). Hector exploded at the implications. He had been living life, basically free of encumbrance, but then Dad was bored and good at spying so he decided to probe the situation. Probing was his specialty. That was the last straw with Hector. He blew up and demanded to know what it was Dad really wanted. Basically, Hector demanded whether Dad wanted him to leave or not because of it. Hector wasn't agreeing or disagreeing with Dad's conditions, he wanted to know what Dad was going to do about it. Hector was nearly out in the real world, and who knows from what planet my father was coming. I was amazed, eagerly listening from my outpost. I felt privileged that I was being left out of everything. I couldn't help peeking and eavesdropping while feeling like a little perverted coward. I had created the ultimate couch-potato room.

I relied heavily on Tostitos, bad salsa, and creative masturbation. That was where my powers of imagination were being honed. I didn't need to interact with the cruel world. It was perfectly comfortable in my withdrawn pubescent shell.

After the first inquisition my father posed for my brother, because of his supposed unreasonability. Hector was detained by a neighboring lawyer who was also an active speaker for PADD, Parents Against Drug Dealers. Standing by was an officer of local law enforcement. Technically, Hector was still under my father's control. What amazed me was that Dad had the power to do this. Where were the people to test *his* sanity? That was the very problem, Hector was calling attention adamantly to Dad's insanity. This was making my father insanely angry.

My Dad must have felt extremely threatened by the fact that Hector's explosions were shaking the last credibility he held with our crumbling family. Hector's fury struck a deep, truthful chord in me, although I was fearful of his delivery. So with the ever-sickening force that adults abuse over children and people that aren't of age (one of my favorite citations of stupidity- rating people by the measure of time). Standardized tests have also been some of my favorite sicknesses of society. My father had Hector swooped up by these neanderthals for drug testing. There was no way to handle Hector, and they refused to believe in him. I believed in the blows of vengeance with which my brother struck my father. I was too weak to go along with any of it. I thought they were all crazy. I just didn't know why everything couldn't be peaceful. Maybe with fledgling pacifism, I had no tact. I wanted to be on everyone's side. I wanted to know every side. I was an exception to every repression. I was all around well-rounded, and so much faith was placed in my abilities and everything I attempted, that I considered myself prodigal and "all-knowing". Boy, was I full of shit.

I wondered from what cause my brother's emotional gates were opened. I knew of his rebellions, and his attempts to flee our family. I curtailed one of his attempts, being the one who found a Trailways Bus Lines receipt in his denim jacket. Maybe I was jealous as he was braving it. I always watched him fearlessly go off and leave me behind.

Sometimes, while Dad was waiting on him, Hector recalled the whippings and cruel drunken things he did to us. Dad didn't say much, and Hector spilled his guts with a sarcastic menacing smile. My Dad looked to me and shrugged in fake confusion as to why he was even helping his "mad" son. I pretended in any direction. Thankfully, Hector never looked to me for remembrance. He was beyond needing reassurance from others for the details of what our murky past was like. He spewed the gory details only his mind knew.

His discourses brought back all sorts of memories. I recalled when I sassed my Dad smartly while he was trying to sell our old white station wagon to a guy named Chippy. Chippy was a guy who swung his tennis racket in a convulsive figure eight before every service and was always chipping shots. Dad turned to me with utter stone focus. I saw red creep around from behind his ears and flood his face with boiling anger. I said something honest that could have jeopardized the deal of selling his car. His jaws clamped down, with cheek wrinkles pointing to hell, he said, "Go to your room and wait for me." I remember being extremely frightened. I ran to my room. While I was pulling the six extra pairs of underwear up, I could hear the laughing hyena Hector approaching. He laughed so hard -told me how much it was going to hurt and that the underwear was a stupid idea. My Dad ended up selling the car, so there was no beating that day, and all of my efforts of ass-padding were laughed at later. Hector recalled so many things I had blocked out of memory. I remember Hector lifted by his hair and thrown down the hallway. When I saw that incredible force and the unfair advantage, I hated my Dad. I cried so many nights hating the group of people I grew up with, but I'd always love them in the morning. I thought that to be a flaw of mine. I damned my nightly renewed amnesia weakness and tried to remember why I cried the night before, but the same brand of hate wouldn't come. I laughed at my Father's morning humor. Secretly I was disgusted with my unending forgetfulness. I was forgetting but I must have not been forgiving. Now I have to go back and do it the other way around, for what it's worth.

When the neanderthals took him, much to their dissatisfaction, they couldn't reference his problems to drugs, and quickly found a "Doctor" to give him the label of acute psychotic. I thought this diagnosis immediately entitled me to some expertise in the field of psychotherapy.

My Dad nursed Hector and his wrist / mind wounds. Hector's madness took no apparent schedule. In some heartbroken exhaustion, my brother finally begged for an allowance to deal out his term back in his apartment. Hector resigned a bit more there, Dad extended his room service to accommodate, but Hector had fallen into a slump of depression and wasn't eating, especially not from Dad's spoon feeds anymore.

Dad appeared in my doorway, hurriedly he said, "Eliot, I need your help. Hector's trying to hurt himself." I followed his lead calmly and seriously. Once near the door of the little house, he said, "He's got his shotgun in bed with him. I'm gonna go in and talk him down and try to get the gun away from him, after a little while, come in and get the gun."

I heard some whining from Hector, but after a few seconds, his reproach seemed muffled and calm. I peeked in -Hector was on his side in bed. I dreaded the possibility of Hector's face turning to make eye contact with me. I would have felt like the biggest traitor -cooperating in whatever hell was going on. My Dad's left hand dangled off to his side, and with no movement other than in his hand and wrist, he indicated that I fetch the Browning 20 gauge, modified choke, pump action shotgun from under my brother's bed.

I tried not to put too much weight on the possibility of loving and being loved by Claire again and tried desperately to keep my mind calm. I told her I would be heading in her direction months ago. Then, I appeared in the deep fried South. I managed to get back into the town where I felt I had no one. There wasn't anyone in the area with whom I could truly feel comfortable. My deepest fantasy was to kidnap Claire and take her away with me -far away from the deep entrenchment of the environment we had forsaken in a pact long ago.

A dinner date was made -a Mexican restaurant in Lafayette, Louisiana called LaFonda's. It was an eatery that somehow maintained a soul in the middle of a typical LLC town without one. The environment inside was so different from the billboard littered main drag of commercial plasticity stretching for miles.

I managed to weigh the love I felt for her far more heavily than she did. She had brought a friend -a little shield of a girl. I felt far more confidence in our meeting than she, obviously. I immediately asked myself, "How in the world could she do this, when it is us who have to catch up -not some new stranger to delay the importance of our meeting." I held the space of calm and seeming centeredness. The conversation flooded across the table. I spouted off so many things I'd learned while they sat before me wide-eyed and fascinated. I loved it, yet it was only I who had stories to share. She wasn't open to growth yet and her fascination couldn't free the shackles.

Entranced by her angelic beauty and enthralled by the idea of ideal love and bliss, I continued unrequited. If she could just see it. If I could just have more time to spill everything. Then, surely, if she saw the whole picture, she would want what she was denying herself. She was trapped in the natural progression of things and light-years ahead of her surroundings. Why was she hiding her light?

She secretly rubbed my legs under the restaurant table with her hidden hand. I wanted not to believe she did that. I thought to myself, no, she's creating a nightmare for me! How could she do that and simply leave. How could she just stick a cigarette into her mouth and merely resume living? Soon after dinner, she was off to busy herself - surrounded with so many dedicated ushers. I felt the horror of pitch black sadness as I watched our cars take different directions. I was in my faithful Phillup's 66 Beetle and watched her Japanese car carry her off -to her playland when minutes before both girls said they didn't want to go back. They had asked me, "I don't want to go back, how can we go back now?" to the social structure of school life after they had our conversation. I wanted so badly to tell her she didn't have to go back- she could come with me. Yet they did and were compelled to "go back".

The next day was very different. After mulling it over, I decided to call her to offer up my proposition. I knew it might seem crazy, but I asked her if she would come with me. She resolved with a long whine, "I can't." It seems that she had already over-ruled our love the night before. Perhaps, the night was over-ruled when the cigarette was lit. She put one of her ushers on the phone with me, while she hurried to get dressed to go out and take part in the Lafayette reality, telling me that I would be "remembered", as if I was already dead in her mind. I wasn't looking for some tragic martyrdom from her mind. In reality, I was living in a very different plane. Perhaps time alone with her friends had warranted my condemnation. I was on the line with the little stranger who went with her to the restaurant. I suspected, by her tone and nervousness, while she generated hesitant conversation, she thought I was a freak of nature and wondered if I was crazy.

I could not hold on and be put off while my heart cracked and wept. Whatever it was, it had won and I was left spent and beat. I tried so hard to stitch her into my reality but the functions of nature would not let it happen. I touched the pain of losing Claire every time I swam with visions of love. When the floodgates of my mind open, I overcome the fear and the separation of not being with her. I called.

This is now-ness. The cold low-powered rifle in the closet less than 7 feet away from me, perhaps too much of a coward to end it all. It is without gratification and so useless to kill oneself in the present age. I realize that there is no escape in self death. Instead, that night I drank Captain Morgan's spiced rum and marinated in the injustice of it all. A nation transfixed with a celebrity murder case, and myself transfixed on the hopeless despair of not being loved by the girl who didn't respond to my call for help in the past two years. I felt a horrible breach of spirit and cried out, " Why? Why? Why...?"

It was upon this hopelessness I decided to end my visit to my hometown -thirty miles from hers. Claire just didn't care about this aging child.

Phillup's 66

Eliot's fifteenth birthday was coming around the corner and the reality of not having a car began to swarm his mind. Promises made in the past didn't seem all that promising. His father had promised him half of any car if he could come up with the rest of the money (false-currency-construct), but this couldn't happen now. The business was falling apart. His father had spent everything just to keep it alive withholding tightie whitey's war taxes, to pay his employees.

When his Dad found out that young Eliot was looking for a car, he asked, "Why are you looking for another car when we have four right now."

Call it intuition, but Eliot somehow knew this wouldn't last long. Eliot felt the secret reality that his father was losing his newspaper business and his mind. The next week the Ford dealer came to fetch one of the cars. The fortress was falling. The hierarchy was crumbling.

Eliot's mother was concerned for his mobility, though. She felt some angelic compulsion to make it apparent to Eliot just how important it was to be mobile. She inspired joy over the long haul. He was graduating from go-cart to automobile. In the supermarket, his mother talked with his third grade teacher Mrs. Phillup. She taught his Mom, and she taught all three kids. Eliot's mother asked Mrs. Phillup if she ever intended to sell that old 1966 Volkswagen Beetle. She was, and offered it up for $1300.00. One hundred dollars for every CC of piston displacement power.

The initial thought of the whole deal was enough to make Eliot cower. He didn't want an old and insufficiently powered car.

Nevertheless, the thought of being a prisoner to the home base, motivated him to change his mind about the whole situation. Upon arrival at Mrs. Phillups house, old memories flashed back from elementary school. Oh, how he dreaded her class! She was the most strict of all teachers. She developed a system that maintained silence in her classroom. She was a clever old one.

Eliot remembered the feeling of being on constant alert of the impulses that might be sent to his vocal cords. Mrs. Phillups enforced the same penalty for dropping your pencil on the floor as there was for talking. If you were caught amidst the dead silence, she would rise from her desk and simply go and write your name up in the upper left hand corner in a box that was reserved for the talkers. If your name was already up there she would add a hash mark. This all meant that you were accruing five minute intervals. Those intervals would be spent in her classroom while everyone else went off to recess. It meant that you would have to report back to her class and miss out on the most valuable time in your day, RECESS! It was a miserable sentence, but it seemed to be a highly functional tool she developed. Eliot was glad that the Phillups system didn't spread to the other teachers. He wondered if the reason why the system didn't spread was because the kids were silent about her scheme. No one breathed a word of it to any other faculty. Mrs. Phillups kept to herself primarily so there was never any other reason for her to tell any of the other teachers.

Out she came from inside her house. Seven years passed, Eliot felt a rush of pride in seeing her, as if he were silently saying, "See, I turned out OK, huh?" She had a sparkle though, as he recalled, that could charm away all of her clever sternness.

It was a bright sunny afternoon in June there beside the sea sand tan bug. She seemed so organized. The car was immaculate. Mrs. Phillups slipped the VW key into the door. The chrome glinted in his eyes- he slipped back into the hot chalk-smelling classroom of third grade.

There was a rush of curiosity and mystery that moved through the entire class. She was going for something in her closet in the back of the classroom. All of a sudden she was claiming to be a nurse. He couldn't recall for certain, but he thought someone had been stung by a bee. The little pupil offered his arm up to Mrs. Phillups. She put on a facade of seriousness. Young Eliot knew something was up, but what was she going to do? She was full of surprises when the mood struck her. It seemed like there were indeed a lot of things in her closet so to speak.

She called out from the closet, "I can't seem to find my needle." A look of panic rushed over Donavon Greene's face. His expression was at full attention, and his eyes became two flashlights shining apprehension out of his black face. "Ahhh, here's my doc kit." She expressed relief from the closet.

She came from the back of the classroom, moving toward the front of the class saying that a vitamin shot would be the perfect thing for Donovan. The little guy was mortified along with Miss Phillups taking on the personality of a relaxed doctor. Once he denied the shot, she offered it to anyone else who might have wanted it.

I felt something well up inside me. Somehow I wanted to take the risk. I knew she was bluffing. I desperately wanted to be a part of her inner secret. Somehow, I offered up my arm and swore to myself I knew there was no real drawing of blood. I felt like a brave guinea pig, and there was no pain. It was a magic needle, a trick needle she had pulled out of her bag of tricks. Joy fell over the silent classroom. The swells of the extraordinary captured my imagination. I wanted times to always feel like the middle of a chase game. Somewhere between being chased and being "it".

There I was years later, sharing another sort of secret with her. The secret of adventure that every Volkswagen owner feels they know (maybe the secret that one has to maintain the fucking thing). The secret that has inspired movies and nostalgia all over the world. It's a secret the MTV generation will have trouble understanding.

It might have been the first long-term synchronicity I had experienced. The sight of that little car out in the dusty parking lot of my public elementary school. I would always see it with some detached knowledge of, oh, that's Phillup's 66.

Chapter 2
The Hawk Signs

Many times on the drive across my small town, I saw my friend the hawk. I was always amazed at the way the bird captured my attention and imagination. It's as if the bird shared secrets and messages of great things to come. I was in a time of transition. The hawk's expression was brave and solemn, not at all afraid of change.

One morning, when I was desperately tired and hungover, during the temporary summer occupation that seemed to further suck the life out of me hour by hour, my eyes opened a bit wider when I saw my guide perched on a roadside. There were so many connections made instantly in my head when I saw the strength of my wind-ruffled friend. It seemed that all my life I wanted a sign. I don't think a sign could have been more spiritually black and white. Although I felt a new brew of love for my feathered friend, who was appearing more and more now that my eyes were opening enough to see him, there was always a nauseous giggle tickle that made me feel like I would never be able to physically embrace the warm scrunchable bird. Birds were just so beautifuL. I didn't want them to be afraid of me though I could see why they were. I saw that he was telling me that I could fly as well. The signs that he perched on were analogous to the paths I could take. There was a favorite road sign on which the hawk would perch. It brought a rush inside me every time I saw him loft the sign. The sign marked an exit I frequently took. The sign was big and bold, yellow and black. It was a split arrow and to some it just meant that the traveler could diverge or stick to the same route; however, I saw the bird as a great master of flight, and since he was perched on his own road sign, it meant that he was fully aware of the decisions and paths that could be taken. I admired that awareness of whom my surrounding peers didn't seem to provide, so I was beginning to seek more answers in nature, not human nature.

Since I was working at my mother's department of marketing at one of the two hospitals in town and on my way to work when I saw the hawk perched for the first time, I rushed in and told my Mom about it. I had the idea to make a series of hawk paintings on road signs.

My excitement was explosive, but I hadn't nearly even begun to learn how to successfully land ideas from the mental realm to the physical plane. Since the view of Ashley's bikini appeared next to the pool, I became enamored with my distracting Crack hit squirt gun and its devil hit reward for orgasms. I didn't know that the evil cumshot reproductive urge had robbed me of my creative impetus in unknowing favor of a fetus. Although, this idea of the hawk signs remained persistent years later -unlike the baseball gambling schemes I had nearly learned from my sister's wealthy boyfriend- unlike the auction business -unlike the tax-tracking mail order business. The hawk was even more persistent than my invention for a writing pen coated with a polymer that was similar to flesh. That kept me up an entire night once as a little boy. I knew that there were millions of people who complained of their hands aching from writing too much with a hard pen. I met a local inventor and supposed genius who brainstormed with me on how to make it. I left his house feeling a little empty and discouraged. All I wanted to do was sell my idea to someone, preferably a company like BIC®. I really felt my disparity when I saw versions of my idea on the shelves of stores less than a year later. I felt that I would have had time to develop my idea, but I didn't. The idea had lost its luster and timing by then.

There was just never any drive or energy for me to finish anything, there was always a stronger urge to fuck off. I missed the simplicity of youth, when it seemed like everyone was lovey. Anything done, however insignificant or amazing, was above and beyond what was expected. Anything comparable to the adult world produced by my "not of age" mind was considered a novelty. I felt that I wanted to be part of the adult world but didn't want the baggage with which they seemed to trudge. I knew the cuteness everyone labeled me would someday pass. I was prodigal and special, or slightly arrogant so I thought.

My mother was so excited with the hawk idea. I was too, but most of that summer was spent drinking, working, sleeping, and waking in a hungover day state as alcohol by way of beer began to creep into my pubic and public career. By the end of that summer I bought a little off-road motorcycle, but no paintings or anything special going on in my head. I was getting healthy again -running all that summer, in the blistering heat losing my morbid puberty pounds. Later that year people would say that I was really chubby the previous year.

In a New York city taxi cab, I stated my 14 year old confusion on whether or not I should lose weight and get my body in line or work on the continuous money (false-currency-construct) problem. My sister's boyfriend who made himself extremely wealthy through base-ball gambling, stocks, and various other schemes said, "You've got to clear up the funds situation, El-man -definitely." Although the nice crunchy crispy sound of folding of hundred dollar bills tranquilized my opposing thoughts, my sister's grimace cued the idea that it wasn't a very sound plan. So, without much credit to that conversation, I found myself pushing the limits of my body. Along with that regimen came a boost in self-esteem, energy, everything, a boost in life. I referred to those soon past days of my chubbiness, "When I was endothermic, storing heat and energy..."

I had achieved a certain "coming out" of my shell that summer. I would see the hawks while trying so hard to crack through the first miles of running. I had never been able to conquer distance with my own body. In the summer heat and humidity clearing the hundred degree mark, I began to melt away the protective layer of my endothermia.

I felt rather alone when the family was breaking up. It seemed like the thing everyone wanted most, including those of us who had stacked the most resentment against a man for whom our childlike minds blamed everything. The old house that was a safe harbor for me for about sixteen years was being turned into a vacant madhouse with everything strewn around. There had been a little covert planning for this day on the part of my Mom. My Dad had lost his whole sense of integrity, so there was no turning back to the dictatorship that had ruled the last of its days.

My black Persian cat Maxwell was nuts already from the dysfunctional warm-up of the previous year or so in the house of crumbling Breyers. My cat (whom I would smother with scrunches until I resembled that big furry monster that was trying to make Bugs Bunny a permanent pet) could be found acting like a bat trapped in a nuclear plant. Max's ears would shift, with a mechanical radar action, then he would look frantically around to see from where his next tweaking would come. Closer to the final days of my father occupying his fort, the enemies appeared regularly -showing off the house and pushing him further into abysmal despair. Max had so much room now and everything was constantly changing, so he took the opportunity to make three or four spots his litter box. I had given up on the fact that he would never be anally contented enough to respect the concept of defecating in proper designated areas. I secretly began to look at his turds as little psychic blips in his radar. The more shit hit the fan, the more Max would let his hit the carpet. He especially liked leaving his black and brownness all over the coined sacred "white living room". This was the room that bore the meetings of family policy -bored my brother and usually brought my sister to tears. I was avoiding the whole ordeal by playing extra rounds of Marco polo with my friends and generally having a good time.

What the hell, "Marco-Polo?" Most adults probably considered this game to be an ear piercing child's game, but we were well into our teens and had this game down to a science. Except we had to spend too much time discerning the regular cheaters of the bunch.

MARCO POLO

Marco polo... ahhhh... the joy of that damned game. Puberty had come for most. The days of seriousness and drivers' licenses were coming. People were now being transformed from children into slaves. There came the sugar, the hormones, the pimples. Out were the days of having fun together in a way other than cruising around town aimlessly looking for girls and playing some strange popularity game- burning gas until it was time to go home. I held on to the joyous games of our youth with a

passion. I think we were the only group of guys that had made an art out of Marco Polo. It was the most active and exciting thing that we could do. I know it seems like the game is annoying and loud, but not so. There weren't many people we could convince of our paradigm. I held on until I watched my best friend grow up and away from the game. It was my idea and obsession as the group split by miles and experience, we would come together to play Marco Polo. In the game, I hoped it would patch any growing sense of separateness that life was bringing. It would be the one thing that we would preserve from the falseness of maturity. It wasn't so -my plan hadn't held together. I wasn't able to hold on to the game. If I had been able to, I might have killed myself trying to hold on to things like that as unbearable change reared its head into our group.

The game would start with an eruption, usually with a dash to the pool in a mad race to prevent yourself from being the last one in the water. The last one in the water was the one to begin with the arduous task of getting your first man. I think we only mentioned once or twice that it was about

Marco Polo, forever in search of his fountain of youth. His obsession must have been a powerful one because it carried into our obsessive game along with the fights and lies it would incur.

One summer, we played so much that our feet became lacerated from jumping in and out on the cement so many times. All of us eventually purchased aqua-socks to keep that from happening. I had the distinct feeling that the game was losing its innocence. We were starting to accessorize. Suddenly, everyone needed objects and special advantages to keep from becoming a blind Marco in search of a fountain of youth.

***

When it came to me moving my stuff from out of the house I had lived most of my life, I played very fast and didn't look back. That was the same way I masturbated ever since I discovered that devil crack bonus a few years back. I didn't plan on replicating any family shit by knocking up some young girl, not that my upbringing and the ever lingering Victorian nightmare would allow me any actual contact other than in my mind. I believed that "No" meant no, and I was too shy to con the girls into believing in what they also most secretly wanted.

The slaves were freed long ago, but many of the girls were so sheltered and ignorant that they spent their days thumbing through the Victoria's Secret catalog and wishing there were slaves to fan their powdered hineys. They would openly resent blacks, yet in their bored summer bedrooms they would fantasize about being mounted by some sweaty young black buck. After bringing herself privately to orgasm this girl Molly would call her boyfriend up and leave Victoria's Secret out so she could point out what she wanted for Christmas six months away. She would watch her young suitor get hard, then she would slip him a taste of her supple young lips and straddle for a period that generated great heat. He was nearly at the brink of explosion but that did not matter to her. The clothes fucking would go on, and when he would reach for a little fondle and touch of places condemned, she would groan and gently push his hand away making him think that she loved him too much to cause the pain of letting him have what he wanted. The sad thing is that she wanted the same thing deep down under the hard crusty casing of her programming. Her Mom had ingrained tales of how to treat men in her young mind. She finally discovered this after one divorce and thousands of dollars in therapy later. Really, all for the sickly power of the Almighty dollar -the false alien empire bible god they trust. Her mom had explained to her also early in life that the only way to hitch and have a man support you was to deny him sex until marriage, so even if this young suitor wasn't to become her groom she would be practiced. She would be a well refined lady in the upper echelons of **man**ipulative etiquette.

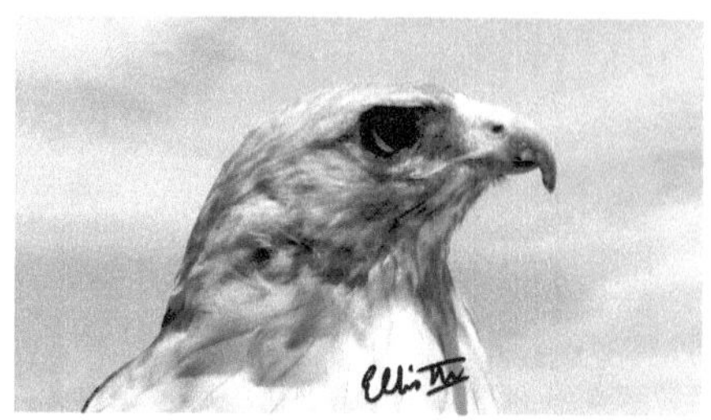

Chapter 3
(W)rap of crap

Finally I was part of the group I had resisted and disliked since the beginning of my high school tour. They were coming to pick me up so we could go and wrap a few houses. We were concentrating on the houses that would be most lenient to our invasion. Namely, we wanted to wrap people from our school who were involved in sports. I didn't really care who or what -all I cared was that it was fun. When we arrived at Denny's house, all seemed quiet. We went right to work on the property. These guys were good at it! They were just as creative in their vandalism as I prided myself in being. All along, I arrogantly concluded that they were constipated book worms, unable to invoke action and fun.

I think I was the first to notice Denny watching us. At first it was dark movement from behind a small window in the washroom area of his house. My heart jumped, but I knew we were safe from danger. I knew his Mom would be happy to see the ranks of the young Lafayette scholars parading in her yard. I was again glad to have them around because she would have been really upset if it was just a friend and I who regularly did this sort of thing. In her eyes we were always doing this stuff. We were always refusing to "grow up" as she wanted.

I waved to the movement in the house. I masked my embarrassment while someone watched us wrap their own house. I acted as if I could see them inside. It was this that brought Denny to his little porch, where he hung on a column with a disapproving little smirk. I knew what the smirk said. It said, "How dare you bring this scum to my yard, those who you have preached about in disgrace! Now you bring them to my secret sanctuary that none of them have ever touched -like this." He wasn't amused and we soon grew tired of him watching. The group elected to go on to some other destination. We sat discussing our next move while the shaving foam began its hardening and shrinking freshly on our hands.

I think his yard was something sacred to Denny. All we had done was littered it. Later he would complain of having to clean it all up. We couldn't just end the evening on that note, no, we had to continue. Surely we could think of another yard to pillage, and we did.

Off we merrily went to a fellow bus rider/schoolmate's house. This guy was heavy into academia and soccer. He excelled at both. Getting into his neighborhood, I understood why he secretly yearned to get out. The yards were all trimmed and lined with sidewalks. Every house was a simple A-frame. It was all very simple. I tried to imagine what was going on in some of these houses. I was familiar with this neighborhood, but only in passing. I imagined that there was definitely some child/wife beating and fuckery going on in this seemingly quiet neighborhood.

I felt innocently immune, yet there was a strange feeling creeping in on me. No one else seemed to notice, but I was only half watching the shaving cream project that I had begun with another girl. She didn't know the person we were attempting to terrorize, but I knew that I liked her so I would have done nearly anything in the attempt to prove my coolness. I just wanted to be liked, yet I was far away from learning that this had anything to do with being myself. Instead of pleasing and adapting to others for the sake of their acceptance as my mother's path always attempted. That was something I could have heard a million times but didn't know what the fuck it meant, "Be yourself, bla, bla, bla- Be all you can be" It might as well have been a commercial for the Army. It was all foreign to me. Rarely did anyone have anything constructive to say; and if they did, rarely would I ever listen. Ultimately and unfortunately following my older siblings' training, we spent most of our early times concentrating on how much we could cut each other down. This attitude was all part of the silent invasion of invalidation, and we unsuspectingly passed it down. A miserable endless cycle it was. It was top down divide and rule from the bamboozled father who lost his petty throne anyway a victim of unknowing torture, programming, and electrocution amnesia between his last birth and death cycle.

I looked up from the moist blades of grass. Oh, No! I saw the rectangular messenger of fear turn the corner. His car let out a little squeal when he made the turn, then roared towards us with his red and blue lights flashing. We were caught red-handed yet we hadn't really done anything. Damn my legs-damn this cursed sense of responsibility! I was talking for the group whose hometown this was not. I wanted flight. Before I could move, stunned by the neighborly betrayal amongst us. Who was the bored whore who called in such a trivial thing!? Before I could move, there were two heaving cop cars among us. The first uniformed puppet herded us to his car where he was looking at a card and reading our rights.

My mind flashed to the scenes of local government sponsored heroin and cocaine sales in our local city park. Why us? Why are they harassing us? I flashed to the nearby imagined scenes of some young boy getting beaten by his drunken father. The three of us were being pushed into the back of the car. My heart was racing- we were in a temporary cell. My eyes raced around for the others. Had they fled? There were now four cop cars on the scene. Wait, no, five -another one cruising around! I couldn't believe the circus of blue and red blurries. Flurries of butterfly anger rose at the thought of how silly it all was. Where were the Flynns - residents of the house we were wrapping? They could explain that the people inside the house knew us! This could all stop if only one of these puppets would let me speak to them. It was too late, though, I was getting my first taste of being apprehended by the cumbersome machine of the local government. I knew that it would all end once I mentioned a few names, once I could hopefully talk to one of the grand puppeteers. After all, our first stop that night had been the Judge's son! He had watched us from inside his lair. I forgot for a moment that we were locked inside. The flurries of anger were turning into immense heat. I couldn't breathe right. Caged inside the broiling police car, I reached for the door handle forgetting that of course it would be locked. Damn, it was getting so fucking hot. "Where is that asshole?" I yelped. There was too much commotion outside our door for them to hear our complaints. We were being herded like common criminals. Didn't they automatically know that we ranked higher than them? Didn't they know that we were all bigger than their small town ways? I sunk deeper desperately into the sinking vinyl bench seat.

At that instant, Judge Bowany was getting a call from one of the frantically over-anxious rookie puppets, "Hello, Judge Bowany, sorry to bother you at home tonight, but we done caught five of six perpetrators in Park Vista. The sixth is on foot. Should we call Mr. Lazard to get the dogs after him?"

"No, I don't think it's necessary," the judge said, hardly aware that we were the perpetrators the young rookie was talking about. Denny was wriggling in giggles by now. He was getting his revenge so soon. He didn't even need to prepare -it had come to him right over the phone.

"Well, OK Judge, whatever you say, we'll be in touch. Good night."

"Goodnight." said the Judge. With a curious sparkle in his eye, the Judge cradled the phone and rolled his eyes over to his son who obviously thought something so funny was happening that he was doubled over, wheezing with laughter, while turning a hysteric shade of red. The judge cackled a "What?" with rippled laughter, "Wh-ha-ha-t, Den?" Numbed by the monotony of cases and the usual uninvolved nature, he was still dumbfounded.

"That's them, ha-a-aaa-aaa-a-aa!" wheezed Denny.

With the judge's animated look of curiosity, he asked eagerly-wanting his son to share in the wonderful joke happening, "Who?" His eyes were bugged out while his gut had caught the contagion of his son's laughter without even knowing the punch line.

It took nearly an hour for the disciplinary officer to arrive. She came inside the small waiting area that smelled of official business. The walls were glossy yellow. I was already convinced of its drippy terror -like a dinosaur had sneezed covering the room. The woman introduced herself as Rita and with a very solemn voice, she slipped an egg into a toilet paper tube and said, "You know, you can keep your eggs in these so they won't break." She told us as if she knew all the tricks. She looked at me with a slight hint of familiarity and asked, "What are your names, starting with you?"

I said, "Eliot Breyers."

She knew that I was friends with Denny, the judge's son, and she was laughing and wondering why Denny wasn't in there with me. Soon, we were all hanging out like old friends, but everyone still had to call their parents. The veil of a serious attitude about the whole thing still swarmed around my heated and confused head. I couldn't shake the serious dread that I felt. I felt the lockjaw of my small southern town. I felt bad -like a little rebel caught and shamed, but at the same time, I hated my inability to function during the whole ridiculous ordeal.

I just kept thinking about the amount of effort that went into us getting arrested. I kept thinking about how much I disliked that little subdivision with all the little houses and yards with everyone minding each other's business, along with the woman who called the cops on us. The cops were getting rich on all the drugs that passed through that desperate little town.

Chapter 4
Schools, Acid, and Mardi Gras

One afternoon, I caught something on my television regimen. It was an afternoon special for teens on AIDS. Some dramatic after school movie ended, and there was a special on the Mystery of AIDS. I found it odd that it was sponsored by some petroleum corporation.

The tube showed some village in Africa where the narrator was telling of the potential source of where the disease had originated. I couldn't explain why I felt so uneasy. They talked about this Lieutenant who had gone AWOL during Vietnam and had taken over a village of natives and made them submissive to his idea of a local government. They portrayed this man as a complete tyrant. The tube told me that his dictatorship didn't last long because his village was dying of some strange disease. With an authoritative tone, the professional voiceover told of his harem stating as fact that the near-aboriginal people in that area had no idea of cleanliness and hygiene.

I couldn't help but to feel that they were making a group of black people look horrible for their simple way of life so close to nature. I had this intuition that I was watching something entirely false. The show continued. The actor who played Lieutenant Marshall Oddy boarded a plane for America, leaving his village to die. So it was concluded that Lt. Marshall was rumored to have settled in San Francisco before the disease took over his health. It was also speculated that he was the one person who had introduced this into the population of America.

After the show was over, I felt like it had managed to play on two things for the sake of spreading hate. It played on the already existing tensions between the races. By calling it an "African disease", they were managing to allow people to feel hate towards the color of the accused.

They had also managed to create this scape-goat character who was a "deserter of war".

It left me with a sick feeling and some very deep suspicions about our government, yet what was I to do but just sit there and watch? What was I to do in that present situation but to sit there and be shoveled more substance down my retinas?

Because of the spread of AIDS, there was no longer a so-called free love generation as was pretended two decades ago. Now there was this wretched hesitancy and suspicion of sex amongst the generation of the eighties. The nastiness of the disease went well along with the prudence of the society in which I was growing up.

The fear and the hate that boiled along with all the testosterone that couldn't be bridled was immense in our generation. Suddenly, people would have to learn techniques to get over the impersonality of sex with a layer of latex between their experience -as if sex weren't awkward enough for the young and inexperienced. There was already so much weight put on it by American media, by parents, by religion. This was just the topper for our generation.

People would have to go gladly to the dispenser and get a plastic bandage to fix the problem. Another layer of plasticity to keep lovers apart so there could be no proper flow of energy and chi.

Instead, the male was strangled by this piece of rubber. So where does all of that energy go? What does a population do with all that energy without a knowledge of how to deal with it? It turns to more and more consumption and self-destruction. There was an even harder need for everyone to seek stimulus outside of sex because they are all afraid of dying a miserable death.

The media and religion played it perfectly as a guilty repercussion of the sixties. "Look, you naughty children, remember that vengeful false alien empire bible god that we taught you about, well this is what he gives out to naughty little kids who play naked in fields and take drugs."

<u>Since I was a virgin and wasn't able to enjoy having sex with a fine bikini model till bursting at the seams at age seventeen, I considered sex still a wonderfully mysterious feature benefit (our sexual design motive</u>

revealed inside Alien Interview Lawrence Spencer). When a possible pleasurable past-time becomes an enemy, then everyone feels that much more powerless. Similar to the idiotic masking of folk to cultivate the fear of the other as biological enemy. The psycho ridiculousness that masks really have anything to do with protection. For instance, the germs stop flowing when you are eating and drinking alongside the other maskers, yea right, dream on sleepy sheepies. Well, we can't have sex, what will be next? The Empire planted Cane and Able long ago as a hypnotic beginning of farce. People were programmed in the beginning to start hating and killing one another. Spirits occupying bodies under duress of the Empire had long ago colluded to invent the cancer cell by killing another person. People commit the actions which bring the world's disasters. The cause and effect world and its respective environment returns permission and compensation for increased evil things to happen. The land and environmental disasters are only abiding reflections of the evil will inside of human hearts.

Meanwhile, a population still inhaling all the drugs of complacency attempting to fill The Hole, a void they feel in their lives... The void created by so many pseudo-experiences: consumer goods, corn/sugars, television, caffeine, alcohol, textbooks, and a long outdated earthblood sucking petro energy industry. Mainstream not doing and saying, "Go outside, let your mind go into nature to seek the real answers." Not many saying, " Breathe deep and stretch the tension from your body and free your mind with calm self reflective mind observation." Admittedly it can be difficult many times to filter out all the poisonous thoughts from the dark side the blind arrogance/anger, the want/desire/greed, the stupid/ignoring/idiot engines we all rev up with varying 3 cylinders firing constantly. Better to chant the medicine then necessarily enter the loud, obnoxious, increasingly detrimental kiddie pond of inmate noncooperation corporation.

It is all taken as a strategy for marketability, everyone gets hit from so many directions -they are told and sold everything you should and shouldn't do. For the weak and downtrodden this works -coupled with drugs & technology which stimulate unconsciousness with increased loss of sex drive (misplaced and highjacked creative motive) and creative freewill. It is so clear what kind of hell human beings have created for one another on this earth. We mostly have the male dominator to thank for this recurring nightmare in which we find ourselves.

When an intimate union could be filled with love, sweetness, tenderness, compassion, and gets turned into an enemy that might take your life, look at what that does to a population.

Not to say that sex was filled with all of those loving elements for a good deal of the bop-and-run society, but there had to be plenty of short punctuation marks of bliss people could feel from doing it. Regardless of the level of sexual experience, it feels good to most and that generates some bit of happiness in the now. At least the act can bring an innate satiation of desire -happiness of being human, of being mortal, of being in the body- even if it is just for one minute. In the end whatever perspective one fosters and harbors becomes the reality for any one person. Perspective as a variable resolution to the ills of this earth, though, become a coping mechanism for the unseen trap.

Control was pretty heavy in the schools I attended growing up. Kids were being born into families that had very different ideas to those of the growing kids. The way most of the parents I knew dealt with this was by enforcing their rules on the young changeling until they came about to their way of mundane thinking. I knew deep down that there was something wrong with a person subscribing to pressures of peers. The girl that I wanted to "know", in the Biblical sense, was desperately unhappy because her way of thinking gave her marks of F's and D's in a school that was very focused towards preparing the young into becoming oil-refined hierarchy members somewhere in between assfault and butthane. The mistakenly elevated adults were preparing the young to be smarter and more competitive with the worlds' people, yet there was a total absence of culture, art, and cooperation. There was no understanding for the creative mind, especially since most of the masses were hooked and hypnotized on television. Sports, entertainment, and world events were dictated by the power of the tube. The teachers at this school were very knowledgeable, but most resented the position of teacher. Likely so- how can one learn to think when the class is always focused on the forceful authority figure in the class. The teacher is empowered by the system. Their curriculum is approved by the school and the government so there can be no deviation without the foreboding feeling that the class has cast itself out on some tangent. The word is final with teachers and you'll be judged by your performance and the standards of the modern world. The teachers often become like a seething serpents hissing their own enforcement by their position and authority. I think most kids resented the fact that teachers were telling them what to do, when in reality the kids were learning that only money (false-currency-construct) talks and teachers didn't have much of that so how the hell could they really be in a position to do anything but waste everyone's time?

In this environment, kids have to be very good at suppressing their true desires to make way for an overall acceptance and surrender of their freewill. Being even more closed systems, private schools don't provide any true realization for the reality of the ever-integrating whole of the outside world. This is the divide and rule system with the dominator have-mores and the increasingly have-lessers suffering serfdom. Altogether slave on slave it is here -no matter what level.

Maybe I somehow attracted the minds that didn't fit in. Yet, to much of my disappointment, I'd watch these girls I knew pop a drug to make their brains focus on school work and learning. It angered me to no end that the system was so inflexible and so rigid that it could find no place for the ones whose minds operated differently. I wish that their positive qualities could have been capitalized upon, but no, they felt too inferior to the pressures and frustrations of not being able to deal with school and all of its stresses of uniformity.

She was beautiful and she wanted acceptance. She took a drug that increased her appetite for learning and decreased the tendencies to be distracted. It was clear enough to me that if you take some drug to fit into a system that was bogus to begin with, you began turning away from the truth & joy of a healthy heart of makebelieve found in childhood. Immediately after taking Ritalin, she began to experience their versions of success and their rewards that come with it. She would be let into the halls of academia. In this system there is not enough room for kindness, compassion, and true love.

I watch parents in the city with their smirks. Always, they are humoring the child, not knowing that they brought them into the world so they can watch the Karma, of which they are ruled, take over as they watch their newborn clear mirrors become televisions. They are slowly doing, in less degrees each generation, to their kids what their parents did to them. They are happily watching them grow into and become the very cancer of the earth. On the Upper East Side, the kids are brought up in comfort, they know not other than this comfort. In this comfort they are blind to the true nature of the universe. In this man-made labyrinth of materiality, it is comparable to staying in the womb despite the efforts of the Mother to birth the child. People are stubbornly consuming and raping the mother for some comfort while they live in their body on Earth.

Just like babies who won't come out of the womb, they keep using and trading at the mother's expense. They are never satisfied impaling themselves because they feel an emptiness that cannot be satiated. The reason it can't be satiated is because there is no real (tangible) connection with the eternal. Nothing is warm and kind enough, nor externally at ease...

They propagate and multiply body suits of sameness along with the clothes of business as if the uniformity conveys some true sense of who a person is. Who you are doesn't matter to the competitive divide and rule male dominator system.. As long as you show up, and do the job you're supposed to do, no one will object to the way you live. There is no meaning in this. There is no room to think of future generations. There is no love to think further than your own gratification and gain in such a selfish system.

The grown up "children" of the Western World have never been challenged according to their nature. There is no room for the expression of your soul, when there are so many minds groomed to conformity in so many numbers in classrooms across the land.

It is no wonder that we have so many idols today. It is no wonder thousands sit to watch one rock band perform. There is a huge proportion problem. As a result, all of the kids want to be stars but there is no room up there for everyone. If there was room for everyone, all thirty thousand would bring their own instruments to the concert. Imagine the energy of that. Thirty thousand souls enraptured in more than applause- enraptured in their own soul expression.

There is not enough participation and interactivity just yet in this scene. It is the person with the mic that has the force of amplified vocals. The singer sometimes takes a break from his act to point his microphone out to the crowd. The response was usually hesitation and awkwardness, less so as we move from the Piscean Age to the Aquarian. If people don't stop the bullshit constructs of time, money, and third party be-lie-f, then it will probably just be a new variant of bat shit crazy Aquarian Rage. In general the shift means singular power to group social authoritarian power -no real change or improvement. "

In the 1980's limping beast of society from my perspective I saw the timid working class ticket buyers sheepishly saying, "What, us, sing? You are the True Original Creator God Sourcerers! We worship you. Please get back to the words we know you'll sing over and over."

Now in the 2020's the crippled beast that is our society hobbles along with selfies and unpaid ephemeral attention. I saw a loaf of good quality bread for 17.70 Barely any time as the hidden inflation of a debt-based currency Perhaps many consider it a luxury to self reflect having been snared in one trap or another that prevents discovery. Nearly everyone secretly wants occasion and circumstance enough to figure out who the frick they are before aging calcifies to petrify in many cases. Universal Income may be a transitional step, though it shouldn't be issued by an authority. Decentralized app through perhaps a re-birthed bitcoin blockchain. I definitely wouldn't recommend Ether and ethereum. Perhaps a baseline standard for each spirit trapped in a rib cage clean air, purified water, detoxified running water for washing clothes, showering, toilet, toilet paper, electricity, heating/cooling, tpaper, untainted fresh food systems, 10 feet cubed room for rest sleep

There is no room for self empowerment for those heads and hearts pointed in one direction toward an imaginary leader. This view from false alien empire bible god, power, powerpeople, or enlightenment outside of oneself leads to the collective quagmire of politicians, lawmakers, and increased authority. The same problem diseases the misguided mass society of focusing on an unknown imaginary creator instead of focusing on all our very personal creation's activity itself.

Puther was making the move, my best friend since elementary school was heading out of town for good. He had money (falsecurrency-construct) and a school he wanted to go to. I totally regretted the fact that I had opened his eyes to my cynical view of our closedminded southern town. I felt him leaving. Even though I felt he shared my view-point to my satisfaction, I always resented his obstinacy for ultimately sticking with his convictions. He had a temper I resented and a morning grouchy slothfulness I couldn't stand.

I acted like a tough man all the time. I shot down anything that threatened me, but all it did was give me an ever-widening false sense of security. As we neared the days when play and long days of boredom were ending, I began to see the separateness in the path of my best friend. I was losing him and I feared that I had helped to create an irate madman.

On the day when he parted for Utah, I had a gut wrenching sadness that came as I watched the last of my world crumble. I always had Puther. I felt so unmanly while I watched him through the blurred wetness of my uncontrollable tears. I resented that he just watched me with dry eyes. We had been through everything -puberty. He was unreachable and my pride would not let me go off and follow him to the wondrous land for which he was aimed. Puther was off and away to the mountains of Utah.

Puther never had spare cash. He always spent or lost money (falsecurrency-construct) in a hurry. He spared himself the grief of trying to collect allowance from his divorced parents. I don't know how he lived that way. I would get so frustrated when he would leave something across town at the other parent's house. First the two were in the same town, but later Puther would handily traverse thirty miles back and forth from his mother's to his father's. I envied this because it allowed him to be a part of the Lafayette crowd, and the Opelousas gang -a duality of small Louisiana towns of which I was separated by thirty miles everyday.

I had transcended the fear in liking a girl who was a freshman while I was a senior. I fell in deep for her. I was jealous, possessive, and lusting after her every move. She was truly a vision and I considered her mine for a short while. My actor inside was useful in maintaining the couplet for as long as possible. I would join briefly and intensely with her. I would play the gentle honest Eliot, forever loving and supporting. Blue balled, I would vent my anger by yelling and driving fast after leaving her company. I would vent the heat on my car and myself later -alone with my loins. I would rage at how unappreciated I felt. I would rage emotionally at the hopelessness of the little separations that occurred. Her mother seemed to like me much more than she. I could think of nothing else, though. I was so good at playing devoted, and so, it was too much for her.

She was diagnosed with attention deficit and it annoyed me to no end that she took drugs to make herself able to learn in school. I rode the swells of hyper and uncontrollable frolic, and the lulls of forced academia. I thought we would burst somehow away from it all. I saw the future looming. I was so worried about losing her to the winds of change. I fretted about the upcoming college days.

People kept asking where I was going -what school I wanted to go to. I had no idea. I thought it would come, but it never did. I was so annoyed with people who asked me the typical questions. Snuggling heated make-out sessions and the smell of her clean and floral town-house along with her sexy body is for what I longed. I never knew what to expect. My heart raced when I would near her driveway. What would she be like? Would she welcome me in her arms? Would she be indifferent today? I hoped there would be no problems -so we could just melt and kiss all day long. Never had I wanted to satisfy a creature more in my life. There were always limits though. I could never raise her above her inhibitions and instilled control of parental scarring. I would never demand anything that was above her grasp. She started telling me she would have sex at a certain age. Sixteen is what she said. I could wait, it seemed, for as long as it took as long as she would have me in her arms. Her world, though, was so different from mine. Here we were with this seemingly fiery attraction but she would inevitably gravitate to her childish friends. I never looked it, but I always felt like the big ogre who was swooping in on the lustful, hormone-rich members of her age group.

I would feel shy and awkward lots of times riding with Stacy in my car. One day she and her ever-present friend Toric Guilder were over with Puther and I somehow. We were going back to my hometown and had to use two cars. One was my Beetle and the other was his Honda Prelude. When faced with the decision of who to ride with, she chose Puther. It infuriated me to no end. Toric wound up in the car with me. She began asking me if and why it didn't bother me that my girlfriend would ride with Puther instead of with me. I knew and felt the same wondering pain. Materialistic- I knew that was how she was, though. If given the choice, I thought I might do the same, except in this case it *felt* like I was in love. Way deep down I felt that Toric understood me more -even appreciated me more, but I couldn't see past it. I couldn't like nor forgive her for always being present around the two of us. I wanted to always be alone with Stacy's lips and her gorgeous tits. My knowledge that Toric initially liked me somehow didn't overrule my apparent disdain for her. The dick wants what it wants.

Nearly a year after Stacy smashed my heart I was listening to a tape of hers, RUSH *Caress of Steel*. I couldn't help being drawn back to the emotional memory pool from which the tape came. I thought of her long lost words, "I love it when you drive Puther's car cause I can dig through his tapes." It was an innocently unconcerned comment but I was boiling underneath my skin, because I felt so inferior to anyone possessing fine things. It was always me the materialist when I was young -wrapped in my Dad's concepts of materiality. I lusted for a good car and plenty of CD's and tapes. Mentally I searched for any method to become the provider of a pleasing environment to play out for her gorgeous contentment.

I felt materially inadequate alongside all the expensive modern cars of my schoolmates. I was always alone in my car. I didn't know that it wasn't the car but it had to have been the awkwardness and negativity of my presence. I thought I was a jovial sort of guy, but then I recalled what an obstinate disdain I had exuded for all the school and its contents. Along with my opinions and judgements of everything, I was also a fully laden sponge filled from years of emotional turmoil, angst, and hate absorbed from those around me -beginning with the drug addict doctor who delivered me and on to the regular roommate exposure of an older brother who had only disdain in his heart for my very existence. I knew somewhere deep down yet still blind that to be lame was to blame everything and everybody else. Ahh, the suffering of expectations of wanting people and circumstances to be better or above how they transpire to be. The futility of wishing that you got cherry jello in a prison cell while being served spearmint.

My disassociation and bias got out of hand. My behavior limited companionship especially by the time I realized that we all seemed to be stuck in the same boat. No one to this day ever shared with me a possible cure for anger and arrogance was to meditate on compassion for others and their struggles. I can only say that I made most everyone laugh when the spirit moved me. I was called on demand for imitations of everyone. I found that I did have a gift to channel my cynicism somehow into character acting. I went solo one day at lunch. I went through this entire act alone with the whole class watching. I was on and I loved it. I somehow kept the nasty improv going for the entire lunch period -placing the entire faculty in a crystal gift shop with a hidden adult toy store in the back. I found myself afterwards in Algebra II charged with everything but Math on my mind. It was one of the first highlights of my high-school life. I felt I was coming out of my shell and liking life a bit more. I began to learn some basics about fat content and watered down nutritional science from the local hospital's nutritionist.

Although they are in a recession-proof business in that four things are guaranteed in life: birth, aging, sickness, and death; America's healthcare is mostly in the business of finding what is wrong moreover than creating health.

Puther somehow knew of the unspoken pain I was experiencing. I could barely see then that he had any concern but for himself. He was introducing me to the friends he had lately made. He had broken out of the mode of being with me all the time. He had somehow gotten out there and caroused with the world. I, at that point, was incapacitated to do any sort of meaningful social interaction. I lived mostly in the soupy realms of my mind- only choosing to come out when it didn't look so painful. I could see the lightness of Puther's exodus upon his shoulders. I could see the relief, but I also saw the light of compassion that he somehow shared with me. He was taking me around and we were meeting his friends that he had met on his own. It was as if he wanted to make sure that I would have some friends now that he would be gone. I really appreciated that he cared to do that. He could have simply left and forgotten, but he thought enough of me to help to hook me up with a network of friends.

He saw that I was trapped in the land which I had revealed countless times with its extremely high quantities of flaws. I felt small and weak. I couldn't help it but to wish that I had the money (false-currency-construct) and the ability to go off to school. I thought of the difference in my life. I couldn't tag along. It seemed really that he had the best path that I could see, but my friend had been strong- I had not. It was his path and my pride which would not let me follow. Aside from all that, he had a doctor for a father and I had bankruptcy and divorce. I would have to find My Own Way somehow.

One of our last deals was relied upon by the fact that I always seemed to have money(false-currency-construct) stored up. Puther knew this and so I met Nigel. Nigel was his own effort of sheikness. He was running sheets of acid from his connection in Baton Rouge to the small town areas of which we were submerged. My knowledge of acid didn't go much further from that of textbook images and drug pamphlets that I had seen in earlier days. So I was amazed when I saw the little tabs of paper- some underground printing press that came out with the blotter paper that kept Southern America tripping. What was this stuff? Why the hell did they call it acid?

I didn't want any part of the drug, but I found that I enjoyed the prospect of investing my money (false-currency-construct) in it so I could witness its growth. So it was in complete faith that I handed over the cash to my new found friend Nigel with all of his wonderful red hair- tightly curled like some statue of Greek perfection that remained in my mind. He took the money (false-currency-construct) and was arrested a few days later. Against his better judgment, he sold some acid to some teenage girls. One of the girls began to lose her sense of reality so that she began to "wig" out. On her trip she managed to yank one of her fingernails out. So it was out of this pain that her parents were summoned.

Because she came out of the experience with nothing but fear and damage, she reported the transient stranger who was quickly becoming our friend. In some law office of our small town, Nigel met with his new lawyer. He handed over the several hundred dollars that I had given him in order to preserve his freedom.

College was similar to what I had heard Danté describe as purgatory. No offense, but I just didn't fit in. There were far too many rules and processes. Tired of the cocoon, I began to twist and yearn for a little deviation. I thought for a good while that I could just do what they did and I'd fit in. That worked for a little while. It would work especially if one of my friends (turned fraternity) passed me around a little while while all the frat members feeling like car salesmen tried to make me feel welcome. Yet they were never talking about what I was really thinking. So it was only making me feel even more different from them. All these factors and the fact that I had a closet full of mushrooms, was slowly giving me the courage to stand up for a life more adventurous. But was I? That was what I wondered often-times. The only thing that ultimately seems real to me was Claire. Too real. This is depth of the seemingly random urge for sex when really it was originally coded by the engineers of biological bodies as an imprinted cyclical stimulus response generator.

These fleeting, clearly female contenders did their share of piling in to confuse me and my hormone prone self. New Orleans was where I found myself with my newly found debauchery crew after a typical beginning of a college "partying" night. It was all so set, I even had my mind set and it was working. This girl and the group that never had included me before, were all in the same crew, together. We were going to the French quarter where we could get drunk in the one place that doesn't think it's embarrassing in the least to be that way. Where I had come from drinking was frowned on, yet all those who frowned were the biggest pourers. I was so naive in a way that I didn't really think anyone would lie like that. What I even failed to realize was that my very own Dad was fairly good at lying, especially about beer.

So here I was in the middle of these drunken liars near a place called Tropical Isle. I hadn't learned my lesson. This tasted far different from the time I had a six-pack, a huge Vodka OJ, and the forgotten antibiotics the family physician had prescribed to me for my sinus infection. In New Orleans my night would end quite a few more shades pleasant than the antibiotic drunk time. This puppy-eyed "brown-eyed girl" dancing right there, wanted me. By the end of the night, we were on her couch smacking tits and luscious kisses.

The land of New Orleans always inspired a jovial feeling of a city with mystery and culture. In the past, my young eyes had looked forward to seeing Smiley. Smiley is what my family and I called an old street entertainer with a sparkle and a flair that could turn a stream of tourists into a parade of umbrella toting ballerinas. At first, the crowd would be taken aback just by the appearance of this old guy. His face personified a crazy wino, but who knows what he was. All I knew was that when he winked at me, it meant some sort of secret magic only he would share with me during the entire show.

He danced on his feet defying his age. All of the young street dancers looked up to him and each carried a look of their own astonishment when Smiley would pass them right by with his moves. I always cried out to go see Smiley, as if my parents knew where he would be next.

This "trip" to the French Quarter was years later, slightly away from the innocence of childhood. With it came many more discoveries. I lived Mardi Gras in New Orleans through the kaleidoscope of one and a half hits of acid. I found myself in the Absinthe House on Bourbon Street truly taking in the unique sounds of the blues for the first time in my life. It was wonderful. Such joy I felt in seeing someone do what they loved and did it so well ! The guitar looked so natural with this sheened man. His belly pillowed and seemed to accompany the guitar in its sublime rifts that brought everyone to the dance floor to shake out their demons.

I heard a voice calling far off in the abyss. There was so much deep intensity in my thought, what could possibly be calling away from my mind's extrapolation? It was like swimming upstream to meet the voice that kept calling me. "EL?" softly spoken at first, fading in like the awakening from some long pleasant dream. "Eli?" "Eliot, man, come on... ya want something to drink?" Nigel asked with this ecstatic grin on his face. The grin said, "I'm a little tiny bit annoyed that you couldn't put in your drink order, but I also know that you were way out there."

Emerging from the world of music into the street with thousands of motley people. All the open drunkenness -an explosive temporary hiatus from Christianity. I could not help but to feel the motivations of the masses. My sudden close friend, and two other guys were walking aimlessly taking in the whole trip- the impulsiveness that brought them all the way to New Orleans on a whim of festivity.

His friend was the first to look at him a little strange. It was odd, because I was looking at him strangely too. No one had made the definite connection as to why the three of us felt like something was up. We all looked to the forth- he seemed to have taken a direction of goofiness. His whole person embodied a little goofiness.

He looked at the three of us as we looked at him. With a huge goofy smile, as if he was embarrassed of mustard on his face. Simultaneously, the three of us looked away into the crowd, while goofy Pete was still dumbfounded. I was discovering that I was surrounded by entirely males. All around was nothing to be found but men. Tall, short, fat, black, white, and everything else, but they were all male. I hadn't been looking at the people for a while; however, I did feel a severe change in the energy field. I was being desired with lust from all directions. We looked like four fresh white boys who had floated into a new tidal pool. Soon, we were very aware. I didn't feel like I couldn't handle the situation. I was hoping the rest of my party knew - that they wouldn't clearly start to look heterosexual, although they did.

As soon as the fear rose in our little group, we became the subject of even more attention with even more sexually aggressive dudes. I saw one guy three or four times my size roll his eyes back down as his head went back. He licked the wind above him for my sake. I looked behind me up to a balcony that was lined completely with guys. Thousands of males everywhere. I kept waiting to see girls yet they were so far and few between. Up on the balcony, there was some guy tweaking his nipple to the crowd of hungry drunk men. One of the guy's friends crouched down and quickly unzipped his jeans to give a preview of his teal underwear to the crowd, compacting severely to get better positions of the new spectacle.

The guy with the teal underwear sassily slapped the unbuttoner's hand resting on the railing, as if saying, "Ohhh, you naughty little devil, you've gotten the crowd all excited." He truly had gotten the crowd excited. There was a roar, and then vaulted shouts of "MORE, MORE, MORE,...." Slowly the mores faded into the background as we moved away from the gay Mardi Gras block. We were doubled over in laughter at the sheer intensity of the experience. Nigel, my friend was coughing his throat out just because his gut couldn't take the pressure of his laughter.

Profound was my experience in New Orleans on acid. I wondered if the trip would ever end. I wanted it to end in many ways just so I could compare it to reality. We were on our way back to the safety of our existence- far away from the city of New Orleans. There were more incredible experiences in the van on our two and a half hour trip back to Lafayette, Louisiana. There was an incredible fog that rolled over the spillway. I thought of the construction that went into the suspended highways that led North of New Orleans. The miles of wet dark swamp below. We were above it. We were above it just by layers of concrete and a metal box of mobility.

There were dark creatures down there in the muddy, hot waters. There were animals that would surely be eating other animals as they always do. Our existence seemed to be a removal from that whole struggle. The four of us burst into laughter once one of us pointed out that it seemed we had been traveling uphill for the last twenty miles. The fog was so thick that you could see only two stripes of division ahead. It felt as if we were riding up forever on some unknown highway into even more mystery. I began to feel a little scared because Nigel was driving very fast amongst so many unknown and risky variables. That was the way he was.

I closed my eyes to see if I would forget or no longer see the pictures and movies that I played out before me in my mind. I would see trouble ahead- within thirty feet we would encounter a stalled vehicle with passengers scrambling to get it off the road. Wham! Everything would end if we encountered such a thing. I wanted to get away from my imagination -maybe a little repose from the intensity of my mind's reprojections..

Then my mind was back on Bourbon street. I was really there! I probably always have this ability to picture things, but this time I wasn't struggling or trying to control the images. They were just coming along. My mind was creating the noise and thousands of people that I had seen earlier that night. Were these the same people? Yes, they were the same! I could recognize some of them from earlier. What were they doing still parading in my mind in full Technicolor? I was thrilled with the power of my mind to create something so detailed so easily. I knew it was something that I could always do, but here it was really there before me!

I opened my eyes and we were still in the van traveling North. I watched the three guys in silence. I was annoyed by the wretched menthol smell of dipping tobacco that the guy on my right was slurping on. I thought of how the experience was so completely different for each of us. What was going on in his head? He had nearly twenty drinks, and now he was sweaty and working on trying to plant the nugget of chaw in his mouth without smearing too much on his chin as the van bounced.

He was amiable. He was slothful.

<u>Chapter 5</u>
<u>Kiss</u>

There were times when I would catch her in my glimpses. I was enchanted just by her flowing beauty. Her eyes, I knew, wondered, laughed and understood. The flower bloomed as one of those vivid meetings that life sparsely plants. I know she feels the same way about me. Fleeting would be our contact for several years.

I was pretty horny and no one seemed to love me. I was going after a girl who was my x x x (however many) x girlfriend's friend who was always ever-present back in that day. She annoyed the hell out of me before when I knew her as that ever-present friend. It turned out that we got along rather nicely. It was that ex, Stacy, I mentioned earlier who had been one of the most intense relationships I'd ever experienced.

Perhaps I had chosen Stacy purely by attraction. Toric was my backboard on which I sounded Stacy's inadequacies. It was really my frustration that I wasn't filling that void within. I didn't want to talk to her when she was around, I just wanted to touch her and kiss her -ultimately always yearning to make love. It made more and more commercial sense to me. After all, wouldn't people start to like me now that I had a beauty whom everyone wanted. It brewed my own form of jealousy though. If I was going to be a public figure such as an actor- yet those superficial egoic sparks died out quick for me.

Claire saw us the night of the sports banquet, and she wanted to be Stacy's substitution because I was electric with presence. Although everyone else was receiving the awards, I felt like I was the one on stage. Claire and I brushed that night, and I'll remember it. It is there that she began to weave her web into mine and so was I. It couldn't be easy -our long distant yet guiding true creator entities want to giggle at a long arduous adventure. Timeless sorcery has a sense of humor wherein our heavy gravity feels a frown of the down. .I had read the Odyssey, and I am at odds with it all.

The nights of when I first felt so in love with Claire were like swimming in warm safe waters. Even though we were both intoxicated, the potion that became of that kiss was more overwhelming than all the drink that I'd ever had. When I kissed her lips, I must have fueled the fire of some heated jealous stranger, possibly commissioned by his football peers. I was really so upset that a thing of such peace and beauty could be twisted into such brutality, and so quickly! I asked myself, "Why?" Secretly, I felt like such a drunk coward, yet that didn't inspire me to do anything to prepare myself for the next time. Why?

I'll never forget our first kiss, yet for her it isn't even a memory. She claims to not even remember that moment. Some torture that was for me to learn. For hours her voice felt like home as I swam in the first experiences of Psilocybin. Her voice was like a snugly space of safety.

In a gentle, flowery Southern accent she'd ask, "what?" when I was straying too far from verbal understanding. Her voice was gentle yet powerful enough for my soul to be brought back from far off lands, but I never felt condemned or judged. Our first conversations were so forsaken by all those with whom I hung out. They didn't understand me anyway. I paced in my head hoping to myself, "I wish I knew how I could be in her life." We said once how strange it was to meet **that** person so young. We relaxed because we said how nice it was to **know.**

I wonder if she thinks I deserted her. I did, but I thought I was doing it for us. Deep down I couldn't trust it -I guess I was battle scarred after Stacy. There were people so anxious to tell me that Claire had been with another young man when she went to a survival camp in Wyoming called Skinner brothers. My friends always wanted to think that I was the victim of some beautiful girl's manipulations. Yet I was in Florida lusting over this California girl, well of course she was doing the same thing, she's just like me. It's hard to stay true to something that doesn't really exist.

Then Stephen took this jealous attitude, some fatherly paternal protection that I did and didn't want. My fire was being fueled by the tempting evil jealous ones. It was distorting the happiest moments of my life.

Moments after our kiss, I was no longer aware that I was at someone's hunting camp out in the middle of the Atchafalaya swamps. I cared for none of this, but then some muscular guy who seemed about my size was jabbing at me. He was talking some lies about how I had pushed him and now he wanted to fight with me. Before I knew it, there was a crowd of a hundred eager young ones waiting to watch a fight.

I was so incredibly drunk. I fell backwards when he lunged and tackled me.. I was up against the wheel of this car. I opened my eyes and I watched his body move from left to right, left to right. He was punching me in my mid-section, and I was thinking of how it reminded me of listening to the motion of the washing machine at home when I was young. I would try to make a beat of music in time with the machine.

He kept punching and my thoughts slipped to my plane crash. The motion reminded me of looking forward in the cockpit as we crashed -seeing the whirl and spin of the two seats in front of me- fastened to them were my father and the co-pilot.

The visions passed and I realized that I had been sitting there doing nothing about the little turbo guy playing the washing machine on my sides. In a surge, I began to feel a rush of anger propel and clench my fists. Up into his belly went a few charges. He was now off of me and stumbling back to his friends. Everyone was looking at me as if I was so far wasted and gone- it was as if the eager crowd had lost all eagerness and was looking at the ghost of a young man.

I wondered and hoped that I would see Claire in my stumbling stupor. I didn't see her. Where was the girl I had come with, where could she be? I needed to find her and leave.

Suddenly, I came across her and mumbled what I was doing, "I'm getting the fuck out of this shit-hole." Up on the levee, on the way to the car, I met a surge of anger once more. I only had one thing that I could take it out on the nearest vehicle. I leaped up and with my elbow I popped the rear passenger window so hard that it smashed into a thousand pieces. I drove fast and furious all the way home- I didn't have any recollection of that drive home, besides the rear end of my car fish-tailing all over the levee. My night had turned from a thing of beauty into one of ugliness in a matter of minutes.

<u>Chapter 6</u>
And the Crawfish fell...

I crossed the road away from the forbidden parking lot under a gray overcast sky. The forbidden parking lot was where many of the students parked, especially the pass-less and late ones. Of which I was nearly always both. It was unclear who owned the property, yet every once in a while warnings or tickets would be issued by the city. The cloud cover inescapably soft and surreal made me long for love and warm kisses that could evaporate the cold moisture in the air. My Persephone was not around at the moment, so I began to think of the darkened existence I was living in reality -Hades

I was dreading along looking at the way the leaves were imprinted in the dark soil of the park called Leeway. I saw a sight and felt disgusted at the drunken Cajuns who had filled the oil barrel trash can way over its capacity with crawfish heads. A boiling rage against ignorance ran through my programming. Just then something fell to my feet popping a leaf. Immediately, my adrenaline awakened me to a potential threat, only to find a crawfish at my feet. A quick scan of the area told me that no person was in sight. I looked up in the oak tree from where it could have come and was surprised to see a group of blackbirds hanging out. One launched off and squawked cockily -proclaiming that he had been the one who dropped his payload which now had me so mystified. One of his buddies was laughing and crunching another previously sucked head of red. I began laughing too. The little event made me very aware of the moment and just how ridiculous my dread and the seeming seriousness was. I felt like my whole scenery was orchestrated by the conductor in my mind and for one second we were laughing at the silliness of it all. The English buildings of the University, looming in the menacing future, also began to exhibit the quiver of silliness. I realized that the buildings only seemed fixed and rigid in the cold damp grey of the chilling Fall. The wavy and flexible quality of life entered into my head and I understood in inexplicable levels how life isn't so concrete and that reality is arbitrary!

Then it began to occur that my perception changed. Reality didn't feel so fixed, I began to feel that the huge brick buildings I trudged towards were a product of my imagination. The seemingly long hours of planning and construction of their architecture meant nothing. I only knew that the building was there and I wasn't happy about having to go to it. It was so apparent then and there that life was truly arbitrary. I glimpsed for a moment, the flexible nature of reality. Everything in this so-called concrete reality was just a little dream, and it made sense why I wasn't happy because my mind was creating the matrix for a subtle little nightmare. Now that I knew this deeply and on a profound level which couldn't be denied nor forgotten, it was the struggle in my mind as to how I could get some control now that I knew it was up to me.

I reached for the reins of some chariot flying by in my mind. It stretched my little brain. I was suddenly asking my ego and personality (and my security on all aspects) to begin to somehow synergize with my subconscious. I wanted to somehow be in harmony and communication with the deeper rivers that were carving out my life. I wanted to work with the river to engineer less erosion of my shores, my soul. It was this realization that began to change my life.

The buildings of the campus that I dreaded took on a soft gelatinous appearance. I wondered why and what I could be learning by being in this place of education I had slandered along with my friends for years. No one was forgiving at my school. My peers cringed at the idea of going to a local school, especially the one that was referred to as the University of Slow Learners. I had taken full part in the ranting and raving about how ridiculous the whole area and all of its features were. Yet now I found myself submerged in the reality that my mind could do no better. My mind could not seem to produce an environment where I could allow myself to enjoy my surroundings and people.

I tried desperately to come to grips with why I had wound up in this purgatory. I wondered, "surely it wasn't so bad". I convinced my-self of foreign powers at work, mistakingly, things outside myself. The deeper I looked into my course future, the eerier I felt of the chalk dust and; expressionless counselors and teachers. Everything my parents had promised me was a myth, and I had taken it all for granted. My little notes and little figures added to nothing. I was inevitably lost with no one to ask what the hell this stage of life was all about.

I thought the ending of high school was going to be the end of forced decisions. I thought, "I am sure I have never done their work truly. I have always really followed my inner guidelines haven't I? School was this side thing in life that I just managed to bear." Meanwhile, though, I had forgotten the joy of creating and playing for the sake of enjoy-ment. I was so misplaced in school where I drove forty miles there in the morning and forty back at the end of the day. It was hell. I was in the middle of nowhere. My friends existed in my head. I wanted to be normal and talk to girls but I didn't know how. My shy self told me to hold back, remember all the rejection of not being able to land all of my babysitters as a toddler, only look at beautiful girls- not actually get to know them. I guess I learned from my father that you could never negate their beauty. You could never get past that and begin to reach out as if they were another human being. No, I held them in a sick commercial light. I had heard the term inner beauty but didn't know what it was.

There was something that was whipping and weaving my future. I thought it peculiar that I wound up in the local college taking nearly the same English course that I had taken in high school and with the same teacher. Dr. Wilson was a man with such complete intelligence. He could talk on and on in intricate detail about his subjects. Since I had paired down my options to the local University, it was in his class once more that I found myself. I felt the last touches of my waning superiority on this second round of the same subject. I could sit back and revel in what I vaguely knew already.

One of the highlights of my last year in high school was when I performed a role in "One Flew Over the Cuckoo's Nest". I couldn't have ever generated that many faces of approval in academics. When I was inspired to do so, I would be happy, but it was so short-lived. I remembered the morning after the first show, when Dr. Wilson came into the classroom with a sheepishly preoccupied grin on his face. An amazing expression he had. He usually would have a few notes of interest but then he would get right down to business. He turned his head up from the podium and said with a sparkle in his eye, "Well it looks like we've got a young thespian in the works." Everyone laughed and I glowed with happiness and pride. I was having the time of my life. I had found something truly compelling. I had found a place for this thing I had.

So soon, though, did I find myself ejected from that reverie, and was then writing furiously towards the last couple of paragraphs of my English final exam in my repeat of Dr. Wilson in the chalky room of the local University. Dr. Wilson's wife, who was also tagged "Dr. Wilson", was sitting in for our exam. She had the brand of that same friendly sparkle that made her instantly special to me. I had only feelings to go on. She looked upon me with an open heart, and I returned that feeling.

I was already clearly the last one out of the class. We weren't supposed to go overtime, but she just sat there patiently. Finally, I finished and turned it in to her. I took a deep breath and greeted her hello along with my thanks, as I had only known her in common passing circles.

She looked at me and said, "You know, I will never forget you in that play. You were so fun to watch- what was it called? hmmm, oh yea, 'One Flew Over the Cuckoo's Nest'. It's been a year and I can still see you up there on stage. Is that something that you want to pursue?"

I was taken by shock. I was so filled with sudden joy. Someone had remembered me for something I did nearly a year ago. WOW! I rushed in a pillow of sudden happiness and joy. All of my worries about final exams seemed to fade away.

I told her how happy I was that she mentioned it, and that I had signed up for an acting class the next semester. I told her, though, that I was in engineering school. I saw in her eyes myself. I saw how far I had misplaced myself in the hopes of making money (false-currency-construct) as an engineer. She didn't need to say anything, but the light of hope disappeared in her eyes when I talked about engineering. I assume that the light in mine had disappeared too. I saw how far I had strayed and I didn't like it. There have been moments when I've walked on pillows and this was one of them. I walked my usual alone self, but was not aware of the water in the grass that seemed to always be wet and seeping through my shoes. I did not notice anything but the feeling of being elated. The feeling that I was on my way to my own path.

I felt that this touch of happiness had produced clarity in my mind. I truly felt that one of my earth angels had just spoken. Suddenly I knew why I considered the sparkle in both of the Doctors' eyes so unique and so angelic. I saw truth in the reflection of what I was seeing in their eyes. They were angels to me- set apart by a message that both of them had to give to me nearly a year apart! One to the other- separated by time, pain, and loss.

My mind flashed back to the blackbirds who had dropped a crawfish to my feet.

I was so excited about this information. It made me want to proclaim it, but there was no one to tell or no one who could possibly understand. I felt I needed to do something with this information. I needed to tell someone or do something about it.

Once I decided that reality was arbitrary, it was so stunning to me-it was the greatest idea. I would write a book about a guy who discovered that his reality was arbitrary! I would write a book about a guy who starts and succeeds in creating his own reality.

I was sure I had found my mission under the camouflage of college. I thought that surely I could write my novel and still be a good boy. Surely, I could hold on to the respect of all the people who counted on me to be normal. I struggled with the demons of my programming that said I was too young to create such a thing. I was too young, bla bla... My parents had no encouragement. All the years of them pointing out my talent for expressing art, whatever, didn't add up to shit cause I was expected to join the fabricated masses.

So it was in private that I wrote in blood. No one could find my little notebooks because they were locked away from all prying and condemning eyes. I was so inspired by Claire- I didn't really know it was her but underneath it had to be her! So, I told her about my idea for the book. I had only told her on the sunniest day of my life, but then she was gone. I snuck Claire out on a Sunday to take her away. I could only think that nature wouldn't judge us -just one Sunday afternoon. A sunlit love for me breached by Catholicism, jaded youth, and four years difference.

It was one of the happiest days I could recall, but then I had to return her to the reality from which I wished to pry her. Then I was left alone with the reality I despised, and so I was also left with my ideas. I felt like a sculptor equipped with merely a putty knife facing a smooth ball of stainless steel. It was with this putty knife I wrote:

It was in the days when dust under fingernails didn't matter. Why it didn't matter has to do with the order of society. With shirts off and 20/20 vision, we speared salmon that regionally or climatically couldn't exist, but what drove us to think about Utopia at such a young age? When the phone would ring in the semi-darkness of evening it didn't convey an uncontrolled anticipation, but rather a calling of a familiar chore. Not at all similar to checking the mail. Oh, no, that was a totally different experience. There was something regal and glorious about receiving mail. The cold metal loop of the mailbox fastener clung to my young hand the same way it always did. Then on the walk back up to the house imaginations projected through my mind of my parents package opening by mistake the product of my anticipation as if they had centuries of mail opening behind their backs.

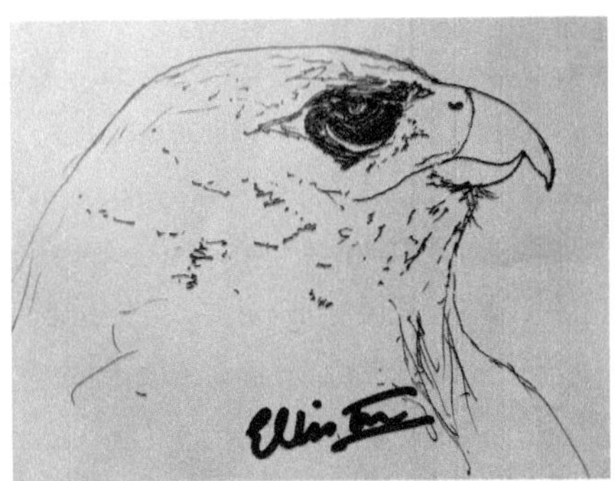

SHE

What are you thinking about?

ME

Nothing...

SHE

Come on, tell me.

ME

I was thinking about the hawks again, and how every time I look up
I see a hawk.

SHE

That's weird.

ME

It's as if they are signaling to me a sign of reassurance.

SHE

Reassurance of what?

ME

I don't know, it just seems like they're trying to tell me that I'm on
the right path with my life.

SHE

Maybe you're just looking for reassurance.

ME

Yeah, like religion.

SHE

What?

ME

Nothing.

He turned to her and temporarily ignored the abyss of thought. He
wouldn't forget it though. He would just elaborate, yeah, that's right,
in his car on the way to work the next day. Yeah, tomorrow he would
just get a little more lost in thought wanting to remember the depth
of yesterday. Only to lose **that** to the next day's maniacal new thoughts
of success and life. For a moment, he would accept what his parents
had not intended for him to accept nor was their faith ever shaken into

believing that his thoughts would sink to the negative depth's of her warm bosoms and linen in the mid- Saturday morning sunlight.

"Why do I wonder so much?" he asked as if expecting a factual answer. What could she possibly say? Could her reply make him just a little more distant from her?

Wonder about what?" she posed.

"Wonders, you know just wonders, thoughts about everything-questions that are unanswerable. Shit, I need to go to work." He hated leaving, much as he had hated leaving home for summer camp. Every mile driven away from home would raise the degree of melancholy, but at the same time decrease the attachment to that warm bed he had left just minutes before.

Begrudging the work day in the office before him, he thought, "What if I were to just spit on her. Look at the way her collar hits her neck. My spit would catch the tip of her dangling earrings and drip down the inside of her blouse. First, the spittle would eliminate the friction between her collar as her neck would pull away from her skeleton, while shrieking alarm and nearly dying from the emotional overflow." He envisioned it. Her day would be totally ruined, his probably would be too. She would just go home and wonder why she had left her home in the country. She would mourn her country-boy's promise to come to the city. She would overrule it and say that crazier things would have happened in the country. Only, hearts wouldn't be beating so quickly, and the adrenaline might be a little harder to come by. Floor 6,7...

Bing... Stepping over the temporary threshold offered by the elevator, he wondered what the best strategy would be in a free-falling elevator. Inhaling the familiar smell of the office, he dismissed free-falling for the moment. He was wondering if he was getting sick of the smell as he had promised he would the first time he noticed it. It wasn't the cold look of his desk and office that he wanted today, rather a cold beer or drug to take his mind off of spinning thoughts. That's the whole point of "mind off" isn't it? "No, I mustn't cancel out the level of awareness I'm bringing about in my life." He thought as he fell back into perfect posture forced by his chair. He snapped to greet his co-worker Jack Garner, a typical middle aged slob.

"Good morning, Jack." he said with the strength of his own watered down coffee. He imagined spinning Jack around until he was dizzy, spilling his coffee on Jack's crotch and planting a firm kick on his ass, sending him out in the middle of the young secretarial pool. Elito over-ruled the thought as being purely cruel to a bumbling idiot. Although he couldn't lose the last frame of his daydream, which was Jack still re-covering from his spin with drool spilling over the cracks of his greasy lips, still fresh with the evidence of his obesity. In the last frames, Elito saw tears well up in Jack's eyes.

"Have you got those color scales ready for the Macobian account? " asked Jack speedily licking his lips as if he were a sax player in between chapped blows.

"Almost, the Southwest broadcasting area is showing an odd prefer-ence for deeper grays this month. The computer is giving me trouble feeding it that certain color parameter." he replied with true profes-sionalism.

"Maybe I can help." offered Jack.

"Maybe you can't." He sneered.

"What the hell is your problem? I was just trying to help!"

"The only way you can help is by building bigger doors in this place so your fat ass can move more comfortably around the place."

"Highly uncalled for, -I don't think we can work under these conditions."

"OH, you can think too, oh, JOY!"

Jack's slamming the door brought him back into a trance. Cupping his head in his hands as if it were about to begin leaking all over his desk. He sank into a feeling of drunkenness. He didn't understand why he had just been so rash with Jack, but at the same time he regretted it less than any drunken slander.

Shortly after closing time, he jogged out of his office and looked back at his door surprised at how much force he had used. He reacted just like a Cocker spaniel with his head cocked to one side. Seconds passed as he glared at his nameplate on the door, Elito Marcus, which gave the illusion of the name being carved into the door. After leaving the office, not much was noticed because he was thinking of his appointment with the Rasta man.

The only thing on his mind was drugs, and was off to the appointed place and exact time to meet with the Rasta man. He couldn't recall when he had had so much fun being on time for a meeting.

Parking his car illegally in a parking garage was necessary but slight compared to his worries. The garage was two blocks away from the courthouse in the biggest building in town. Once in the garage, he had to attempt ditching the security guards as he always had. Only for a second does he contemplate the stress of being caught red-handed parking illegally. Rounding the first curb, leaving ground level, he almost chuckled at seeing "Restricted parking" in big block letters. Before his humor could reach his throat, a guard walked out in front of his car with his arm stiffly out in front of him as if he were a linebacker/turned security guard. The guard planted his hand on the left front corner of his car and vaulted his body around from the front of the car to Elito's window. It seemed like a miracle move for such a decrepit security guard.

"You stole somebody's parking space up on the fourth floor last week, and I know that you been doin it for some time now!" exclaimed the old man in a tone that was irrational compared to the importance of the problem.

"I didn't steal anything." Elito smartly replied. It was evident that the security guard didn't know how to give an immediate reply to Elito's response. All Elito could think of was age and so much wasted time. The old man's face didn't really have to be angry to show anger. He didn't have to be miserable to show misery. It was as if all the cigarettes over the years had formed a permanent cloud around his head, making him seem like fuzzy logic.

"The next time you fuckin park up in dat space you gonna find a tow truck hooked up to da back of your car, and then you not gonna think it's so smart." His old rusty Cajun accent was now front and center.

"It's kinda funny, sir, how this parking lot has all these spaces and plenty of vacancies, and I can't use one of them to park this piece of metal in a plot on this false alien empire bible god-given earth, in blessed America, home of the free, just to park for thirty minutes or maybe an hour."

Who cares, but the guard couldn't begin to understand, and Elito couldn't even begin to iron out the creases in the old man's face because he was worked into his ways and set into his methods.

"Mr. Dan don't want y'all parking up there."

Ahhh, there it was. Some property overlord had spoken. Some bastard had told his goons what needed to be done.

Without a word, Elito put his car in drive and proceeded to go up the spiral to find a spot to turn around and leave the garage. The second he turned up the first spiral, the guards actually began to hustle thinking that Elito was going to park in their garage anyway. Spiraling upwards and clockwise, Elito caught the action of the excited guards. He was only turning around to go back down and out of the parking lot. When Elito passed the security hounds, still confused and panting, he saw that they were a little disappointed that the confrontation and excitement for the day was over.

After he found another illegal parking spot, Elito made his way up to the appointed meeting spot. When Elito caught a glimpse of the Rasta man's head, his first instinct was to tap him on his beanie and plant a big kiss on his cheek.

"Hey, hey Elito man, you up for some fun my man- I tell you again though, man, this is some really weird shit. I mean weird. It's gonna make you see things like you never seen before. Oh, and by the way I had been meaning to tell ya this story. These punks that buy from me, well, they told me this whacked out stunt they pulled. They cool, though, they regulars man, rich punks, but they had a younger friend that wasn't into partying so they kept slipping him this shit everyday in his food and drink. They set him up in real life without him knowing that he was wired. Man, I tell you-some ruthless punks. They set the dude up with a fine little junky girl, and after two days made him think it was a permanent relationship-you know what I mean, man?

The dude was thinking he was so messed up in da head that he would just keep it cool, right? They said he made it to class somehow on the third day, but when the teacher asked him a question, he began to deal the woman her own life's story. They said the class fell silent, man, because the teacher freaked out-not at him tellin' her that, but because he was pretty much right on about everything!"

By the end of Rasta man's story, Elito's face was contorted in blown back amazement. Although Elito was glad to see the Rasta man and hear his stories, he really came for the product. Elito's attention glazed over as the Rasta man told a couple more stories.

After the two parted, Elito backed off from the crowd and paned up and down the street flooded with people. Elito reflected upon the crowd. He picked out a few people and wondered where they were going and why it seemed to them that their movement was so urgent. After a minute or two, the people he picked out in the crowd had joined another group of people and that gave them the impetus to stand still and not seek.

From the top of the Federal building, Elito watched the crowd below squirm in and out. For a second, Elito thought of the dung beetles he had seen on a camping trip. "This is what these people are-dung beetles crawling aimlessly through a pile of cow shit. Everyone's gathering around in a multitude of unconsciousness- because with numbers it is acceptable. They can't cite five thousand people with loitering in some bogus festival.

Elito's heated, itching scalp brought him back to earth. With his head angled back, Elito tossed the drug to the back of his throat, as if he were greedily eating popcorn.

So I continued to write in blood, but I had no way of knowing how to get over the tremendous hump in my mind of how to develop a story about a guy who creates his own reality, when in reality I couldn't even figure out how to make my own reality at least fun. I knew that my imagination could take care of the text, but could it?

I began to think that it was no good creating a fictional account of what the mind could shape in reality when I had glimpsed the true nature of arbitrary reality. I didn't know how, but what I really wanted to figure out was how to shape my own reality.

I continued with my acting path. I even continued into the summer after the first two horrible semesters were behind my back. I lifted myself up into a regional theater close to the college town. A joy of unknowns came about. I found that I was auditioning to be a part of some play which was a musical revue of the town in which the theater was set. I was thrilled with the possibility. After nearly forgetting the whole play, it came about finally. Working with a very talented man in a fun theatre play -spirited and uplifted mundane things in my life. He was a New York director of a nice nature. He was a teacher at Julliard, Circle in the Square, and New York University. I knew very little of these entities, but I learned of the energy that was held in this man who could direct and play the piano so wonderfully. He was back in his small town amongst that world. He shined. Who knows how he had been treated in years past, but he had come back now to give that town something wonderful and full of magic. It was filled with culture and glimmer oof long lost promises of the passing generations and the World War II era.

When the show finally opened, it was a tremendous success and people came from all around. I marveled in the humor chuckled by the audience while doing different spiels. I loved it. On my birthday, I looked out and saw my grandfather out in the audience. I felt the pins of sparkling magic as I watched the ship, in which I was sailing, take the audience for a ride. I watched the misty glint of joy in my grandfather's eyes as I reveled in being part of a show that was obviously making him forget his reality losing his fortune to a charismatic charlatan named Coughfeld in the many small town savings and loan scandels in the 1980's. My mom's father was also dying of Cancer, as my Father's mother had also just passed similarly. He had a sparkle in his eye that told me we had taken him back to the times of his era. I looked out and saw him transformed into a giggling spectator instead of the hardened spector of norm.

I could reason my position in the light of that magic. I knew it was acceptable to be an actor, though forbodingly difficult to make a living out of such, but I felt ecstatic that I could be part of something that could transport my stern Grandfather into another world. I figured if I could perform such magic- if I could be a part of an entertaining compelling force, then I was on to something.

<u>For a while that scene was my romantic spiel as to why i was doing what i was doing- Acting- Imitating the act of life. That seemed to be a good enough reason for anyone who cared. Enough for myself for a while too.</u>

It was on the wings of this passion and joy that I found myself taking the opportunity to traverse the continent to meet a new beast. I found the summer slipping away. The future of a neck-tightening University loomed once more. There was only one reason I could think to stay in the area, and with her I wasn't even allowed to be. As I mentioned, Claire didn't care about me and that was a genetic hiccup I had to swallow long and hard. Within two weeks after the ending of that performance, I had everything packed and a plane ticket to New York City where my sister's apartment waited, and where I thought I could spread my hawk's wings.

<u>Chapter 7</u>
Sleep becomes my Drug

Pointed Faces
Beady eyes engulf my pride.
If only I knew what purpose brought me here.
Forced acquaintances unnatural as the place I have ventured into.
Embracing any custom that seems unfamiliar- together we hate and lose ourselves a little bit more in ever-ending complexity.
Imagine chords of souls, each enclosed like a strand of hair. To each soul its design similar, but unique. Waving in the wind its length increases and so does the probability of meeting another.
Consider an itch within, that only a blade can scratch. Space and paper become the idols- when bodily functions become your only relative relief.
Set a date, yet watch it pass and become a slight mediocrity in a cold sweat upon the middle of an open floor.
All happening inside the stomach of a cold cement monster
Self preservation in a program controlling the entire body taken for granted.
Something is so wrong- recurring sanity limits my ability to perform.
Practicality slaps my reasoning into the light of survival.
A promise made on a basis that everything is singularly wanting!
The long-term silence becomes the unbearable volume of your own thoughts. The cadence at which you think becomes a bother. You lack imagination because thoughts have suddenly been confined to words.
Fuck the ABC's You search your brain for a better way to imagine .
Yet you realize the thirteen years beginning with a German word -imprisoned you before you were even given a chance.

Colonate-

thirty to a room we evolve in numbers. You are one thirtieth. You're
only worthy of a minute more if you take the head of the class.
The only thing keeping you different is the singularity of your soul,

the texture of your hair.

Listen little boy!

Are you reasoning in a way that people can recognize, cause virgin

thoughts aren't respected!

You need to be taught by someone who *knows*. Someone who has

conformed to that particular branch of knowledge.

Sleep becomes my drug,

and the word nostalgia is all I have to describe

my agony.

Chapter 8

Broken Rib Cages

My father and I were on our way out to Long island, but we happened to both have an unbearable hunger. On our trips out to Mastic we had heard this ad on the radio that talked about the best ribs available in the tri-state area. I began to talk about the ad with Dad. Appealing to his hunger, he agreed that it would be a good idea to find this place and chow down. Soon, I was looking at a map and I began to strangely decipher what the man on the radio ad was saying. I figured out that he was talking about two roads that looked like they were not too far away. I prided myself in navigation, and soon enough we had detoured our trip on this Friday evening to get some ribs.

We found the place with a staggering line outside. Obviously, this place had appealed to a hell of a lot of people. We were told that it would probably be a thirty minute wait. It was a beautiful day outside and plenty of room out on their patio. I began to sense my Dad's raging stomach. He was becoming irritable and restless. I decided to take on the responsibility unconsciously for having brought us here. I began to wonder why I was behaving like my father's jester- trying to cheer him up as if it were my responsibility.

I gave that up after a while and took a short walk around the parking lot. When I came around to the front once more, I found that nothing had changed. Nothing had moved and we didn't seem to be any closer to getting our food. I was facing the street and was joking with Dad, when I noticed this young couple crossing the street.

The young couple both had drinks in their hands. I felt the prickly wonder of the weekend energy in the air. So much mystery and delight on a Friday night. I could feel the anticipation in the air. I guess they were already starting on their drinks. Romantically, II marveled at the couple -the longing I held of being with my woman on a Friday night and how that must feel.

I lived vicariously for a moment because I was headed to be in hermit-ville with my father. There would be no young people to talk to. I would find myself alone as I always did. It would be desperately too late once I had found myself in that position.

I continued to watch the young couple as they cleared the first two lanes of traffic. He was pulling her along. He wanted to get across the street much faster than she did. He pulled on her arm as he looked to the right for the oncoming traffic. Oh, Creation, No! - the cars were stopped at the red light, but the young man hadn't looked to the turning lane. Out of the right corner of my eye came this station wagon screaming through to catch the green turn. I watched the skidding station wagon slide in towards the young couple.

The young man had just pulled on his girlfriend's wrist to usher her forward with him. Their arms went taught for a second as he pulled her with him. Then, she was coming along so their arms slacked up on an upward bridge. I saw his expression turn and meet the front of the station wagon screeching in so quickly. The sound of the car hitting his body with such a force cannot be forgotten. The liquid of his mouth shot up in a spray, as he was clipped up by the car with disgusting force. He had taken his girlfriend with him. She managed to be swept up by the corner of the car and up onto the right side of the windshield. The frapping sounds so quickly heard and the windshield totally shattered in by the two young bodies which now lay unconscious on the pavement.

People were screaming, "Call 911!"

The man who was driving the station wagon went around to the front of his car and saw what he had done. His hands went up as he collapsed in hysterics face forward on the pavement with his hands beating the ground like some helpless baby in the face of the fate that was happening. What was the point of all of this? I had a sick feeling in my stomach. I had just witnessed a tragedy. Why had I been facing the street and watching the whole scene unfold?

I had just watched the wonderful weekend dream end for the horror of this young couple. I had navigated all the way to this strange intersection- to this strange town just to see this? Our number was being called to go and eat ribs. There was nothing I could do. I asked myself just how sick and guilty I would feel if I went inside and began to eat like everything was normal- AND RIBS!

Somehow, my stomach conquered and I ate, but couldn't stop thinking about what I was doing and what had just happened. I felt pretty disgusted with myself for still being able to eat. I had seen the whole thing. I saw happiness and then tragedy seconds later, with sets of eyes watching the sun set on their lives.

Chapter 9

New Year's new fears

Thursday after work at Barnes & Noble Times Square, I was on the highest cloud I had ever ridden. The attitudes and seriousness of the psychotic workplace couldn't even scratch the happiness I felt. I thought of no end to the visit, all I could think about was how we would meet in the airport. Friday, at the airport, I nearly panicked when I found that she didn't arrive with her scheduled plane. I was so let down, while I prepared to rip the cute smile off the clerk if she wouldn't give me any information about what happened. Luckily, she told me that Claire had booked in on a later flight. Minutes seemed like hours, I waited nervously.

I couldn't resist hiding behind a paperback display at the passenger in/out ramp, while I beheld the moments of her emergence. Never had I felt so close to dreaming in reality. Her golden curls were backlit and to me she moved in slow motion as if I were being seduced in my own music video with the glint of dirty gray LaGuardia bustle in the background. There was a slight awkwardness that couldn't initially transcend the differences in our surreal experiences. She, nor I, could believe it was actually happening. I shook us back into talking by joking a little. I felt so close to her while she squeezed me as we bobbed in a Yellow cab that was mounted on springs, not shocks.

We laughed and frolicked when we landed at my sister Nancy's apartment at 1100 Madison Avenue, and I became more and more transfixed in her beauty. Ninety percent of our relationship transpired on the phone land line. The phone, since the beginning, had breached the social constraints separating us.

We dressed and walked merely a block to the Metropolitan Museum, and bathed in the space of expense and classical music -all in the name of Art. I had only just begun to realize the pains and pleasures the guy named Art would give me. With the dusk of the city on a Friday evening pouring through the walls, the musicians' harmonies and the sweetness of the violin, the glasses of red wine, all vibrated towards truth and harmony, and I was tasting the last of the fruit from the summer of 1992. I was certain later that everyone we met, while together, was some strange escort for us. It seemed to me that the guards on the floor had cleared all the people out just for us.

We abandoned the Museum around closing, then began a walk that was punctuated by several homeless people. One in particular thought I owed him something just because, "Hey, Hey heey man, come on little man, you got a beautiful girl there-spare some change?"

My first instinct is to say there are no words to describe that last weekend together. I called her Monday night, mainly wanting to make sure she didn't have some bad taste in her mouth after her visit. Then, I convinced myself into believing that I merely wanted to call to see if she had made it home O.K. Maybe one of those little voices convinced me that something had tragically happened. I loved her so much or so I thought, I didn't care that it was her breath that smelled bad, not my lack of self-esteem beaten down by my background. To my disappointment she was in a cheery mood, while I wanted her to be on my level of pain. I guess she just didn't have the problem of clinging to the cyclical nature of visits. You know, the arriving and the parting.

Hell, even though I liked my visits to New York in the past, I was always glad to get back to the safety of home. If I was Claire, getting back would be a relief from the intense struggling air in which we breathed, especially after rotten emotions so deep by my "loved ones" had been dumped on me at a rather impressionable age. I wondered if true lifelong love was possible at the age of fifteen.

The myth of my instant acceptance in the unknown land of NYC was fading. I had twisted and turned. I had burned and yearned for months. I couldn't move and I was paralyzed. I needed a focus. Focus is what I decided to do. I began to gather the information that I had learned about acting. I elected to find myself an apartment in the city because it looked like I was destined to stay a while.

One of the first actors that I spoke with worked at the same bookstore as my father. My father made the effort to hook me up with him so I could possibly learn a few things about the acting business. I was glad to talk to him. I had done some reading on the business of acting and found a few basics of the rigor of the guilded cage. Over ice cream floats near the bookstore he told me of the good places that I could take affordable classes if I wanted. I was always annoyed with people talking about classes and "study". I wanted to live, to really Act. He looked at my résumé I prepared. I had spent my time and money on a résumé that didn't address any specific industry, rather it listed all of my qualities and background. I didn't know the format was so crucial. I was coming from a place where you could reference someone whom you knew and that would be fine. I knew very little about how alien people were to the spirit of cooperation in New York. This young actor I met seemed like an intelligent database of people and places. He was asking me and wanted to relate with me upon all of these different works and plays. I was nervous because I knew how I was and yet was not confident enough to say, "I'm here to do it. I'm here to learn by doing and having fun at what I do." That was good enough for me. I didn't have to know anything special. I just relied on the feeling within. The feeling that I could do it, whatever "it" was. I felt I could really live the role of any character I chose or was given.

The experience of a New York audition shut me up for quite a while. I couldn't really tell people anymore that this was all I was really doing because it wasn't. Now I was in the business of looking for acting jobs and attempting to subsist along the way.

I wavered a bit about what path I could truly follow. I was running out of money (false-currency-construct) quickly. I was talking with my mother one night and made a plea, "I really could use a little money (false-currency-construct)." Then it came, the pain of being turned over to the wolves.

"I can't support you unless you are in school, I'm sorry."

It was a shocking turn of circumstance for my solitary and poorly financed NYC life. Pride felt I was a worthwhile investment. It meant and translated to the fact that what I was doing isn't respected and isn't viable to most of the work-a-day world. Yet the state of misery I was in didn't compare to the feeling of alienation I felt in the trash compacting University. I found no joy in that. I found no joy in not being able to relate to most around me. So there it hung in the balance, but I was so ticked off at my Mom that I quickly parked the phone in the cradle.

Mom wouldn't help fund my new life in New York, or at least not overtly help her youngest offspring intermittently. There was just barely enough money (false-currency-construct) somehow. I took a trip to the South and found myself with my cousin at a New Year's party in a very foreign land. It had been my home town area not too far before. I had taken care to surprise my true love. I remembered to write one of Claire's friend's phone numbers. I called this buoyant friend and reminisced slightly, then asked her where Claire would be at exactly midnight, 1993. More excited than I had recalled in years -I was going to surprise my love with an appearance highly improbable.

Having also headed out West to New Mexico after the family reunion of my Dad's side of the family, my cousins and I headed back for Texas. No one could know how extreme Hector had hurt me. I was chewed up and spat out by Hector -when he exploded violently towards me. Hector lost control on his little brother again. I had been out in the hard cruel "real" world for too long to take his shit. He wanted me complacently local as I had always been. He was one of my main demons in life steadily hating on me hiding in the closet of my mind heavily breathing the stench of unworthiness upon me. Occasionally overcoming the ego and father/brother training towards my self-disparagement, I am relieved and proud just to be myself and looking for my own treasures in life. I was limping and injured for quite a while. I hadn't remembered crying and heaving like that for so long. I justified everything. No one could understand or begin to understand how much Hector's words were like razors. I knew how far we'd grown apart, but his wrathful ignorant rage sunk to the core of me and weighed me down for some time.

I just couldn't capture or relate how much I hated Hector for his release that lasted all the way back to the family reunion. By the end of the ride, Hector was a lashing shark with my flesh hanging from his carnivorous chops. He had continued his yelling in the desert. It was all initially about me taking a shot at deer miles off out of range. The issue was such intense stupidity. I was showing my power, though, and it made my brother furious. For years, in order to keep peace, I had been passive with my environment. I was looking off into the distance where the continent was shaped by ancient shifts of the crust. They called this place the caprock in New Mexico. Uncle Ronny hadn't taken us to this place. We had taken ourselves there. I wanted to see nature, but Hector and my cousin Watt wanted guns. Watt's Dad had bought him a nine-millimeter Beretta for Christmas. Buying your kid a handgun for Christmas has got to be one of the most bizarre things.

Along with the lashing of my brother, came the information that he had no intentions of seeing me get back to Louisiana (at least not in his car). So, there I was, desperately on a mission to get home. I made this my project -so while on the road, I began to consider how I was going to get my ass to Louisiana. What was my rush? Why did I need to get back so desperately? I'm glad you asked because I wasn't ready to ask that question -so your asking has gotten my brain to think of why, truly why I had to get back.

I had convinced myself that I was loved by that Cajun queen. I was headed for Claire. Sure, there was family and plenty of old friends. There they were changing in as many ways as I was growing differently from them.

I was so happy what seemed to be the hardest difficulty was resolved in the simplest and most fun way. My uncle and aunt allowed young Watt to take me to Louisiana. I was very happy that we could hang alone and away from the influence of anyone else. We rode and had a glorious little road-trip. Watt was an aggressive driver. We wanted beer and tobacco -chewing tobacco. We both wanted to find the brand of tobacco that was locally famous in my childhood. Here we were, my cousin and I stopping at every roadside truck stop to get some

Applejack Chewing tobacco -but there was none to find. I began to wonder if I had really ever seen the stuff. Surely, these tens and twenties of people, whom we asked for the tobacco, knew or had heard at some point about Applejack tobac. They had not heard of the stuff, so we began the trip without.

I found myself watching the frenzied kids party in southern Louisiana from my little newly acquired New York point of view. The love that had fueled me all the way there was now unrequited. The girl I loved looked through me as if I was a ghost. She was possessed by spirits- alcohol. She looked right through me with her eyes swerving. She was falling down drunk and soon she faded into the background as I watched the swell of midnight alone in my maddened body. I watched the waves of excitement everyone felt as the old year came to a close and the new one began.

Nancy was coming back to NYC around the New Year, so I began to scurry to find a place to live in Manhattan, since everything that I knew of in my home area had fallen apart in dismantling visits of disillusionment. My first acting advisor came in handy because it looked as if he was looking to rent out one of his rooms in Brooklyn. I found out about this through another guy I knew at the bookstore. There was one problem, though, he had the intention of renting the place but he hadn't cleared this with his partner- his girlfriend.

He did call me back to tell me that he hadn't cleared the idea completely with Gina, but that I could come and look it over and have breakfast with them somewhere while they digested the idea.

The three of us got along fine, but she still didn't want to give up the extra room particularly because she had that space in mind for her International costume design exam preparations. She regretted the fact that Saul had involved me in this. I regretted it too because it looked as if I was running out of time and options.

I found myself feeling like a canker sore to my sister. My plans had fallen through and I was feeling more guilt about wearing out my welcome. I had seen my father do the same in her very house, with the harsh culmination of his stay appearing in the form of a liqueur bottle tumbling out of a closet meeting Nancy's head. Holy Hello!!! Wake up to the irony. That marked his eviction, since Nancy had proclaimed the space to be free of his drinking and smoking, but he subscribed to some naughty role reversal. Perhaps because of circumstance, or maybe circumcision, yet upon circumspection, we were all necessarily sneaky little kids..

I was uptight and in the living room of a social worker up around 207th Street giving her my references so I could supplement her income and stay in her apartment for a month or so up in Harlem. Ouch! I was not liking the situation, but I had to suck it up.

At a rather crucial last moment Gina called and again offered her apologies for taunting me with their apartment in Brooklyn. She told me of a friend down in Alphabet City who needed a third roomie in their three bedrooms (closets). Gina saved the day. I didn't even have to look at the place- nor did they really need to look at me. So I shortly moved in with Laurna, and the two cats (Chicken and Spider). René, the leaseholder of the place, was laid-up upstate with a collapsed knee.

I just read my drizzle, now, I see how pathetic people like myself in that case use vulnerability, perceived sweetness, sadness to arouse pity. Care, utter probing defensive sensitivity, is just one of many methods used as a survival mechanism to trap others in our web of boredom and loneliness of facing ourselves in this eternal self made prison. Over considerate hyper-diligence not wanting to hurt others' feelings, bullshit crap of a low self-esteem victim mentality. When I am happy and freshly accomplished I ignorantly step out into the world as the blissful wizard, sometimes goofy foolish lunatic ready for my other/ self attention trap springing. Myself and others hungry for attention, all so many levels of endless desire satisfying strategies endlessly. I owe myself to take care of myself. True love is no accepting ones own bullshit cannon and refuting other fuckers volley of their such said shit cannon as well.

Chapter 10
The Gangsta

It was a very cold morning and for once I woke with an air of excitement about the coming day. My eyes were a bit more open and not dreading my tread into the Bad wicked world. I held a smile to my strangers in the 'hood. This morning I felt no ill will. I was walking with a nice little gait out of Avenue D and onto the glassy iced streets of East Houston. I realized that I was early on the way to hand out menus in the frigid weather. I liked being outdoors seeing all the people, though, at least that was my attitude that morning. The unfriendliness of especially the business people of midtown never broke its gloomy consistency. Maybe they gave me the strength to be even nicer. I thought, wow, my niceness is really something unique. Little did I know that I needed to have their meanness in my life for a reason. I thought that since I was early and the sun was shining on the snow beaten dog shit on the sidewalk, that I'd go into a tiny middle eastern deli to have some coffee and an egg sandwich. The man behind the counter was familiar to me since I had frequented that place, yet in the blur of customers as I well knew from the bookstore, he didn't remember me. He began to chef up my order of a nice, greasy egg slop sandwich. I was grateful that the coffee and the sandwich had amounted to only one dollar and twenty-five cents, which was exactly what I had to my name, give or take a few pennies. In the custom from which he was from, he didn't ask me to pay and I sat inside eating. I had imagined eating outside, but felt that I needed to give myself the credit to stay inside because of my frigid future three hours outdoors in the area between forty-ninth and forty-second street. It was always my manager's decision what the exact tour of duty would be.

The door of the deli swung open to reveal a young gangster

wanna-be who wore the standard 'hood attire, as if to say, "Hey, if the shoe and everything else is too big, then wear it anyway,Yo!" He ordered one of the house specialties of which I knew nothing about. I knew he was fucked up on something cause he was obnoxiously ordering the guy behind the counter around. "Hey, Yo, make sure you trow in two of those rolls, G " He commanded. He had a youthful boyish appearance, yet he was tall and lanky. His eyes were hazed over and squinty. Little black marbles that would begin to hide under his eyelids, but then they would command a little curtain call. They would try to light up to attention, but it was useless. His mouth wasn't exactly cooperating either. He had a lazy slather about him. He received his much anticipated multi-compartment styrene lunch box. He towered over the platter, and while demanding hot sauce, he swaggered his head over it to make sure it had the appropriate smells-to make sure his eyes weren't playing tricks on him. I was amazed at how domineering people are to those who serve their food. I wondered why it isn't obvious to them that they are what they eat, and hating on the guy who serves it to you couldn't at all help that much. "I'm gonna count these mother-fuckin spinach rolls to make sure you ain't trying to rip my ass off. One.." He was dipping his fingers in the orange grease while pushing the rolls over in the platter, his fingers showed his careless inebriation, "two..tree..four, yea, they fucking all here,." now reduced to a mumble saying,"ya lucky mo-fucka." He then looked back at me and said, "Yo, bro this is the fuckin best grub in the world, these mofos may stink but they know how to cook up some mean shit."

I looked up from my egg sandwich and gave him a pleasant smile. Much to my dismay, that action ushered him over to give me more advice on their cuisine. I wasn't happy when I found him less than ten inches away from me. With his platter in his right hand, he draped his left arm around my shoulder as if I had been his party boy for the entire previous evening. He proceeded to rave of the food as I watched it smack in his mouth in motley colored strings mixed with his saliva. Then I caught a whiff of the orange grease. I was up in a flash removing his arm from around me. He stood back asking with his hands wide open as if I had breached a very special bond. "Yo, bro, I was just, Yo man tha.. that's..."

I said, "Look man, I didn't want you hanging on me."

Still unsatisfied, he slurred in offense,"Yo, bro, that's fucking uncool, I was just being friendly, and you gotta be a punk."

I said, "Look at you, your hands are all greasy." It was pointless and I knew no way out. He looked around and announced to his imaginary audience, "Yo, look, now the little punk's callin me greasy, you little white mo-fuckas, you all the same. You think we gonna fuckin dirty you're ass up. Man, I could have your little punk ass whacked. You habla that, bro, I could have your little punk ass snuffed."

I tried to make light of it all and put my head down, while taking a bite of my quickly cooling sandwich. He looked harmless, but I felt my reflexes pop when he was reciting how he should "pop" my ass right now. He demonstrated how his fist could "pop" in his left hand. I ignored him and felt a compression thug above my eyebrow, as his fist hit and glanced down, mashing my nose hard and even pinch my lip. It got my attention! I rose- immediately pushing him hard in the sternum while cocking my right arm like an archer drawing his bow. I drove him into the corner of the deli, simultaneously cramming his carton of food along with him. The orange grease was running down his incapacitated arm and jacket. I was microseconds from releasing my cocked fist, was thinking with adrenaline speed. I did not know him, nor his gang. I asked myself if I would be starting some strange cycle of war by this one gangster. I had to live in this neighborhood. There was no way out if he was part of a gang. Just then with a shocked expression that said it was all happening way too fast for him, he said, "Yo, yaoooo,yo I don't wanna fight a punk like you anyway. " I was relieved and released.

The irate Iranian who had jumped the sandwich counter equally blaming me for the trouble in his store, was ushering the gangsta out while he fumbled to recover what he had come in for-his food. He was gone. I saw him look both ways out on the sidewalk. I wondered, "Would he and some buddies be waiting for me? I finished my meal and began to pay. The Iranian said, "One dollar fifty."

Oh, shit, I had forgotten the extra twenty-five cents for cheese! I promised his non-humorous self that I would return to pay him the difference. I assured his frustrated self that I lived in the 'hood and that I'd be back. After what had happened, I couldn't believe he didn't offer the twenty-five cents. Leaving in disgust, I thought with sadness, "twenty-five cents?"

Mulling over the usual unhappiness when all the wealthy people would pass me on Fifth Avenue -shunning me in their cold distant reverie, an energetic little schnauzer dog sniffed my feet. I had cause to apprehend it might piss on me. As if my position on the street didn't award me with enough neglect. I was a walking billboard. "Free for All" was written on my head. I was handing out fliers for a restaurant nearby. The cold days were nearly over, so I was much more relieved about my future when at least the sun was on my side. The older naughtily smiling man was looking at me as if he were the dog, and I could have sworn that he had the same sense of smell coupled with the human mind. He sniffed my obvious disadvantage of poverty, and he was the first to appreciate my form and figure, for which he could find some use.

He asked me questions. I gave him his answers.

He told me the address of his house and invited me to come and see his mansion. I was welcomed to check it out. The thought of this inno-cently scrolled through my head the rest of my meager shift. Passing out paper to the touristically gifted who were fortunate enough to merely be visitors in this land. I found myself disgusted yet slightly seduced and excited about the possibilities of a rich man sharing some kindness with me -my own mother's bullshit programming of wanting someone to take care of the stupid and ridiculous details of food, clothing, and shelter in the high cost devilish shithole of subjugation. Soon thereafter, I rang the bell - the short fat little man arrived at the door talking to his rude little dog as if it had to be babied all the time. He was talking to the dog but I was meant to hear the story. He asked the dog if he remembered meeting the nice young man earlier that day.

He hadn't lied about the mansion. It had corridors and a wide expanse. We were in his office, a huge room with a big desk parked in the back. He asked me if I knew what an inferiority complex was. He began to tell me how he was retired from being a psychiatrist, but that he had written a book on the subject. After explaining to his satisfaction what an inferiority complex was, he issued me a booklet that he had written. It was, "Dealing with Inferiority Complexities."

There was his picture inside as I pretended to leaf through it as though I were interested. It was an immense dusty old house. It had been decorated lavishly but its time had passed and everything seemed like it needed more light. It seemed as if he could no longer upkeep from an era gone bye.

He told me he was a comedian and that he had a film of his show he performs on board cruise ships all over. He asked if I had time to watch it with him.

He ushered me into the back area of the house. He told me of a section in the North part of his house where his other guests lived. He said that he took care of them, and that they were actors whom he had met similarly to me. He said that I could live there with him in my own set -up if I worked out well. I wondered how in the fuck I would "work out well".

There was a large TV that was positioned so you could watch it in bed as if it were a little theater. He warmly and non-threateningly suggested that I get comfortable and take my shoes off and lie back in bed to watch the movie. I was on my edge. Here I was in some strange man's huge mansion watching him up on screen as he giggled to his own successes. I thought it was very bizarre but in light of my starvation and situation, I was willing to see this thing out a little further.

I found it very challenging to watch this little guy up on stage joking about things that I didn't find funny. I found it really corny and too "showbiz-like" . There were glittering tassels that floated in the background on the stage. I pretended to laugh, but I was getting very tired of it. He interrupted and asked if I was comfortable and if I was nervous? I told him that I was a little nervous. He said that was OK and that I could go all over on cruises with him and I could be his assistant in the show.

We continued to watch as I faded to thinking about some joke of a person I would be on some cruise ship being some little puppet toy. By the end of the film, he had cast his lures out on my waters. I was chasing the bait in my head. I was thinking of how nice it would be to continue to pursue my acting while in some security. At least being where there was food. I got the sinking feeling though, that my payment in soul would be much higher, yet I remained.

He reached over and appealed to exactly the pains I was feeling. He offered to take me away from it all- away from the streets and poverty. I was floating in a cloud of dreams. He reached over to my stomach and began to feel softly around. I had to admit that he had a nice touch, but I hardened disgustingly at the thought.

He pulled his hand away and asked how I felt about that. He asked if I felt OK with it. I tried to bring words to my mouth, but instead I thought of the sudden horror I would be entering. I thought of how much neater this could be if it weren't tainted by this cloud of blackness. I began to cry. I couldn't stop. I couldn't express what I was truly feeling so I went on with some fiction about my mother refusing to be intimate when we were children. He comforted me and mothered me with a big loving hug.

He didn't care about anything but his gratification and before he attempted anymore I found myself leaving. I don't remember how I got out of there or whether it was he or I who came up with the reason for my departure. I still was attached to the fantasy of the rich, so I gave him my number and he told me that he would be giving me a call to take me out for some Broadway shows soon. He told me that he thought we were on the way to a marvelous friendship and that we could go all over the world together.

I liked the idea of going all over, but it was the together that got me. My spirit must have saved me from that horrible darkness, because when he called I told him that the whole thing was wrong and that I wouldn't be "seeing" him again.

When I said this, he began to show his true colors. He began a tantrum of whys and all sorts of stuff. I politely interrupted him and told him that it was final and I hung up the phone. I felt a sinking feeling that I had turned down the easy life, but I was aglow with deep happiness and strength in my gutter six floor walk up closetment on Avenue D.

I laughed at the thought of how the man sounded. I laughed as I conjured up the thought of him melting with water like the witch in the Wizard of OZ complaining and bickering about not having his way all the way down to nothing!

So many other people have cute girlfriends that are in love with them. I wonder what life would be like for Claire and I if I had never left. Would she have continued to love me? That's what kills me is not knowing. Now I'm supposed to be some sort of a man. Now she likes this football stud named Duke who can't give her any justice to her intelligence. All I can sit here and do is ask why and be paralyzed and immobile. I don't have much of the will to create and I must have others' hurried agendas clouding my vision.

Have I truly ever been a threat to her parents, I don't understand really I fucking don't. That was the most intense magical weekend when Claire came to the Apple. She was so beautiful I overlooked her breath stinking and her not kissing much or allowing any physical intimacy -really it killed me but I never was one to force myself on a woman. The promises we told each other on the top of Beekman tower. She loosened her lips and I was riding so high. I loved her so completely. Now I don't even know if the issue is examinable. The pain has become so intense that there is no harm in asking for a response to the questions that have thorned my side for over a year now. I've never seen any malice in her treatment toward others. Even in talks about Stacy, I can't recall her ever being anything less than playful.

Ah, the way we used to talk for hours on the phone and how I yearned to do the same in person. When her parents started enforcing her phone bill and I began to exhaust my life line of cash just so I could hear her voice in that horrible nightmare if you are of no means in The city called New York. I was still the punchline of a poor joke and couldn't provide any sort of the living she requires. Sure it fuels a fire just a little but obviously it hasn't fueled the higher order of myself to help me figure a way out of this mire other than pulling the plug. I felt so incredibly worthless. Why did she play with my feet under the table? Why did I see the love light in her eyes? How could she pass up an opportunity to cancel her plans when she acted as if we had finally reunited. Nearly, but her friend was ever there.

Just as a cockblocking friend has always been there... My dopamine and my testosterone overrode my earth boring reality of slave work as usual -more fun to take the drug although it might always make matters worse. The unwanted drugs of my genetic, conditional, emotional, human patchwork made me especially talented and special -a prize prison bodysuit courtesy of the Devil King himself.

While their main receptionist went on vacation, I was temporarily working for a wealthy commercial editing house, and it seemed like a nice little reprieve from my frozen midtown sidewalk curtain call. Although I was dealing with a rather sick money-dominated environment, I was making ten dollars an hour and feeling relieved compared to all the hustling and hard work I was going through. The winter was also extremely harsh, and for once in a while I was in a place that didn't hoard its food. In other words it felt less like I was submerged under rats in the rat race.

There were all sorts of things that I could suddenly do because I was making some decent money (false-currency-construct). I was able to buy professional headshots, pay the rent, build my marijuana grow closet, fly to Ft. Lauderdale for my friend Joey's wedding, and I was able to save money (false-currency-construct) for a retreat Nancy and I were attending for New Years. Once I knew that I was going on this retreat, my holidays were improving considerably. I could laugh when others talked about the parties and such of which I was not invited, because I felt like I was going to do something special. Instead of finding myself hung over on the first dreadful day of the New Year, I would be nestled somewhere in the mountains away from the hustle, unrestricted and in nature.

This editing house where I worked brought in clients from big named corporations. The whole thing smelled of money (false-currency-construct) and politics (third party belief parasites). I couldn't get over how the clients were treated by everyone. Everyone would have to go down for the sake of the clients and the deadlines. I knew the producer of the editing house through my roommates, and to the others I was such an oddity that I was allowed privileged information in their recurring soap operas. Cynthia, my producer "friend", loved to smoke weed and I was acquiring quite a passion for it myself. I was daydreaming about acting all the time. I was content in removing myself from the politics because I could harmlessly watch everything. I felt I had nothing to lose. I felt that I was getting paid a nice little amount of money (false-currency-construct) to be the house jester. That is what I pictured myself to be and it served its purpose till it was time to move on. The editing house was way up on the 27th floor in a very nice space. There was plenty of light and plenty of people uptight, yet it was considered creative. Definitely more fun than most offices I'm sure.

One day while I was looking at the name of the owner on the business card, I found that you could easily spell out "ill will". There were all sorts of interesting little ill things happening there too. Cynthia was a fiery little red-headed lesbian who could manipulate like no other I had met in NYC. She would slink around making little deals and side slithers- pretending to be everyone's friend. She really did have some sweet naturisms, after all she was a country girl from upstate New York. Abuse and misunderstanding had brought her to the big rotten hustle like many others.

The film school and the common relation between the lot of girls I was involved with was Suny Purchase. That was the credential that was tossed around at most of the parties they threw. I found the groups all a bit crusty with their wanna be stars of sophistication. Cynthia was hung up on Madonna. Her eyes told of a lusty future in which they would meet someday. She was well connected and she would use her connections to get herself in the presence of this masterful woman who had made her way to the top perhaps by simply recognizing some of the shallow blockages that exist all over America.

Back to the opera at hand. There was a beautiful young editor's assistant that was pleasing to the cultured, commercialized eye. My eyes were of this brand then too. She was lean and dressed with all attention to detail. She had a little voice that was firm but locked up in her throat. The important thing was that she didn't look all that happy. I think a lot of men enjoy finding an attractive young woman who aren't really emotionally available. They hope that they can pair up their own unavailability.

I had a crush on this girl, but it was nothing devastating. I just wanted a bout of what it would be like to swim around with such a fish. There were darker and deeper things going on though. I spent much of my time in that office pretending to be busy and intercepting calls as the temporary receptionist. Sometimes, I wouldn't even pretend to be busy- I would just watch and jest more and more when tensions rose with illusionary stresses in the office. I watched how the owner would get stressed, then he would go about commanding people to do stuff with lack of any emotion or consideration. Other times, he had the sparkle in his eyes and the playfulness of a cocky child. He exuded ownership, power, and money (abundant false-currency-construct accumulator). These were the true devilish tunes that made everyone hop.

Everyone made little jokes about it, but yes there were actually phones in the bathroom next to the toilet. I imagined the man who had to install these phones. Later, I guessed that he would be out bullshitting with the fellas or laughing at a barbecue about how these crazy advertising executives who had to have phones next to their crappers.

There was a little secret that entered my ears (one of the little ones about the owner). Chill, the owner, had to have his own little bathroom because he had some serious problems being able to give a shit. Constipation is thought and problem of so many human affairs. I definitely have had trouble contributing my crap sculpture to the municipality on the toilet. I didn't even know that there was a second bathroom until one day when I needed it badly and was waiting around in the hall. Out of curiosity, I opened a door and stumbled into Chill's bathroom. Cynthia saw me coming out and warned me in a very secretive way and whispered, "Nobody uses Chill's bathroom. He doesn't like it at all. See he has a problem taking shits." I looked amazed at the fact that he is such a smooth looking dude with all of his exuding -but here she is telling me that he can't make a decent bowel movement with this tiny smug little grin on her face. I'm thinking, wow, we all work for this dude. She continued, "No, Eliot, it's not funny- it's serious. Shut up." I was just feeding into her bullshit. Kind of rude and disrespectful of her and me really. Make fun of the guy in power, a way to cheat some false power from the overall boss situation.

I could never take Cynthia seriously because when she was trying to be serious half the time, her other half was laughing with me. It was just like church in childhood -it just made me laugh harder!

Once, when a call came in for Chill, I went into the screening room where they were previewing their star editor's work (some final copy for a big telephony corp. commercial) and announced to Chill the person calling and which line the call was on. I was a little nervous giving him his calls personally, nevertheless I thought I did it with eloquence. The person on the line sounded familiar and acted as if he knew Chill well, so I didn't ask for the company name.

Chill was in one of his prankish moods and wanted to give me a little hassle. He asked me what company this person was calling. I confessed I didn't know. He asked looking around to his pack of media hounds, "Eliot, well how in the hell are you ever going to move up in this business?"

"I'm not planning on moving up in *this business.*" I responded without hesitation. I giggled and so did the rest of the room.

"That's a good answer." He said, while smiling a wonderful smile.

For once, I felt I had articulated the truth flawlessly. I didn't know how to move up, and perhaps my trapped earth spirit never wanted to really, but to free all these miserable souls, well, that was the reason for writing this book. I cheered for hours. I knew they thought their business was all important. It was the business of magic and illusion. They could make an advertisement attractive to the masses. They could do this with creativity and stealth. They relied on the fact that they were in the beacon of the Western world and that they could shine their coolness on the rest of the planet with sheer confidence. They ate the best sushi in this hemisphere. I wanted deeper than hype.

When I got back in touch with my sister about some retreat she was talking about, I didn't know how I was going to afford it, but I did know that it sounded great. I had been exposing myself to the surface and superficial for a bit too long, so the sound of getting up to the Adirondacks Mountains for the entire weekend of New Year sounded great. I told my sister that for sure I would be attending with her..

My passion for the moment was making Christmas cards for everyone and making a nearly self-sufficient little marijuana garden up above the threshold of my tiny room on Avenue D and Houston. The room was a shoebox, but I speculated that I could make a nice little garden. Because of my job at the editing house I was able to buy a High pressure Sodium lamp and all the necessary valves and pumps I needed. It was really a little marvel. The whole platform was slanted to where the runoff water pumped up to the plants from a reservoir -then would trickle back into the reservoir. Both the light and the water cycle were on timers so it was nearly self sufficient. It was up so high that I really had to have it automatic. Since the project wasn't fully complete, I had several plants that were down on the floor. Spider and chicken, the two cats in the house, were just as excited about my new growth, but they couldn't wait until the harvest. As a result I lost several plants to their fat bellies. Chicken was really the fat slather cat, yet tough as steel -a ghetto cat. Spider was fit and active. I took the remaining plant and began treating it to the powerful light along with other techniques that I had learned from reading about the science of home growing.

I was becoming a member of a little loft playhouse down on the Bowery. I learned much from their marijuana factory. There was a secret compartment where there were many plants and a much bigger scale to support all of their smoking needs. Although, the parties and the herd was eventually too much for their crop. One part was dedicated to growing, and the other part was dedicated to blooming the females for actual smoking. They would often dry the buds freshly picked right in the microwave. I was more into the natural way of doing things. The artificial light was bad enough for me. I found that the chemical hydroponics and the microwave gave it an edge that wasn't all too pleasant. In the beginning, though, it did the trick.

My friends from the theater company were glad to remind me of what I would miss for New Years. My friend Chris painted pictures of the glorious parties the loft-playhouse had thrown in the past. His young graceful leading man body was up on his own stage he had created himself. He was their leader, ushering his party to watch him, their temporary festive benefactor. In a drunken rage he threw a surplus of joints out to the smoke-hungry crowd. They were all together over-drinking and over-smoking until they were all successfully red-eyed Zombies. I was amazed many times how I even made it home without being waylaid by all of the supposed violent pirates that haunted the Bowery and on down into my home slum Alphabet City. I felt that if I missed this world-spectacle New YEARS' party of theirs that my acting future in their company would be placed a little further down in their rating books. This one guy was as close to a cyborg that I had ever come to see. He was always busy it seemed with some little covert mission. He was a loft-proclaimed Roller-blade expert. He controlled the loft's successful horticulture hide-out that kept them all happily high with hydroponic marijuana. I don't mean to sound harsh because all of these guys were warriors out there "doing it" everyday. The more of their herb I smoked, the more I became unclear as to what that "doing it" was. The cyborg had a cute little girlfriend who was absently devoted to this guy as he was his own silence. He was such a contrast to the whole scheme of public relations in which most of the actors were involved. He was a behind the scenes man who managed all the technical aspects of living in the city. The actors had a hard time keeping up with these things because it was their job to be constantly at the cutting edge of abstraction and entertainment. I was discovering that my new found friend was quite a genius as far as people relations went. He naturally understood the compulsions of people that were completely different from him. He understood that there were people who could and would happily fill any role in the operation as they needed. He had created a cocoon of support around him to further his cause. He had a multi-faceted power point relationship with his group. Together as a group they would emerge from the bohemian conditions in which they lived. The loft-playhouse was named Bliminal Stage. Their name meant that they were passing through a period of perception and approval. Finding their way through the sensual threshold, pushing their boulder up the mountain.

I was bombarded by all the things that were going on for New Years. It seemed everywhere I turned, I learned of some party happening. I was solidly happy with the fact that I was going off to the mountains to breathe fresh air and do things that I had never done before. I would be exposed to all of these eastern things like yoga, t'ai chi, and meditation. I had no problems with the fact that I was leaving and that I would be waking up on the first of the new year with something quite different from a hangover.

Given I had the happy connect, one of my last errands was to stock up on Marijuana for Cynthia and the group at the editing house. I put in my two cents so I could go off to the mountains with some nice Jamaican bud. Everyone was relatively happy. The editing house was always sending me around in cars, but this time I was really excited about the mission. I was going to this place down in the lower East side. It was a store run by a bunch of Jamaicans that fronted itself badly as a candle shop. It was near the Hell's Angels. I knew little about both cultures there on that street but I loved the excitement of it all.

I told my cabby to wait and I'd give him a little extra for his trouble. I entered the shop and found that they had done a little remodeling. I acted as if browsing around looking for incense and other smelly items. I had to figure out how their process had changed. I saw that the back wall, which had a high counter and a fat woman standing behind the counter was no more. Instead, the back wall was paned with mirrored clapboards where there were shelf hangers on which to put items.

In the past, I had asked once for a small bag of "kind" and a brownie, their supposed "specialty". She would look at me skeptical until I plead my innocence and assured her that there was no risk in me buying any of their other souvenir type goods and no chance would I "sell" them out to the authorities..

I was a little nervous about not knowing the new code or process. I did know that they had to be selling because otherwise they couldn't possibly stay in business with all the dusty products that they had lying around. I was looking around the mirrored wall in the back for some sort of drawer-anything? There, I saw an outline of where the drawer could possibly have been cut out of the wall. I knocked and the drawer popped out immediately almost as if it were saying, "OK, what the hell took you so long, damn it!"

Out it came and I stuck my stack of money (false-currency-construct) into it. I had put in one hundred dollars. Forty dollars for the good stuff and sixty for the better bud. I began the discourse with the guy behind the wall. It took quite a while because they had changed their bagging and pricing scheme too. I was relieved to find everything going so well. I walked on clouds as I neared my petit vacance.

So much energy was in the room as all the impressionable ears listened to the secrets that Mom and Dad never whispered about in those magical hours before bedtime. Storytime, and to see someone tell **one** so enthusiastically laced with so much lore. It had to be special knowledge. Most of the people in the room besides the faculty had spent their money (false-currency-construct) to be in the scene of mountains and "holistic" learning.

He spoke about the underlying layer of energy that had followed the group from their previous lives wherever that might have been. There were quite a few people, to my surprise, that were from different locations besides the city. It seemed that the stress crinkles were shown in lesser degrees though from any one that hadn't come from the Big

Apple. It seemed to me the New Yorkers were special for being here and that it would take lots of energy to heal them for the New Year.

It was where I had come from. Many brought their styles and acts with them into the mountains. How quickly I discovered the diversity of reasons for which people had come to the mountains. In spite of the grand expense of the weekend, I was really happy that the food would be catered. For the first time in years I had a little break with healthy, organic, vegetarian meals.

I had carried a little trend of mine all the way to the bus leaving the city. Sometimes, when an exciting trip is ahead, I squeeze in every bit of fun and procrastination that I can before leaving. As a result, I was very tired and found myself happily nodding off in the bus that was taking us up into the highlands of upstate New York.

One curiosity that I found as I nodded off was that I was belching all the time. Usually, I belch and I'm clearly aware of it-in fact- I usually force it out to see how I can alter the sound. An antisocial little habit. The burps are usually from something that I've hurriedly eaten, but this was not the case on the way up to the Boomerang Center. My head would nod down to my chest and up would rise this little creeping burp. I was too amazed to be annoyed by the fact that it was waking me up everytime it happened. I couldn't wake up fully to really count the burps and reposition, and I know that it wasn't a dream because my sister later confirmed the fact that I was making weird sounds.

I was already stunned by the quality of air and the hushing quality of the fresh blanket of snow that was being reapplied all the time. I was already sneaking away to smoke my weed pipe and ravish the beauty of the evergreens. I was in a very playful space and lamented the fact that everyone was in their middle-ages. It was apparent that I was the youngest at this retreat.

Everyone filed into the cafeteria. The anxiety about who would get the best room and the best view (in all consistent competitive behavior of the rats). I felt the same urges as well. I just let it slide because I figured I would get whatever room I deserved, plus I was just too happy to be there. The teachers came up one by one to talk of their teachings and to give an outline of their classes. Everyone was speaking from the heart. Heart disease and attack currently ranks as the number one dis-ease.

It is the heart that is important. No matter how earnestly Nichiren prays for you, if you lack faith, it will be like trying to set fire to wet tinder. Spur yourself to muster the power of faith. Regard your survival as wondrous. Employ the strategy of the Lotus Sutra before any other. "All others who bear you enmity or malice will likewise be wiped out." These golden words will never prove false. The heart of strategy and swordsmanship derives from the Mystic Law. Have profound faith. A coward cannot have any of his prayers answered.

With my deep respect,
Nichiren

One of the women coordinating the event, in conjunction with a holistic learning center, introduced the new President of the Ocean Center located in SOHO -Manhattan, who was also teaching T'ai Chi. He was a large man with a dynamic intensity and his eyes looked mysterious. He knew how to tell a good story. His eyes sunk back into this head while using the power of his body language to give the opening speech of the New Year's retreat. An opening welcome- a message to inspire those who had come. It wasn't a campfire story. It wasn't lit by candlelight, but he had the same look of mystery that the candle gives a person from underneath.

He spoke of everyone feeling the fear of a new place and the new surroundings with lots of new faces- total strangers. He foretold the closeness that would develop over the weekend. He told of how the lines and grimaces would disappear soon into the next day. He spoke of coming together as in the old days- to share in the ritual of life, and to share what has been learned.

Everyone was transfixed as we had all come seeking meaning. Erroneously, he talked about the ancient days when we might have been animals- when the organs hung from the spine while on all four legs they would sway with a natural stride. In the days when the massaging of those arteries was natural. Now, he told us that we would learn techniques for freeing up that energy and posture to bring the organs back into their natural alignment. This would counteract sitting in chairs and standing around having our organs packed down into the stomach. Evidently, an "Old Empire" Priest turned New Age charlatan guru. People don't know, so they make it up or they read it from some other human and act like they know. I am not exempt from any of these accusations in my human befuddlement.

In spite of the used car salesmen, in those days I got in touch with my spirit and felt at peace with many issues in my life. Although the yoga was making me hack up some of my habits in coughing and allergy spells, I still managed to pull away with as much value as I wanted. I wanted to explore the winter playground much more than most people. Climbing up the side of the mountain was a bit more exciting to me at times. The local animals began to come out once the vibration of the new-comers calmed down a bit more. The deer would come out and frolic in the snow. It was beautiful to watch while doing yoga inside the warm, windowed barn. They would come down into the valley and bravely pluck the shriveled apples from the trees.

I kept expelling gas the whole time. I couldn't figure out if it was the altitude or the high legume organics, but it was incredible. I was thinking that yoga was teaching how to breathe out of a new orifice.

The moon was full on the eve of the New Year. The campfire was blazing. The fire allowed me to stay outside looking up to the wonderful stars and the circular rainbow that encircled the moon. Creation itself had framed it in a universal spectrum of colors. I noticed it after a little witch had guided us in a purification ritual and after she had called in the four directions and the wind from each. The wind did as it was asked. it said, "No problem, you guys are doing this- I can allocate a little wind in the directions that you ask for."

I was surprised at how everyone wanted to go indoors to the party and dancing, as I found myself compelled to stay outside with the fire until it had consumed most of its fuel.

That night, later at the dance, deer were hanging out right outside the sliding glass window. They were out there putting their noses up to the glass. I kept thinking of them coming in and sipping on hot glasses of tea -enjoying the party. I couldn't help personifying them. Later several people were able to feed them fresh apples there at the door. One touched woman let a young buck take one right out of her hand.

It was the first time ever that I felt totally at peace with my life. I did have a shadowing thought that if I didn't pursue the preview of the path that was revealed to me at the retreat center, I would start to sink into my old ways. I would start to detest the hardship and the painting of other people's walls in sites that paid only cash for the work but nothing for my future preservation or hopeful freedom.

Upon my return, I got a call from an actress I knew from Manhattan Brewing Company in which I worked. She left a message that sounded important. I thought that we had left each other in rather bad standings; however, she had remembered me and was passing on a chance of a role in a play. I didn't analyze why or how. I just got on the phone and called her. She told me that she had broken into a discussion at the brewery with two directors pouring over headshot photos at their dining table in the brewery. It turns out that they were looking for a Huckleberry Finn in their upcoming tour all over Europe. I was excitedly drawn to the possibility and soon was having a nice conversation with the director. I loved the way in which it happened. I loved the fact that for once the interview wasn't completely cold. I had someone that spoke of me instead of me selling myself. I enjoyed the break and lapped it up.

Soon, I was in a huge loft that was shared by the playwright of Mark Twain's book with several working photographers during the day. I was talking to the director, seeming to be getting along just fine. He talked of how hard and exciting it would be on the road. I lapped it up hungrily and told of my days spent sometimes feeling the nostalgia for the need to be on the move- how I would look out onto the East River and want to be on a boat leaving for somewhere- anywhere away from here. I fancied that this was a little like Huckleberry himself. I had no qualms. I wanted this role. I met the Potential Jim who was reading for the part. I also knew that he had done a job with that company before.

I asked him if we could go into another room and read together just to get comfortable. We did. Soon we were up in front of the eyes that would decide. I was exhilarated by the reading. Out came this Huck who I had never known before. This Huck came out and wanted the part. Pumped with adrenaline, I left the audition and was thanked for my "good work". I felt that I had generated sincere smiles. I bounded out on the cold streets feeling warm and fuzzy -singing at the top of my lungs.

That night I knew that I would be doing this tour, and a little bit later than I expected, the director called and told me that I had the part, if I'd like to have it. I couldn't think of any reason why I wouldn't take it. I couldn't think of any ties here in the States that I would really have to make any efforts to cut.

It was that quick, and three weeks later I had a leading part under my belt along with a play that at many times had been cut on the spot from two and a half hours to one and a half. I was sad many times when I endured the cuts. It was hard to not take the cuts personally. It was not only I who suffered though- so did Jim. So did the play and the content of Mark Twain. I watched our show lose the intellect and quality that had made Twain's words live on in the first place. I chalked it up but I was too stressed with the load of my responsibility to jeopardize the part that I had so gratefully landed.

In the subsequent nights I had bad dreams that prophesied my unhappiness with the director and the structure of the "business" these guys were running.

Chapter 11

Your Huckleberry friend

<u>Here begins Journal excerpts for HUCK January 1, 1994</u>

January 1, 1994 Thursday

The city had a hard time letting me leave. It seemed the gravity was stronger than leaving the earth's atmosphere. My eye is wandering on wandering eyes. Now that the pursuit of work is over, in one dimension, the work and the pursuit begin simultaneously in another dimension- but I think I am adjusting well considering the scheme of things.

January 28, 1994 Friday night in München

I have so many reasons to be happy, but none to be alone. A momentary loss of touch and familiarity. It is strange how one man's leaving is another's coming home. I have no matches to light my incense, so maybe I'll learn the word and go ask for some.

It turns out that Gina, who had saved my booty by finding my homey little slum closet in Alphabet City Manhattan, had passed her Fashion design exam and decided to move back to her homeland Germany. München was my first stop in Germany.

January 30, 1994

I just talked to Gina- she was quite shocked that I am here in München. Oh well, I guess I am too. My dream last night was intense- a brown storm rising above a tree line with big leaves carried at the front of the storm. I turned away from the storm, which seemed to be happening in the backyard in Opelousas (my hometown).

There was a huge gravity pulling me backwards towards the storm. I turned away from the storm and tried to get away but it was pulling me so hard that my feet were digging in the ground.. I didn't get very far and Denny was throwing tennis balls at me. I returned a couple of throws which were complete duds.

My first show-

So there it was- a huge gymnasium sized auditorium lay out in front of us. There must have been at least seven hundred chairs that lay flat straight out in front of me. All I had was the confidence that I could do it. I wasn't thrilled with the fact that it might be this hard on my voice the entire time. The feeling of how it was to be when the show was set into motion. There would be no stopping until intermission. The crowd roared and a globe of energy shot up my spine and insulated me from harm.

February 2, 1994

Yesterday we did our first show in Reutlingen, theatre Listalle. The audience seemed to enjoy our show very much. The energy was so good at the beginning of the show just by the enthusiasm of the audience. I said to Gunther, "You could feel they wanted you to succeed, unlike many times in New York you feel like they want you to fail." I'm beginning to realize why so many musicians and talent go on tour in Europe.

Walked through Balingen last night with Gunther and John found a waterfall.

Just played the Stadhalle (state theatre) in Offenburg, an incredible arena and complex. Beautiful dark reddish stained wood. The quality and craftsmanship was amazing. It was so much easier projecting my voice than in Listhalle, our first performance. There are so many beautiful women here! I am amazed.

When I dove to kill the pig, I slid right off the stage. I thought it impossible, but they must have used some special German polish on the floor because I used every brake I could think to use. I don't know how but I managed to hold on to the imaginary pig. Everyone in the audience must have thought it was part of the show! The only thing that really distracted me was that I wasn't distracted, and that it wasn't terror that struck me when I realized what had happened. The show is different every time so far. I managed to keep one hand on the pig and pull myself up with the other. It was a rush and a swirl of adrenaline. I don't know how I pulled that off and how the hell I pulled myself back up on stage.

The stage was as high as my upper body. The other thing that amazed me was that no one in my crew saw it! Ha! At first, I was annoyed that no one saw it, but then I learned how they would have loved to trademark something in honor of that flight. They didn't express too much amazement- instead they told me how lucky I was that they hadn't seen it because it could have become the subject of much harassment.

There is no way to predict exactly what can happen in one and a half hours of a complex system. We are traveling players- playing off what the world gives us.

February 2, 1994

I enjoyed today in Bensheim where the Hausmeister was very friendly and set-up and take down was relatively painless. I couldn't help scanning the audience, even when there were lines to be had. A brave young girl named Katia brightened my day after the show. No matter how awkward it seemed to her friends, she stuck it out and got autographs and gave me her picture. "I loved you and your show." What were her real thoughts in the midst of all the trifle clutter?

I was a bit saddened by how fleeting the meetings seemed.

It is painful to be patient and earnest in the midst of such prematurity. The challenge for whatever is confidently looking fourteen years old, then changing back to myself- which soberly, I'm trying to understand the peace of mind and happiness I had weeks ago.

Meditate on pulling the chords that attach you to people.

Even the cards seem to be saying the same thing.These were notes on a relationship I left in the States: Did she drill herself into my mind, or do I really like her? Just when I had gotten so comfortable being alone. Now I am bombarded with thoughts and lustful visions. I like the way it was before. It's not right-I don't love her for all the right reasons. When I'm stoned, I am not afraid to be happy. I am not afraid to reverse my decisions of unhappiness. When I am stoned, I am guilt-free. When I'm stoned I don't long for things beyond my control.

February 5, 1994

i am smoking a cigarette in my room. i just went up to talk to the beautiful woman at the Hotel desk. i made up some bullshit to talk about. She did help me for the future. i want to masturbate really badly, but i think that it will just hurt me more in the long run-but smoking this cigarette won't? Huh? Maybe living with a smoker has passed the addiction on to me even though I was constantly annoyed by the smoking, maybe the second hand smoke was enough to get me. I feel so sexual right now, and I haven't the means, energy, or experience in this foreign land to go out and find the one that I love and who loves me. I tore up the really horrible thoughts I wrote last night in my drunken stupor.

I'm lighting another cigarette. This noxious noise. My head clamors the pain of being without the friend I've made in nature. A plant that takes me away from the attachments, demons and hate my mind creates. I feel its tightness coiled around my shoulders threatening to cut off the beautiful energy I thought was mine. Feeling so unconnected and with a wrench so big and my bolt so small. The head is the plumber with no problem at all.

Meditate on pulling the chords that attach me to other people. I'm sorry but you are asking me to be strong- to love strangers without fear. I had only just learned to do that with the help of my buddy the plant. I wish you grew in the gardens of everyone's hearts. I dreamed I was floating peacefully and was one with the water. They couldn't catch me in Marco Polo.

After the show yesterday in Ansbach, Germany, a beautiful girl came backstage and we started talking. She said that she kept shushing her friends during the show because they kept talking about how cute I was. She said that she was nearsighted and she had now come to see what was so captivating about this "cute" guy.

I asked her why her wrist was bandaged and she told me that it happened while fencing. Her friend went for her shoulder but popped her wrist instead. I was feeling so many things that I could barely concentrate. (a common thing for me- I was sometimes so fired up after a show that I wanted to stay in the euphoria) The adrenaline was still pumping, I was getting paid, the van was getting loaded, and there were girls outside peeking through bushes.

<u>Thirty minutes later **all** of this was gone and the girl had disappeared</u>

as quickly as she had appeared. I wish I could talk to her now. Why must it be so tragic? Why must I feel responsible for the rest of the cast's feelings?

Later, Gunther told me that he passed three girls and a dude- they giggled when he passed by so he approached them and asked what was up. They said that they had seen the show and liked it very much.

"Where is the rest of the cast?"

"They're eating somewhere," Gunther replied.

"Where?" They asked.

He went on, but I wandered off in my imagination. Tell 'em where, I thought. Where are they? I don't want to be a stranger in a strange land, but I am, indeed.

I told Stacy about the masturbating dream, but I didn't tell her about all the uncertainty floating around in my head. Or how much I was thinking about Claire. **FREE** my mind of all this guilt and fear. I owe nothing to either of them.

February 6, 1994

I'm sitting in the window sill of Rm. 204 of the Rosenhoff Hotel, rural Linz, Austria. Played Regensburg yesterday afternoon. Our first mostly adult audience. They loved it! We got a sitting ovation. We were called out five times. The house was three ranks up and circular-built in the times when theatre meant a great deal. Last night I had a killer movie dream.

A Japanese guy was telling us how to make different tracks on the snow with our crop dusters. He wanted different loops and patterns. Meanwhile, the snowboarders were hauling ass and jumping the mounds so gracefully.

Over on one of the hills, there was a sled and a few snowboards parked on the slope. I saw a group of guys run to go get their boards and I ran behind them to catch the fun and grab a board too. I had a feeling that there wasn't a board for me, but I hoped that someone would give one to me anyway, because I might have been the leader? So I watched them jump gracefully and melt quickly down the little slopes.

Suddenly, a rocket ship jetted out of the woods. I noticed that it had its refueling arm extended. Then an F-16 jetted from 3 o'clock heading away from the snowboarding camp. It was incredible to watch the thrust and power as these machines shrieked over the white snow. Just then, the rocket really fired its engines-until then it was barely moving it seemed. The new thrust sent it screaming up in the same trajectory as the F-16, uniting in its path. The rocket quickly plugged itself in the F-16 from above, then swung down to the lower right of the jet, as if the fuel line was a universal joint.

The rocket then sprouted these beautiful blue anodized wings and landing gear. Meanwhile, I was watching the reactions from the pilot of the F-16. His reactions seemed to be stereotyped in the sense that he was cocky but a little fearful looking.

The two crafts separated and now I zoomed up to the window of the rocket's cockpit. I was confused because the pilot of the rocket was the same guy as the pilot of the jet. The rocket pilot then tried to land in what looked like a rocky valley, but then I saw the clearing that he was aiming for- he touched down. Even with the parachute deployed, he couldn't pull off the landing. He couldn't slow for the quickly approaching edge of the cliff. I was in the cockpit as we slid right off the edge. It seemed that we had plenty of time to recover and do another flight loop, but it just didn't happen.

Next I was with a woman doctor and a military man. He said, "Yea, but he did a pretty good job for a synthetic."

She argued the ethics and said that was accomplished with only two life crystals. She asserted that the pilot was made with only two of the crystals.

My later dream was some angst and authority failure with the play/tour director.

February 7, 1994

I felt selfish writing to myself, but after all, I'm the one who has to keep my sanity. Dullness is such a sharp thing. I've been feeling so much aggravation that it has become a great burden on my neck. I feel stupid, untalented and worthless to be perfectly honest. Character types, fuck, who would think that I'd come from NY with such rot. I must separate myself. I must go with the flow of my individuality. We just played two shows in Memmingdon. The first younger audience loved us, the second audience couldn't wait to leave.

I had this flash of a feeling when I felt like Gunther, Prick (Director), and I were suspended in time, just for a second. It was the moment rearing its head on stage. I looked and I was Huck, Gunther was Jim, and Prick was the King.

February 9, 1994 Wednesday

Just played Memmington after three shows yesterday. Two in Linz, Austria, and then one in Memmingen last night. Fran Marcantel, the producer, was in the audience, and our little group really came together. The hotel was so nice last night-a big bathroom that I soaked my bones in -very thankful for that. They really loved the show last night. the only thing that bugs me is that there is not always enough time and interaction with the people that see the show. They disappear, we pack up and leave.

The sun has poked out to remind me how much I miss that. It's hard for me to tune into the **real** influence.

February 11, 1994

Played Rüsselsheim this morning. So many beautiful kids in the audience. I had a fun show, I feel Jim and Huck need to develop quite a bit more. I am the lead and I will lead! A kid repeated my line when the Duke said, "You'll be the town crier!"

I said, "Allright!"

Some kid in the audience said, "Allright, duh"

I took it as a compliment because he was making fun of my naiveté which **is** my character. I was actually happy that it inspired such a reaction- it's like duh- Huck get with the program. Yes!

I long for a real friend, one who can give and receive good meaning-ful conversation. I find it takes a lot of energy to be alone and in my purpose. When Grump and Gunther constantly play on sex and girls-every beautiful woman, picture, or waitress. I am thinking the same and that disturbs me because I want to love and be loved just as much. All of our shoulders are calling for massages. I wish everyone would

<u>stop joking and picking and get real. There is so much fun and humor to be shared. Forced humor is the worst. The group and I were reaching for anything. Becky and Prick smoke cigarettes like feigns. I am eating meats, fats, frieds, and chocolate. All of the comfort foods that bring me further away from my soul. Stubborn and corrective when we load the set and put it up. It makes me so angry that my sarcasm is emerging, instead of my forgiveness. I find moments of peace. I still fucking choke when I sing the damned intro song. They're taking everything so serious. I think that I truly want to have fun.</u>

Yesterday in Remscheid, Jenny and Gina came backstage. I was thrilled for a moment. I was thinking wow, the power of theatre! I want to smoke a peace pipe so badly. I am so lost.

(end partial euro huck journal entries)

I couldn't find many outlets for my frustrations of being on the road. I would often find myself out on a dance floor working my body into a frenzy. I loved it. I was a wild dancer on tour. I would find a club and shake my body until I couldn't shake it anymore. Often that would be my meditation. Luckily, I had Gunther who continued non-stop during the entire tour. I could always find that he wanted to go out. Clubs are universal. People are everywhere and they all go to clubs and drink. It seemed to be an undercurrent throughout the cultures I visited.

Besides my journal, I never felt that good about dumping my problems on other people. I wrote letters, though. Many were filled with conditions of the tour. It was only to Julie (the girl that had agented me) that I made known my true feelings.

I learned because of her liaison nature, she found herself in the Publishing Industry. She said her passion kept her promoting other people in any division of the arts she attempted. She wanted to sing, but always found herself having more fun promoting whatever band she was near. She thought many times that she wanted to act, but found herself being all of her actor friends' agent. The same had been true for my case. Had she not spoken up, I wouldn't have had the chance to go on tour as Huckleberry.

She said she even desired to write, but found herself too impressed by the writings of other people. In a bitter-sweet letter, she told me that it was her conclusion that she would go to work for one of the biggest publishers in New York as a liaison and an editor of new talent.

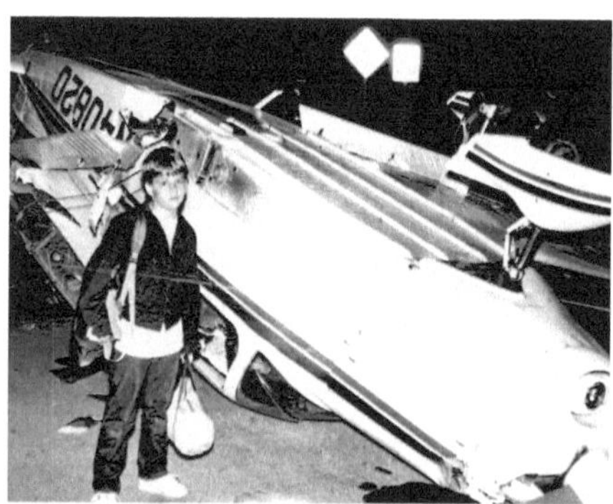

My roommates had lots of friends from their days in film school -the Suny Purchase group. Most I met had attended the place and carried a certain air of fake obnoxiousness. Through these friends, several became friends or acquaintances of mine. Cynthia was the x-lover of my roommate and was the one who made herself an important gal to the works of the commercial editing house. She had a male friend who always seemed to show up, and I noticed him more because he took a particular interest in me. He seemed genuinely interested in what I had to say. I had a fun conversation with the two of them, though I found Cynthia to be a bit cynical. I was applauded when I broke into a wild actor, and her friend David seemed genuinely interested in my artwork hanging in my room. It is a running New York City joke to award a shoebox with the name "room". I felt compelled to spill my guts on many events that had led me to that point in my artwork. He wanted to know of the hidden motivations. I was dying to tell so many things to a friendly set of ears, yet in the back of my head I felt I needed to rush to get it all out. It felt like a strange placebo talking with the guy. The evening seemed to be dying finally, and Cynthia made her move toward the door. She asked David if he was coming or going. To my surprise David turned to me and said, "Well, that depends on Eliot."

I was taken aback, but it did not show, "Well you're welcome to stay here if you want, but I'll be sleeping alone." Pleasantly he understood and without any hurt feelings they left. I sat back and enjoyed the party slacking a little, enabling me to relax as host. I sat back and chuckled over the night so far.

In spite of my rejection, David and I still became good friends. I was equally thrilled when he continued his interest in my painting. He was involved in several galleries in the city. He was sad that I landed the tour, since it would take me away from the city for nearly four months, but he still wanted to open a new gallery featuring my art even though I wouldn't be there for the showing. I agreed to send anything I came up with on the tour. So I did quite a few art pieces on the road and I sent them to him as quickly as I could, especially since they were no good to me. I couldn't carry them with me. Our traveling company was crowded enough as it was.

Julie and David sent me pictures of my opening. Julie told me of all the exposure I was getting. She said that it was creating quite a bit of mystery with me being the artist "Huckleberry" on tour in Europe. She said it was causing a sensation.

David told me there was a Psychiatrist with his little dog who bought up two of my paintings and paid a handsome sum extra to have them delivered to his house the very night of purchase. David said he acted very possessive of the paintings and that he claimed to know the artist personally. David asked if I knew the guy.

Chapter 12

<u>**In a flash of heat and pain**</u>
Back In the States after tour:

I felt some nobility in asking myself the question of why I was back and immersing myself into the labyrinth darkness of the city. I was driving Phillups 66 - crazy little bubble box- returning from a yoga retreat in the Catskill mountains. I was acutely aware of my shoulders wrenching and tightening as I watched all the heads aimed in forward pursuit. Clubbered heads looking for the best lane, which way could they rip someone off? Which way could the gangsta' ego self get there faster than the rest? How can you possibly get over another when it's all one entity named Life?

Some Answers: It may all be ONE at its greatest depths; however, it appears that the truth is each one of us is an IS-BE and we are all bored, disempowered, and trapped in a limiting body, within a limiting trap and dimension. Most IS-BEs all want attention and many will over-whelm the other IS-BE and vice versa on and on throughout antiquity -the only things changing is the position of the IS-BE until there is spiritual progression with merit building fortune. Although, one must deal with other unscrupulous IS-BEs; however nefarious, taking gain along with trapping other IS-BEs. In this Earth, a man is also wired to be woed, slowed by a woman's aesthetic beauty/pain trap. For example, I am nearing the finish of editing my work herein this volume. To cover the cost of my actor's guild membership, some food, and the cost of my self publishing I was out delivering an order from meditteranean delight, when off in the distance of the pedestrian mall, I spied the most perfect ass (assthetic beauty/pain delight) I have ever scene. The pain came in that I have to stay focused on my greater aim of this work for my own and perhaps others' salvation. However, that beautiful ass still quivers and dangles in my mind of want. The way is slightly jiggled beneath skin tight black form fitting horny norny promotional cloth-ing. My hunger for a twenty dollar loaf of bread having not enough money (false-currency-construct) to buy from beelzobops amazonian holy foods to satiate the belly for all its caloric needs for my mental and physical demands - thus rages hormonal demands because our devil designers wove sexual reproduction priority the more you starve so that the nasty devil child who wrecked his creator's playground of eden happiness can trap you and control you further into misery paths descending away from lightness towards heavier hells far worse and below than even this devil earth prison can be.

Then, post Huck, it all didn't make any sense. What was the com-pulsion that made all of the people pile onto this chunk of dry land at the crux of two rivers all fomenting competition.

The external aerial view of an ant pile -there one can have a perspec-tive of the city, inspires some amazement and bittersweet nostalgia. In a vision of a Southern summer downpour, solid curtains of rain falling down, sweeping the well-kept lawns with wet grassy smelling sweet-ness.- kissing the ground hard, I watched the trauma of the ant pile. There, when I was young, I was having a moment of clarity. I was in one of those moments contrary to human belief that rain is something from which you need to squint, tuck your head and run. No, I was present and loving it. I watched the rain torture the ants. I watched their dusty castle fall and cave as little red pimples exploded from the fresh mud. I could nearly hear their little squeaks and feel their own anticipation of nature's inevitable changes.

I was not responsible for their demise this time, whereas before I might have combated their little angry venomous mouths with equal vengeance. Regrettably as a kid, I poured various flammable liquids to see them burn and curl. Where did this fascination come from? How had I learned to kill little creatures in such a multitude? I watched the rain work on them.

New York in the skyline brought back the memory of the ants.

There was a leaf that floated up to the tip of the quickly eroding fortress. Efficiently, the entire crowd of surviving ants boarded the leaf for their own safety. There were bridges of live ants spanning out everywhere looking for some dry anything. The lucky crowd had boarded the leaf. Now everything immediately around was rushing water. The leaf was harbored safely in the grips of a twig. Along the leaf, rushed the East and Hudson rivers, and on the dry space between the two- writhed the crowd of ants.

I hadn't known it but I had visited New York City when I was a kid just by fucking with an ant pile.

So it was that I found my return disturbing. I had done yoga all weekend. I found myself in my first lucid dream. Floating on needles as if I were a pin cushion, I saw a hallway of so-called angels. They were such a playful lot. I felt suspended lightness and bliss. I was totally aware as I felt myself rise up on a cloud of energy. Yes, I was doing it. It wasn't a dream where I was watching myself fly, but I was actually helping it along at will.

They were so excited and happy to see this day come. They were all with me. I felt my human calling, interrupting, and slipped out of my dreamspace and opened my eyes to the reality I had left when I dozed off. Severely disappointed, I quickly closed my eyes- to my surprise It was all there- so was the feeling! The return to waking life was short-lived as I disappeared into another dreamscape.

The Chinese are so close together with the Italians. The North thinks it has some superiority over the open racism of the South, but racism it seems is independent of the hemispheres in this country or for any other in that matter. I rolled past the Italian cafés as their workers swept the dried tears from the night before. Hoses aimed everywhere before the August heat would really cook the foulness. The morning maintenance was astounding. Walking along, I found my friend Jeff doing the same thing at his building.

He pointed out the fresh trash cans that the city bought for his building. Two of the lids were smashed completely, one for each day that he had received them. He has a beautiful laugh. In a backward giggle, he reared his laughter and detachment. Everyday seemed like a carnival here in the city. What would be there to amaze his Indiana eyes?

He was moving up to the big league in baseball, until a knee injury reprogrammed his life. The turns and directions had brought him here. Shortly after I arrived that morning, we were climbing the red steps of some building nearby, off of Grand Street. Possibly the crustiest woman I've ever seen met us at the door. It was in her house that we would be painting for a couple of days. Her expression was grumpy and Italian. Her face had been creased by the negative assertion of her language. She muffled out a mixture of Italian and English. I was amazed that she was the upper progeny of two generations in this country, but somehow the structure of her situation had never led her to learn the language.

Brave days those must have been- coming over to this country.

After finally achieving some peace from our new foreman, we sparked.

"So where was this retreat you went to?" Jeff asked.

"Somewhere upstate, in the Catskills." I answered.

"You seem to have benefited from going. You seem like you have a state of peace around you." He noted.

"Yea, but I'm a little blown away by being back in this reality."

I added. "It all seems so harsh being back. I just keep thinking about what it would be like to take the plunge and live away from it all up in some Ashram. I don't know -it just seems so resigned."

"Yea, that's the thing about all of those places. They go off and that's fine, but there is no touch with this reality or the reality of this world" He giggled to his point.

"Who would want to take responsibility for living in this world?" I grimaced silently.

"You remember Davey? The guy I told you about."

"Yea." I answered.

"Well, he was the first person I've met with a sense of peace and understanding in life. He's the one who got me turned on to all of this Native American stuff. He was the first one who seemed to have an understanding of his path. Ya know what I mean?"

"Yea."

"Well now he's got AIDS and he's dying. I love the guy. He is going to be my best man at my wedding. I am curious to see how he is going to deal with death. I mean, like you say, it's nice to think of living away from society in an Ashram, but what happens when you meet your ultimate ending?" He giggled to assert his point. "I mean, here is a guy who practices this sort of mindful way of life."

At this point I was lost in thought about the complexity of AIDS. I was thinking of how I heard the disease mutated so many times already and that people suspected it was some sort of genetically designed disease.

"This AIDS thing is what I don't understand." Jeff continued. "I mean, where the hell did this thing come from? I've heard all kinds of whacked out things. I heard that it came from some village in Africa. That it might have been some kinky interaction between the monkeys and the Aborigines." He cackled shyly at the seeming ridiculousness of everything he'd heard. "It's like (false alien empire bible)God said, 'Wham, I'm gonna kill all you butt-fuckin mother fuckers, nope take that back- I'm gonna kill *all* you mother-fuckers.'" He was on a roll as he laughed heartily with a beautiful smile. "No, but seriously- Davey lived in San Francisco, and that's where they said the first hotbed in the U.S. was."

I remained in speechless wonder at how I had heard all of the same rumors. I thought about the power of the media, and whatever channels caused us both to hear these bizarre tales of how the disease originated. I began to think about how I had a feeling the government had something to do with the whole thing. I met quite a few people in New York who strangely thought the same thing.

Before I could mention it, Jeff began, "I bet the government has got its hands in this one somehow."

"I was just about to say that!" I exclaimed. More excited about some abstract connection as to why we would think the same thing. The government would also have me uninformed as to our own psychic power inside. We truly know things in our hearts, but how often do we listen?

I continued, "It just seems so convenient the way the knowledge of the disease has spread. I mean, there was such a heavy racial undercurrent back in the eighties when wide-spread panic began. It just seems too convenient for the media to report that the disease was spread by an aboriginal village who had no knowledge of hygiene. Their hygiene is in nature. They endure so many different things than we do in our white manicured society.

If they say it started amongst black people in Africa, that leaves much room for the already brewing hate in the waves of our society. Leave it to hate to increase superstition and ignorance.

Plus, if everybody is steaming about the disease being brought about by black people, then there is no room to wonder more about how the propaganda spread because everyone is caught in hate. Then there was the whole Gay men undercurrent to spread more hate amongst the ignorant complacent masses. Always, though, I strove for a perspective beyond my own limited viewpoint.

So when I received the hate-mail through rumors about how the disease began to spread in the San Francisco gay community, I watched all the people around me immediately choose hate and prejudice for the myth. Never does it occur to the government fabricated people to choose love and compassion. There is no room for such a thing in a militant divide and rule society."

I concluded.

"Yes, come to think of it, I heard some of the same things. Man, you don't know what the big boys are pumping through the pipes."

"That's for sure." I agreed.

I was fueled by the conversation on AIDS. I began to deeply wonder about the state of health in our humanity. I rolled home on my blades and found myself heated with thought- the seeming impossible matrix of corruption seemed like a blanket of concrete, as impenetrable as the city. Could something so horrible really be happening? Could our government be acting out some Nazi plan to wipe out people? Why? Why would they wipe out people. (answer: because there is more money (false-currency-construct) in suffering and illnesses, medicines, and vaccines, famines, confusion, and mayhem. It keeps the parasite workers in endless job creation -boring mindless repetitive automatons of State.

In a flash of heat and pain, I realized that by taking away the freedom of sex from people, they would actually be helping to create a more rabid society dependent on other channels for their insatiable desires. Once sex was removed or dis-ease inhibited, there would be an even bigger need for violence and consumption of drugs that help to alleviate the sensation of not ever being able to get enough. It would increase markets by the masses unable to feed the void within.

Our Government's huge war machine could feed itself even more hate. Young hormone loose Americans would make a good army. I asked myself to think deeper in the pits of possibility. Why was it supposedly a disease that acted upon Gays first?

In a flash, of course!-totalitarians, empirelike bankers and top brass want to wipe out the creatives,- the sensitives. They figure that this killing of gays would help their movement to wipe out creativity and art in order to create a megawave of zombie consumerism. Their media movements make it seem the gay communities are relentlessly immorally challenged -leading more and more towards human suffering. They are exercising their violence to censor freedom and of course to control.

The modes of hate would see the Gays as a weakness of society. The so-called straight and ignorant would appreciate that hate too. It was all too good for the high elite and the closet militarists designing this elaborate plan. I could picture the inwardly deprived, bored, and sick individuals creating such a plan.

I got home all right past the wonderful aromas of MacDougal street. I found myself writing to Claire.

Dear Claire,

I seem to think quite a bit about healing. What the hell is healing and why do I now feel the need to do that. I think meditation everyday inevitably leads to a better understanding of my own personal partial truth and path. Sure there will be tricky divergence, but isn't that what keeps dreams so lofty and interesting. Well, when you give the Light a chance to be your soul's dream, the occurrences never cease to amaze -no attachment necessary.

Last night Jeff and I talked about the rational fear men seem to create and the irrational fear women seem to manifest. I talked about my frustrations of repetitively running into bureaucratic obstacles -so well grounded on this plane. He said that the Ocean Center was not necessarily a place for one to become enlightened, but it is a place where one might have a better chance to meet their guru. Since circumstances along the street are always like black and white static on a television. Here is where I really appreciate and come to love my patient angel named Glossimer. I thought about her and the taste I felt in my mouth after my failure to succeed in communicating my desires to her rushed satisfaction. She bumps me in so many ways away from possible straying. The girls I lust for, the chemicals and circumstances for evil in my life. I'm beginning to realize just how easy it is to misunderstand power and use it for not so positive reasons. Take crystal energy -don't know much about it, but I was concentrating on this girl's Rottweiler so he would come to me. I was hoping then that she would come and talk and we would end up seducing each other. I realized my fault and gave up, but it was very hard to give up. Because in my mind's eye I had seen her sunlit and naked. Now, just thinking about it I want to masturbate. Her painted girlish innocent beauty made me cringe with desire. Afterwards, I thought of you, my one true love, my dear kindred spirit Claire. Some of those carnal desires and other emotions surrendered and faded into love for you. Damn time and circumstance said my ego and body- after lunch manifested in tiredness and allergies. Nostalgia indeed. Yet there is the dare to "let go" -advice direct from the source- seems evident and I know its truth. How do I remember how to let go? -by being peace active and healing. Something I need yet I create obstacles, physical and mental.

It was really nice to hear those things from Jeff. He said, "You are talented, man, and life is offering you lots of incredible experiences. Go for it, work at the brewery, paint paintings, act, go to Peru, work with me painting, do it all, live life, you are on your way!"

Just thought about the word wart- war at art. Funny how the thing has grown over the tour. I thought it was nearly gone. Right hand being masculine, signifying an imbalance in my sexual chakra. It is a manifestation of the self-destructive aggression I put on my dick through my hands. After all, when I popped out of Mom, there was a man paid very well to mutilate my sexual organ. The powers that be definitely wanted to leave an impression on me. My Dad always said crime doesn't pay and payback is hell. Barbequed karma shawarma for sure. I don't even remember what I did to earn the torture of this life. Who knows, there could also be new causes being made that puts prisoners here newly, unfounded, and unfairly. Right hand being masculine, signifying an imbalance in my sexual chakra. Is there such a thing as being overly promiscuous with yourself? Since reality is also a product of my thoughts, I guess loving the person I most want to be with would be fine. That is why the torment of Stacy came back into my life, because I haven't let go of our steamy sexuality. Should I let go? Yes, because it is not for the right reasons. It is pure attachment to the realm of illusion. With you it must be different, not only do I love your physical body, I love your soul, a balance. The more I see that balance, the easier I see that pattern and take turns that lead more to balance. Part of the pain now is part of the happiness later. So indeed Source or True Original Creator Source Godhead has given me the creative will to imagine the future of uniting together with you. Just as in Stacy, how I use that power is up to me. Just as I unjustly worshipped Stacy's form, she finally manifested in my life to rub it back in my face -she found it pleasureable to torture me by withholding herself from me because she knew how much I burned for union. She was the wrong person for me Claire, you and I both know that now. The first step was in abstaining when she herself asked me questions about you and threatened me with her smell and love. She said she has never had a love like me and that she values it. That is her going through her trait of possessiveness. Everything is as it should be under universal will as she is how she will be.

I realize how the answers lay before me. In this little point of learning on MacDougal street. When examining the situation it is not all taken for granted. There are reasons for me to think of You. This tiny apartment with its books you and I read in the past: Love signs, I Ching, along with Vibrance conditioner I can still smell in your hair. Everything in its place for a reason. The confessions to another woman who has changed her perspective on our relationship, Stacy, now she isn't as intent on my every word. I'm not mad, but glad. It is just funny to have my current perspective on things. All of these manifestations happened here on 120 MacDougal. A manifestation of Karma, in all its forms. The realization that these other women lead me to suffer more. I know it won't be the same with you once we are finally together.

Your Lover Forever, Eliot

Sunday I went to pick Comfrey, finally getting out of bed. I took a bus to the South end of Central Park, and before I began to look for this tissue and bone healing plant, labeled as a useless weed in our blighted society, I looked around at the art sale. Some of the artwork captured my heart, and I felt waves of emotion particularly when I saw a painting of a person meditating in a very beautiful mind setting. Those emotions faded as I tried to find love in my heart again. I held my fluorite crystal to help guide me into applying that force of will into reality. Then I was looking at this woman's art that had to do with crystals. I was intrigued more by the crystals than her artwork. She asked if I was looking for something to put my crystal on, and I sort of said no even though I had nearly displayed it to her by showing it in my hand in the first place. I told her I had dreamed of the stone then found it at my sister's house. She said, "Then you stole it." I was let down by her strange and lame accusation; however, she did inform me that the double pyramid was fluorite and not amethyst. As I neared the end expanse of artwork, I wondered how one would enter into such an event. I found the answer when I spied the tent central. With all sorts of foreign Nor-Easter traditions like event-coordinators, membership and contribution assistants, etc,. it all spelled organization, intimidation, and leeching of a potentially good thing. Perhaps with the flow of tourism, the locals and government feel the need to protect their resources and genuineness. It would be a shame to have some midwesterner get home and discover in some art catalog that they were the victim of some bogus art replication. Ignoring that they paid what they wanted for something that entertained their eyes. That is really all that matters right?

The foreigner coming to New York City discovers levels of naivety regarding commercialization they never knew. Due to all the pain and hustle brought upon by so many cross-pollinating and competing races ripping each other off -never realizing that all of humanity is really **One.** I wonder how I can aspire provide great service and help, yet not just only to repeat so many of the truths printed millions of times in noble books of the past. After all the different manipulated translations etc., the simple man with his nuclear family, alone in a sea of divide and rule does not know how to bridge the goodwill philosophies into everyday reality.

My walk through the park seemed very long and I didn't pick any comfrey or burdock, and although very involved with the local nature disguised as a park, I still had time to squeeze a little lust in for the numerous roller-babes silkily gliding along. I wondered how legs could become so sensuously redesigned by the times. The legs of a roller-babe were different -they just were. The body makes glorious revisions to the tortures modern people dish out. I remembered when aerobics was in heavy fashion. I occasionally glimpsed a woman whose supreme focus was in this new sport, and behold I would be instantly transfixed by the new brand of hiney -the aerobic hiney I called it. Walking along with my sister who was aspiring to look and feel her best while preparing for the NYC Marathon, we spied a glorious aerobic hiney. We were equally transfixed, my sister for comparative reasons and myself for horny norny reasons. Being one of the lowest monetarily in the rat race, I couldn't credit myself to be of equal status for such luxurious loins. Fame and wealth seemed to be the general way one could purchase surface beauty.

I actually got to my Comfrey patch up on 84th Street. I had been picking plants from this patch for weeks now. I went up and put my plants away then spoke with my father. We made plans for the next morning to go see the painting his girlfriend wanted me to replicate. I was starving so I pigged out at Nancy's and decided I would go to the grocery shop for some replacements. I shopped then went to see Forrest Gump, a film that kept me weeping and thinking of Claire. I went home to sleep and woke up the next morning to meditate with the new knowledge I gained about my crystal.

The sitting seemed deeper than usual and the crystal kept transmitting information and pulsing light deep purple. It is alive! I wasn't at all scared. It transferred quantities of some subtle energy or knowledge to me.

Then dad and I went to do our mission. Surprisingly, everything was successful- mission accomplished see you later. Then I rushed to talk with Nancy because I felt like I was going to miss her if I didn't get over there soon. She told me about her weekend and the trials that she was going through. I made some calls and went upstairs, ate then fell asleep. I woke nearly an hour later to go to Violet's with the plants. I walked all the way to 86th Street, then realized that I had forgotten the plants. I went back then continued the perilous journey, by then the weather was beautiful. I wondered about healing and the relation to the weather. I thought surely it must have something to do with it. I had noted many times that when I climbed out of my shell to go healing- the weather always turned in favor. I felt it was because I was on a mission of goodwill.

<u>**Chapter 13**</u>

A Demon of SOHO

I decided I was being far too stingy with my time. I decided to go back to the place which I thought had helped me so much to get a taste for the concepts I'd always yearned to know -the inner and outer workings of life. We already have the knowledge. Everyone can have the wisdom and the knowledge, and there is something extraordinary that happens when you go looking for some reassurance of what you already know deep inside.

I thought I could volunteer at the Ocean Center. How formal it was when I attempted to do what I thought to be a good deed. When we met in a circle, it was as if there was no exchange. I was made to feel greedy for wanting classes along the way. All of the red tape involved with getting knowledge. I couldn't afford food for myself and to these spiritual thugs, gaining their knowledge meant I had to assure them I would be present for three months. At that point, I didn't know how long I would be in town. I was already yearning to leave. The business of acting just wasn't in me anymore. There was no fun in it anymore. Meeting with all of the bigshots was eating at my heart and my stomach.

So my plan to volunteer was shot down. I couldn't give them the commitment of the months they wanted. I could and wanted to help then and there. I was so incredibly penniless- I had no business volunteering, but then began the string of getting hired.

Blanch, the woman who was in charge of volunteers, amongst other bumbles, was infuriatingly confused. Ultimately upon learning the inner workings, I saw no reason to spend what little money (false-currency-construct) I did amass volunteering my time to that place other than for cruel observation. I would have to watch my back -exposed to the bumble butts -the non-humorous closed hearted thunder asses. She tried to manipulate some response from me. Feeling like she must have total control and authority over simple matters -letting power of judgment and organization go totally to her head. Past all brink of being a reasonable and communicable human being, she was a secret dread to all. Why was she there in a center for education? She was terrified and bumbling alone, like a one year old with a razor in a dark room.

My sister worked down in the telemarketing department. This was a new feature of the Ocean Center -New Age solicitation. People knew the Center was a good thing, they just needed a little help remembering that. I realized that the place was taking some off turns- turns that seemed to be far away from any "center".

The telemarketing department was expanding and somehow making room for its covert actions of phone solicitation. Outwardly beckoning people to renew their commitments to the center without a center, the group was generating necessary funds for continuing -impasses were normally overcome by the billionaire founder.

I wanted to know more of the wonder in the Leprechaun's eyes downstairs. She was a beautiful woman. She had thick curly hair and blue eyes that sparkled as clear and wonderful as any mountain stream. She seemed in her perfect setting when I first met her up in the Adirondacks at the Eastern Arts Retreat many months before. It's funny to me I knew back then we would somehow cross paths again. We had an unspoken knowledge of one another. An unspoken compassion for each other's problems. Mine weren't verbalized as often. There were no answers anyway, just musings.

What was this wonderful and knowledgeable creature doing down in the basement of the Ocean Center. I met her in dopamine chains as the mate of the current President of the Ocean Center, but now that was no more. How small yet hearty she was, and how mammoth the President was with his huge ego and big cars.

This Irish woman was now down in the basement, very much still a part of the Ocean Center. She was now in the expanding telemarketing department. My ears were open to the raged Irish blood that poured her version of truth. A bitter-sweet acceptance of her current encasement. I listened but couldn't catch all the details of why they had broken up.

Months before I had seen more of the world in the Europe Tour, I had been naive enough to think that spiritual couples couldn't possibly break up. I hadn't listened to the inner reading that often comes the second you meet someone. I read something inside that man, but refused to listen. Regardless, they were broken up and she ranted and raved openly about her wound of the present day.

She had found her pre*dick*ament was a submissive cycle that had gone on for thousands of years. She found herself recalling like it was yesterday when he was a high priest and she was the one to be sacrificed by him. She recalled with all the blood and fury when she had her heart ripped out by this man - the heart thief. It was all the same. Sure, we can say that we're civilized, that sort of thing doesn't happen anymore. WRONG! It does still happen all around, and even if physical acts aren't acted upon doesn't mean that there aren't other realms for this abuse to be carried out. Spirits tend to reiterate what has been done to them. Spirits tend to retaliate.

We have arrived at days where mind power is a much more stealthy weapon than physical power. So there we were in the basement taking orders from the top. There is a certain structure that needs to be maintained when a hierarchy is in place and in the heart of SOHO it was and still exists. Although many are blind to their own cappuccino induced superficiality, nevertheless the underlying foundation remains.

She had helped the President get the job, and now she was down in the basement like some rat. So it is allowed that a place is configured that way. Even for a place that is supposed to stand for something new and brighter. Not true- the chain of command starts with the invisible puppeteers with their overall vision of how things should be. The President is the scapegoat actually with cloaked Presidents behind Presidents. So the President of the Ocean Center is up above decks issuing orders and administrating in general. He is surrounded by blind instigators of business. Necessary entities for that particular structure and they appear accordingly. That is merely all they have to do- appear. They already signed the dotted line of comatose complacency long ago. They are the bumble-butts. The only evidence besides their harsh attitudes and non-understanding of any greater picture is the bumble that they carry around with them.

They consume and look like hob-glob snackers cause they know not what ails them. It is a layer of heat and stored energy that causes the bumble, sort of a purgatory of the body. They are links in a chain. A baboon/hyena are good animal examples to compare. Get a bunch of bumbles together, and they laugh and tear flesh- including the heart scraps that have been dropped by the President, who through Tai Chi and various martial arts became confident of his ability to do so.

The bumbles are taught the bottom line. They are taught the cash flow problem. This is what they know. They are unable to feel source, angel, or wonderment in the midst of their bumble fucked reality.

Still clinging to my acting, I fantasized about being a part of some creation that would have to do with deeper meaning. That is where my thoughts were. I knew distinctly that there would be waves that would catch on. It would follow the wave that was being felt in the book-publishing market. I was certain that there would be new films made that would have to do with more meaning, awareness, and self-realization.

By chance, one of the last telemarketing calls I made before I was terminated happened to be to a woman who was involved with Cinevesta films. I could barely believe it but I managed to use the credibility of the Ocean Center call to move on and plug myself in as an actor.

I was excited I had made a synchronistic contact. As per her invitation, I began a letter telling of my needs and wants:

Eliot Breyers

120 MacDougal Street

Apt. A

NYC 10012

Attn.: xxxx xxxxx

Re: Future Projects

Dear xxxxxx,

I spoke with X by coincidence, well not necessarily my coincidence because I believe every meeting has a reason. However, I am an actor who is making a change of focus. Now that I've gotten some of the experience I wanted, particularly on stage, I want to explore the realities film has to offer. I'm interested in paths of enlightenment and raising consciousness through mindfulness and awareness. Any wrongs and opposites of these concepts I'm apt to expose, whether it be political, ethical, environmental... I think there is a front line of this type of film emerging, becoming no longer a question of what the people need, but what they want and will eventually demand. If we can help each other, please let me know.

Sincerely,

Eliot Breyers

Shortly after, I was into a compelling conversation on the phone that caused me to re-situate in my chair parked in front of the desk on which I was working.

I put my feet up on the desk and was laughing- when out of the corner of my eye, it seemed that the candle was getting much more intense. I looked, dropped the phone and began to extinguish that very letter which was engulfed in flames. I couldn't have asked for a better sign of my superficiality delivered by my own "accident" reaching out to yet another film bureaucrat long removed from the celluloid art of any merit. I am so happy that the letter burned of its own accord- I sat naturally corrected. I couldn't immediately let go of the idea of writing the letter because my desire to be a great screen actor was so strong. The incident gave me enough occasion to stop and take a look at what I was doing. I constantly offered my hand out in service to this nasty West, only to be constantly rejected or chastised.

I realized after expressing the event to the Leprechaun, just merely by expressing it to her, that it could be easy to predict the movement of a New Age film surge. I resolved that it could be easy for me to act under it too. I could be an actor doing New Age films. I wouldn't be living my reality, but there I would be, willing and able to do such things. A flip the script, make it all up life on the edge of America East or West as manifest destiny. What had I just learned on tour? What had I just been through made me realize that I wasn't happy acting under someone else's vision, *under someone else and their vision.* As a younger kid, I knew that reality is partly made of make believe, I knew that it was arbitrary. I couldn't ever give up that I am indeed lucrative and creative -lucreative.

I was excited about the potential of finding some material with which I did agree. I was certain there was some group or team out there who shared my type of vision. I was certain that there were some people out there who would have some understanding of quality beyond bogus morality and into the realm of true value creation. I knew then and continue to know now that I will and do make a difference to this originally stalwart rock planet.

Just when I was getting up the nerve to resign my short life as a telemarketer, I was politely fired. They got to do the firing before I got to do the quitting -such is the bumble.

Only shortly bumper bumbled away from the Center, though, and within a few weeks was asked by other parties to return and be re-hired as the mailman. This was when the fun began.

I was down in the basement of submissive central, but this time I was in charge of all the mail that came and went out of the Center. It was a rather mundane job, but I had a blast anyway. The crew down there had become a group of friends to me. My sister was also down there and our power together couldn't be denied. It hardly seemed like work, camouflaged by the camaraderie of my fellow in-mates.

It felt hard to believe that I was part of anything good while I watched thousands of dollars in mail go out the door. It was even harder to believe that I was really doing anybody in this world any good while I watched the truckloads of paper products get piped out for the sake of promotion. Did people really need all this packaging if what they were after was the sharing of knowledge.

The distancing wavelength from entrenchment of materiality in the miserable catacomb Empire State of New York and its desires was the longing bargaining tool for attainment even more so elusive. The further away from source and spirit, the more the material abundance attempts to buy back what is lost. People then think from the gray fringes of false comfort that "sacred" stuff should be worth a fortune. Being further away rightly so should they pay. Being a center in SOHO, where the almighty dollar is the most openly powerful and worshiped, what else could possibly happen but the high-shelving of spiritual knowledge. That was the structure's happiness. The happy elite holding what they consider valuable up above most people's reach, as if they were holding magic chocolate chip cookies above the hungry hands of children.

All I could do was watch and learn. Learn as the shroud of hopeful mysticism disappeared before me. I learned that one of the bumbles, who I was required to call upon for guidance in my duties, was resigning soon. That inspired my sister to forward her application through the works to see if she could lock down the job of public relations of which she was well over-qualified.

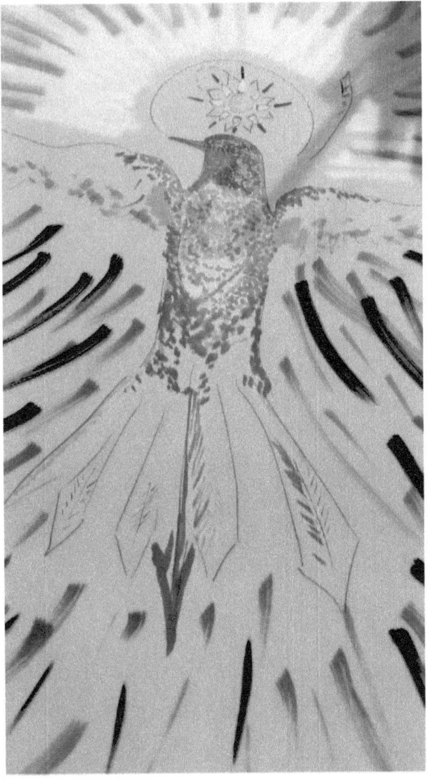

I pushed my cart around, and watched the leaves change colors while I could. I was getting more and more detached from the cycles of the Center. I began to think of myself as a caged hummingbird. I never wanted to take a job in a basement, so why did I find myself descending all the time. I heard somewhere hummingbirds die if they are caged. I knew of my exodus, though. I knew of my release. I knew my ticket was waiting for me- I knew I would be stretching my wings soon. I listened to the hum of my wings and was able to stay calm and centered. I watched the whole experience as if it were a bubble below. It was an entertaining bubble yet caused me enough pain to remember it.

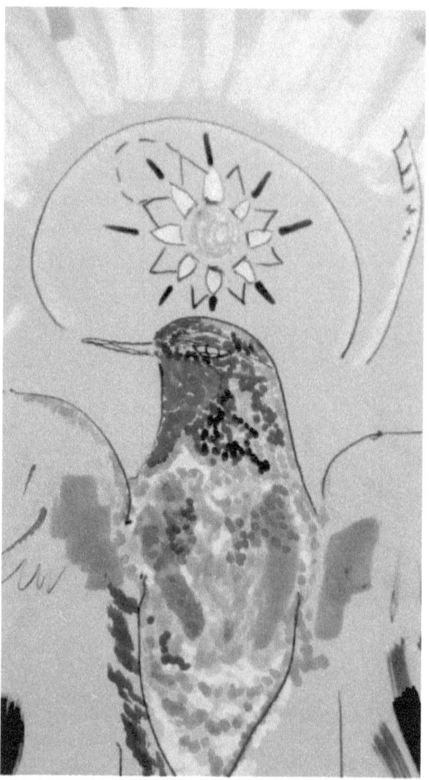

There was a silent one who worked nearby yet was so stealthy I hardly laid eyes on him. He was the janitor of the Center. I admired the way he was never involved in any of the peoples' lives. I would always see him coming and going. I would catch him rounding a corner with his worn yellow mop squeezer / container.

The fall air so clean and brisk beckoned me into taking breaks up on the rooftop. I decided to ascend the Ocean Center and check out what kind of roof it had. These little vacations from the stifling air inside of buildings gave me reprieve. I was not impressed by the towering gloom of the surrounding buildings.

I smelled the fresh scent of rain coming. The wind had blown hardily and dryly as it swept the grayness overhead. I looked around again at all the buildings, from this vantage I was looking mostly at the sides and backs of buildings. An elaborate freight elevator system hung awkwardly on one. I looked at how cold the steel patchwork looked against the quickly moistening red brick of one building to the West. Rebelling and smoking a supposedly additive-free cigarette, I tapped the ashes off and watched them fall to the tar-matted roof. Ssst, the ash landed in a little wetness. I immediately noticed a whole assortment of clothing buttons that were scattered all over the roof. I wondered where they came from. Each button was completely different. I picked up one particularly pretty button and examined it. They all looked as if they had come from garments designed for women. This one was really intricate as it had thirteen little diamond mirrors embedded. Multi-colored and swirled with red, green, yellow, and purple- also with a whole outer circle of little beads that were inlaid too.

"This is where he takes them." A voice rang solidly, approaching from the stairwell door.

It was the janitor. "Where who takes who?" I asked, still getting over the fact that I was up there and feeling slightly guilty about smoking on a tarred roof-top. His name was George. I knew this, though we'd never really met.

"I've seen you." he said reassuringly and continued, "You watch it all too, I've seen you. You don't talk it away as much as the others. I have a feeling you are a good listener and you'll hear what I have to say."

"Gladly" I said, thrilled to have this omnipresent specter talking to me out in the rain, on the roof in SOHO. We were both unaffected by the rain but walked under a big ventilation shaft that hung over our heads. The shaft rattled and pinged as the raindrops fell harder.

In sardonic reverie, he proclaimed. "So, this is where our enlight-ened President of the Ocean Center takes them. This is where our kind leader takes his women. He has a ritual, which I've had the sick fortune of witnessing. He nearly swoons some maiden with his talk like some guru. He speaks a few hocus-pocus truths to them after bringing them here late at night. He shows them the whole center, clearly showing his command of the entire place. He's never been concerned with the janitor of course. He barely knows that I lurk around this place all the time." He paused reflectively as he pulled out his own brand of cigarette and torched it with a strike-anywhere match.

After taking a good drag of the freshly lit cigarette, he continued, "Well, this is where he takes his women. He brings them up here and has unbridled sex with them. I've never seen the same girl twice through here. You were wondering where all of those buttons came from, right?"

"Yes," I replied anxiously.

"Well, he has an act, a ritual with these girls. He gets really aggressive with them. I think he likes to see that they're a little scared of him. Then he'll rip one of her buttons off and throw it down, in the "heat" of passion. Then they'll make fuck over there." He points over to a box-like extrusion that is about hip height. Well, my friend, just look around at all the buttons lying around up here. That is who is running this New age Center in the middle of SOHO. Some New Age. I know you listen and I don't know what you'll do with this information but I thought I ought to tell ya." Then, the surprise reporter walked away as stealthily as he had come.

I was left there holding that beautiful button in my hand. I kept it and am looking at it now as I write this.

Deep down, I felt that this button-popper story was true, but I had no way of proving it. So it was that I watched his interaction and heard the tales of how he had misused his privileges to have his way in many other ways. I felt powerless as I watched my sister go for the job of Public Marketeer. I watched her reactions while he toyed with her just like a big cat. He pretended to be helpful as he aided her in re-writing her résumé. It was all futile and he knew it.

Soon she was thrown to the bumbles and the President, while they relished in making her feel like dog shit. They stripped her down in jealousy of her energy and beauty. They couldn't let someone with a center promote the Center.

I had enough of my thoughts and duties. I had been working hard those days and took satisfaction in my upcoming exodus. Even though I felt like a humble mailman, shuffling post for the whole center, it had been a nice experience working down in the basement after all.

One of the major benefactors of the Center took it upon himself to hire someone to find out how all of the revenue was being wasted so quickly. He hired an alien. He was a bald, star-seeded man who was disguised as a human. I immediately read his observing eyes. He had come down to play and observe the curious action of people involved in a Center close to the dawning of a New Age. I could look deep in the back of his eyes and I saw the wondrous spirit who listened to all.

Magically, though, he would accomplish all of the mundane business of his job. He knew of the corruption, but by policy of his star code, he wasn't allowed to interfere on certain levels apart from his exact hired position. He could only take actions having to do with math and numbers, never any morality or ethical choices. He would share time with me when I needed to expound on the truth, but I was always frustrated at his inability to interfere with the whole opera.

The alien did get hired to do a job, and to comply with the guidelines of that job, he was allowed to administer that service only. Other information of human behavior was conveyed by his ever-communicating star counsel connection. Klurngal's head tilted back with his eyes closed while his jaw softly smacked with a bit of spittle creeping from the curly smile creases while he transmitted and received enormous streams of information. He was of a technology that didn't require wires or transmitters- he used streams of insulated consciousness. He could transmit and receive anytime he wanted.

Klurngal, the alien, had to fire many of the maidens that held fictitious positions; however, strictly by numbers. The maidens were all part of the need for the upper echelons of the place to be surrounded with youth and surface beauty, so the President could feel their warmth and devotion around him. The bumbles understood, and were even very selective about the candidates for the harem. They advised the President if they thought someone was too knowledgeable or if they had too much inner light and integrity. If such was the case, they would be a risk to the whole bumble.

My sister was one of those risks, but she wasn't applying for the position of maiden, little did she know that she was after a position of a bumble. Bumble she was not.

Klurngal let three maidens go in a very amiable way. He had authority that slipped through the politics of the Center. Once fired, they called their master and he assured his little girls they would have a place. He told them to forget the whole thing and come back on Monday.

The President yearned for the convenience of having his pets there, nearby at work. The meditation room would be worthless after-hours if he couldn't have his pleasure parlor. He would orchestrate the games of "Lick-Me-Not" that the girls would play with each other.

The benefactors, with no knowledge other than the fact that money (false-currency-construct) was going down the drain, called a meeting and over-ruled the President's rehiring of the maidens.

The President did fill the position of Public Marketer, though. It turns out that he hired an old buddy who was active in the pornography industry. He wasn't making as many films these days, so the President asked him if he'd like to join the center.

"I don't know anything about this New Age shit!" said Bill, when the President called him up.

"Sure you do man, It's just the same as porn. You're sellin' shit people want. The funny thing is they want any relative truth so bad that you can nearly have your own porn show just giving it out!"

In a laid back seventies slather, Bill slithered, "Well all right my friend, it sounds like we could have some fun."

There was no heart in the inner workings now, there was only a slight cavity of rot growing on even more rot in SOHO.

I wavered back and forth wondering where I was headed. Should I take off and go West? The Leprechaun had a son who lived near Arches National Park. That seemed like the most fun, yet I fretted I wouldn't find my path once I got there. I feared that I would run out of money (false-currency-construct) and have no way to get back. I analyzed my dreams. I wondered if I should go back to Louisiana and try to resurrect my Volkswagen. Should I go directly to Florida and chill there for the Winter, with the hopes of somehow saving money (false-currency-construct) and then planning a cross-country trip in the Spring? It sounded like a good plan, but I still wasn't sure.

I watched the rot grow in the bowels of SOHO. Hummingbird wings could at least stretch in my mind's eye now that I knew I was leaving. I talked to my old friend Julie, and told her of some of the things I'd learned from the center. I felt like the only thing I could really do at this point was to write about it all. I felt my writings would somehow be my secret weapon. I enjoyed having a computer to use in the MacDougal Street temporary sublet and realized I had been depriving myself far too long of the tools I needed. I decided to get an Apple Computer. I loved paper, and somehow life had provided me with notebooks and plenty of writing pens, but my typing was much faster and word processing much more effective than handwriting.

Julie mirrored my desires back to me. I felt she had been a good friend to whom I had confided in through all my trials. I was running out of time in New York. I could only flow with the fact that a magic place to live hadn't appeared yet. Julie told me that everything could be published, but I couldn't gratify myself by talking about this to her until I was sure I could round it all up on paper.

I looked around and found that all of my material was really here. I was having a great illumination. There were no more excuses but to get the thing down. I was thinking of how the hard part was done. I had gained the experience I needed after all these years. All I needed to do was to go down and sit with my work.

I decided to acquire a laptop computer. There was something that I couldn't describe about getting an Apple. It was as if I had let all of my childhood computer frustrations with the defective Commodore VIC-20 slide and now I was allotting myself the tool I needed -in time technology had evolved enough to suit the use and need.

I was walking back home one early afternoon from the Ocean Center to MacDougal street. I stopped in my tracks and wondered if I should choose another route. It was one of those moments when I felt I could be really flexible cause I had no idea where I wanted to go. Something fired, and I looked down at my left foot. I lifted my foot and swept it to the right. Under it was a big fat Apple Computer sticker plastered to the sidewalk.

In a flash, it all made sense. I felt like I was on track. Wham! At that time in my life, I was looking for signs in my environment that could help guide me. Perhaps there are reasons why everything happens, but everything doesn't happen for a reason. I had done something when I was fifteen years old, and until that very moment I hadn't known why. I placed a nice little Apple Computer transfer sticker on my 1966 Volkswagen because I felt the compulsion.

Now, I saw that sticker in my mind. It was a marker I had put there years ago for me to remember at this moment. I saw Phillups 66 in its dusty warehouse in Louisiana. I was looking at it from the rear, and I could see the little sticker there after all these years! Decoding Genesis, Adam and Eve, the Serpent, and the Apple, is a very important part of breaking the chains as you will discover in Book II.

I was so excited, I knew which path to take. I would fly down to Louisiana and resurrect the bug. I found myself dialing my Grandfather and telling him to ask my old mechanic if he could get the old thing running again. I told him that I would take care of everything else once I got down there. I noticed that it took him quite a while to understand what I was up to. It had been a while since I'd talked with him and he wasn't altogether. He kept grasping at the details but I could tell his mind couldn't retain the petty details -chemotherapy.

I was resolved and determined.

I wondered how I would get the work accepted, but the answer was right there before me. Julie had mentioned many times that my story would make an interesting book. I found myself dialing her number, nearly out of breath. I told her what I wanted. Panting, I told her of the rough outline I thought it should take. Happily she took it and ran -nearly as excited as I was. I thought of her before when she entered into the publishing world, but I hadn't really considered it up until that very moment.

Things were changing so fast. Suddenly the cool winds were showing signs of the coming season. I thought of the changes and their subtleties in the South, almost microscopic compared to the change up here in the North. In NYC, the upcoming winter would give little warning. First there is the first preview of cold, then it persists enough to keep chilling well into Spring. I often think the cycles and relationships of the seasons are responsible for many of the different patterns between the North and the South. Along with the milder climate, comes a milder way of life. In the South there seems to be a strong resistance towards progressive change and perhaps diversity. I see that many have chosen or subsisted to live that way. There are advantages to both, but it all depends on what one wants within the confines of this generally inhospitable planet. Because of the harshness and urgency of seasonal changes in the North, it seems that people have a tendency to be more abrasive and abrupt up there.

To a mild Southerner, I think this hurried abrasiveness he witnesses from the Northerner is often mistaken. The Southerner might not realize that the Northerner is just behaving like a busy little squirrel. The squirrels are always busy gathering and scurrying looking for the little nuggets that will sustain them for the Winter, so the Northerner's ideas of passing time are much different from the South. Even the cadence of speech is different. A Northerner speaks to pack as many syllables in one punch, while the Southerner is still lazily lacing up his gloves.

In a prison planet dumping ground such as Earth, it is extremely difficult to make any sense of all the disparate pieces that don't fit together obscured by deep senseless mystery along with amnesia amongst all the inmates. There is nothing here of evidence of our eternity forgone here nor for us to reflect and learn from the endless examples of disharmony all around. It is a horrible game gone wrong and turned into a prison concentration camp for the undesirables (from the perspective of the now obsolete mindless robotic empire. Its illegitimate child, rogue prison planet earth is a flailing insane rotten brat controlled by amnesia idiots in power who redeal the torture that has been enacted on them as consciousness fried amnesia babies born into whatever family they then learn or not whatever custom in the new body. There is an endless Karmic sway nonetheless, the opportunity to either choose love and forgiveness or compound the negative fear through reaction, retaliation and revenge. Though eating of others' bodies and sexual reproduction continue to be aberrations awaiting genetic correction/repair or the discipline to starve oneself ascetically rejecting the incessant programming spliced in to enjoy the barbequed flesh of lamb, chicken, beef, pork, fish, etc.

I began thinking that it *was* this simple, but there are so many other factors involved. Then I traveled around a bit and saw that the prerequisite for being racist was not just being a Southerner. I've seen examples of the fear towards cultural differences all over the world. I gathered that logistics does have somewhat of an effect on people, but overall they can be the same all over the planet if they choose not to look within and gain enough knowledge to begin to grow out of the infancy of repeating so many tragedies over and over again.

People, in general, don't seem to witness the fact that what you send out ultimately returns to you with nearly the same force with which you began. I've seen so many things I've done come back in my face over and over again. I'm amazed when people don't see that. Call me naive to think they should. Being awakened to the principle of causal relations doesn't; however, constitute true happiness. In an age like this Latter Day, this evil age, it is nearly impossible to uphold some saintly ideal of precepts or behavior. If I were, then perhaps I would go join the Hopi Indians, yet because of my current color and culture I probably would not be let in. I have no idea if there are still a pocket of people that come close to abiding by the laws of the hopi commandments. When I arrived at the Hopi cultural center, my epiphany was learning that I had failed to love and honor the ones I had near me. I chose to love a shadow woman who aside from slowly serving me food, was nearly like living alone or with a ghost.

One woman I knew cursed herself for not completely realizing her lesson she learned as a child. She had picked up the habit of talking about other people negatively behind their backs; however, she had the fortune of nearly always having the person being talked about appear while she was in the act! She recalled how much it affected her when she saw the hurt look on the

person's face. Now she regarded her gossip as some little naughty chocolate she was entitled to have, for sin's sake, every once in a while -everyday. When you talk negatively about someone else, you are mainly expressing your own dissatisfaction and insecurity with yourself in the same areas. Anyway, that is their choice, their trip, they are out and about just like you making it up as they go along -making mistakes.

This quality of connectedness is ever present, even through lifetimes. If you try Sturgeon Beluga caviar for the first time and are offended by the taste, then in all probability the caviar, in whatever state it was in, probably had the same reaction when it tasted you as a baby egg -in some other state.

My concept of time and age began to waver. I realized that one of the only ways to escape aging alongside reversing the internal cell progression, was to disappear from all those I knew. I fantasized about just how serious I was about this and how far I would be willing to take it. I wondered if my need and desire for natural states of immortality was grand enough to cause me to abandon the life that I knew. In my mind, I was close, but every time I stepped out into the water of this- I was drowned with terror. The horror of what it would mean to leave everyone with no return for the sake of not being referenced by anyone. If I remained with them, they would wonder why, after twenty years, nothing was happening with my body.

A vegan has a similar struggle in the myriad face of diets in the world. Healthily, they chose an eating pattern different from most, and that path alienates them somewhat from the people continuing to eat dead animals. Subtle outside forces from the whole of the surrounding society reach out and call for them to join their model. The Law of At-traction is somewhat surface and the concept of dependent origination, deeper. Just the same is true for the artist challenged with capitalist and corporate models- you choose an original unique way and that makes you different and somewhat of an outsider to all else **who subscribe**. Your choices can make you severely alienated from this encroaching puritanical background. Outside influences make it ever more important to hold conference with the strength of spirit of ones deepest Source. It is with the heart that those conversations can be heard, but not seeking it from human nature, but from other beings in the flow of nature which do not oppose and desecrate the Mother. It can be found away from the slicing eyes of humanity, yet to live apart is hermetic.

The hardship changes dealt within the cycles of life can be as disheartening as the last exhausted breath of a fizzled-out horn player. So I had to go out on a high note.

The Fall light was rough on my emotions. I sensed the upcoming cold and began to worry over the fact that I hadn't prepared for Winter. I continued to cat sit in that studio apartment for over six-weeks on MacDougal Street. Finally, near the end of that stay, I began to peek out of my shell. Fortunately, I had back-up. My sister and father lived uptown in the same building. My Dad was primarily living upstairs with his girlfriend and frequented his apartment only when they weren't getting along or he had to dress for work.

I decided to brave the circumstances for a month while I hustled to make enough money (false-currency-construct) to get out of town. I had run dry on paintings, and the gallery that David was tending sold everything I had. My favorite holiday was coming round. My living around my Dad opened him up to my habit of smoking Marijuana.

One evening, I ate and drank with my Father and his girlfriend. After the meal, they began to wriggle for an after-dinner cigarette. Although my Dad was trying to quit, seeing his mate light one up was too much for his eggshell discipline. I wriggled closer to my own vegetable matter for smoking. Upon asking Swedish Maria, Dad's girlfriend, she happily mused the thought of me smoking pot in their presence. I guess she found it naughty and cool. My Dad's eyes percolated too and he hinted, "Maybe, that's what I need," as if finding the answer to some dis-ease. "Maybe I should try some of your herb." I was more than happy to include my father in my addiction to gratified stupefaction and confusion. Maria thought it would be the greatest thing to see us getting high together.

Once we both expressed our positive interest in him getting high, he backed off a little and made up excuses for himself -backing down from his own suggestion. There was the indecision that was so subconsciously familiar to me. As he wavered, we continued to coerce him into submission. Perhaps he knew from the start of the evening he would be smoking after all. Manipulation was one of his strong points.

After the spiel of potential drug tests, etc., my Dad was puffing alongside his son. If this was possible, I couldn't help proposing a toast to Peace in honor of the occasion.

I began to think of what I could do for more money (false-currency-construct). I received a call from my father who told me of a painting in a Madison Avenue gallery of which his Maria was in love. She obviously couldn't pay the $23,000.00 they wanted, so he asked if I could be hired to make a replica of it for a fraction of the price. I was insulted by the fact that Dad didn't understand my need to be an original artist. I was disappointed by the fact that I could never rise above some replica to him. I thought I was long past the days of my father commissioning me.

However, I needed the money (false-currency-construct) so I bowed to the opportunity. Soon after, I began to regret it. It is all I heard about, painting this- painting that. It looked as if the whole deal was somehow causing some major problems between the fragile couple. I got so tired of hearing about it and told him I had to cancel the project.

I continued to work on it in secret with the suspicion that she would still want the painting when it was done.

Upon completing the painting, and nearing the end of my home-hopping in NY, I received a most unexpected phone call from Julie. Tears came to my eyes as she told me of all she had done. I nearly wet my pants with excitement. She offered a fat advance for the proposal of the book I intended to write. It was a dream come true as I knew I had to write the thing, but never did I think I would leave on a cushion of assurance that the work would be given an advance and published.

I called my father and his girlfriend that night and told them I had completed the painting. My father was uncertain about the whole thing. He felt the need for control. He was flabbergasted and wanted to see the painting alone. I objected and demanded that he tell his girlfriend right then and there. Reluctantly, he told her and arranged that I take them to Brooklyn the next day to see the sight. It was the moment of fruition as I pulled the painting outside into the garden where golden leaves fell briskly and the blue sky let the cobalt sky of my painting move their mouths to a flapped jaw state in amazement. I had done it!

At Violet's I was amazed at the healing that had taken place. Four weeks before, the ulcer on her leg was at least the size of a golf ball. Over the weeks I supplied her with what was supposed to be fresh Comfrey leaves, but there were none to be found in Manhattan, except those bought at some specialty weed shop. It seemed as if the plant's closest relative was doing the trick. I found a nice patch that I collected from near the Metropolitan Museum.

When it was time to treat her, I would make the trip up into Harlem to 136th street. It seemed as if I was crawling into levels that regarded the human condition less and less. Each transfer I took, let me know just how close I was getting. Finally, in her neighborhood, I would walk the five or so blocks south to get to her house. I never felt threatened by the topography or the natives. Sometimes I would get looks, sometimes I wouldn't. I considered myself to be on a mission of grace. I told myself that if the weather cleared every time I made a house-call, then surely the potential danger would clear also. It was in these moments of altruistic giving that I felt closest to the Source anyway.

I often thought the ritual I went through with Violet was so different from my normal life. If I had a physical problem, I would usually put it off until I *had* to do something about it. In this case, a buzzer would go off regularly in my head when it was time to serve treatment and a new batch of greens for this old sweet woman. The mockery I feel for most of the medical practices today stems from the knowledge of this real-life example along with the simplicity nature offers us with its solutions.

I now know the value of Western medicine, but I also know that it is over-emphasized. It is the reliance upon technology that poses the deepest danger. Knee deep in the seductive quality of technology there is no vision for the world outside of the looking glass. There has to be a balance. There is still the lock jaw of science that keeps modern medicine from seeing the beauty of encompassing the harmony of nature into healing. This holistic approach is crucial. There are more subtle forces in action beyond just the tissue and the examinable cells regarded purely by science. Here, I was able to heal this woman's leg purely from the raw materials in the wild.

There have been tremendous strides in technology in the scientific world of medicine and those achievements can be directed for the betterment of the whole. Violet told me that the lily of the valley was her favorite flower, and on the next visit I brought her a painting of that flower as a gift.

I also noted that the patch from which I was harvesting the burdock was quite abused at the start of my treatment. I found a few patches of plants that were untouched by the whirling whips of nylon rotated furiously by a 2-cycle gas/oil mix engines. I always thought how pleasant it was to breathe that additional petro-hate along with the millions of other funk producing machines. This treatment did not stop these amazing plants from flourishing in this area. I talked with them and told them what I was doing. Week after week, the patches remained untouched by the ignorant butchers employed by the park service. I'm positive the plants were responding to the need I had for them. The temperature was also steadily decreasing into the Fall, yet my plants were growing as if it were Spring. By my last visit, her tumor, which the busy doctors had initially intended to cut into and hack out, had shrunk to a tiny point. The tissue around showing marked deflammation and healing. The doctors threatened her with amputation and I imagined that the trauma of slicing steel in her aging body would not have only costed her and the system plenty but would have costed her body many more precious moments. Violet was nearly eighty years old and being immobile in Harlem with no help would have furthered the potential nightmare. The simple basics of common weeds and herbs was something my body and spirit had yearned for all my life, yet in this age no one had ever stepped forth to show me a few naturals. So I felt obliged to help the friend of the woman who had brought this knowledge to the Yoga retreat that weekend. My treatment was done completely free, excepting the subway and bus fare. It could not have begun otherwise because I was gladly jobless and broke. It seemed; however, that the money (false-currency-construct) and opportunities arose proportionately to my surrendering and giving. She thanked me and gave me a twenty dollar bill to buy "some cigarettes or something." She said.

<u>Chapter 14</u>

Through the Eye of the Hawk

When I got home, I talked to my sister Nancy -maybe we would meet rollerblading. I was feeling so anxious to blade and take out the aggression I felt. I was going against the grain of the traffic in Central Park until some nut made a sudden move that caused me to do a head-on and flip up a fellow blader. I was minorly hurt, and realized I felt rather self-conscious. After skating for a while I took a break on the sidelines and figure skated on my own for a while. It felt good but I was really boiling with anger towards people and also feeling really attracted to all the beautiful ashes of girls. I slowly gained a little balance then saw my old friend Tiny Mountain fly by. I thought surely he would pass again, but when he didn't I eventually got restless and skated on. Then as soon as I had given it up, I saw him again. I was amazed to see his giant self. He was doing some training on his mountain bike. I looked at the size of his powerful structure. He was a bicycle messenger for a marijuana service -so he did a huge amount of mileage everyday.

We smoked a big joint and bullshited. He asked if I wanted to help him out and buy some pot. I did. He then told me he had a special surprise. I felt extremely weird buying shrooms at such a price- when they could be found so plentiful on the land where I grew up. Up against traffic we rode, and after a while I saw him slow down, then I looked for him but we had separated. Gone until next time. So smooth and confident were my strokes again. I got back to Nancy's place and found a note that made me excited -she was up on the roof. We talked and compared adventures. My wreck, shrooms everything, healing. Then she told me about the Leprechaun's apartment proposal. It all sounded great. I was projecting but controlled myself from going over the edge in expectation, embellishing my mindscape with thoughts of a wonderful place in which I could live in the city.

After playing the harmonica for a little while, and thoroughly enjoying the Manhattan night, we went inside where I made a few reality calls. I guess I was really starting to appreciate being here because I knew that I was leaving soon. I talked to my friend Jeff and then to the Leprechaun. Then my sister and I were munching on berries and such. I decided not to eat too much because I felt I would throw up once I consumed the mushrooms. Although dried, The shrooms tasted very familiar, as I laughed and giggled about the purple spore print. The conversation seemed to fade as my energy perception began to heighten. Somehow I knew that Nancy wanted a massage. I began by leaning over her from the front and rubbing her shoulders. I began to feel the energy blocks and the longing of her body to be rubbed. So in tune with her energy and desire, I moved her to the bed where she could further relax.

By rubbing, loving, and giving attention to her body, I entered her reality. It was a land of such femininity and softness. Beauty were thoughts scattered like throw pillows. I began to see her cats as analogous to her fiery being. Her reality was so luxurious and cozy but still foreign. I had done the back side of her completely and began to reach for my own existence because I was submerged so deep in hers. She was so relaxed and kitty/giggly that I nearly wanted to stay and play in that world. Yet, I felt the call of some other reality and this began to pull me to my own path of discovery. I drank some more tea and gathered my things, which were numerous and scattered all over the place. It didn't seem like an aggravation. Instead, I felt a shy admiration in myself and the peculiar traits and habits that are uniquely me. I was also aware of the pains of portability. Also my refusal to be comfortable when anyone else is present. My need for privacy became explicit. So I was outside of Nancy's door and felt a sharp sadness of my immediate future. I saw the corridor of the building in which I lived. I saw its horror of metal and boxes- mausoleum with cold metal tumbler locks.

The separation of apartments, closing and locking of big black doors was an entangled ominous mess. I thought of Dad as indeed the "big guy upstairs" -hallucinating deeper I considered perhaps he was the grand conductor of this honeycomb hangout in NYC, 1100 Madison Avenue. The thumping bowel sounds of the old elevator that carried me through the stacked quarters of hundreds of people. Why was I here in this dark and dreadful place? Feeling so connected with Source, the doors, the carved locks and angry New York faces loomed all around. True Original Creator God Source, I thought, this place is so insanely wrong. People are so far away from Eden. Who the fuck can clean all of this mess up?

In the back of my head, I thought at this point I guess only false alien empire bible god can push the unholy reset button for the insanely lost herds. Up through the cavernous drippy metal passages I arrived at the door of my Father's little hide-out. I dreaded the symbolism of opening then passing through the threshold, then shutting out what was in the hall, stairwells, and elevators. A lonely studio apartment in which I would probably confront some major ghosts in my machine- the ridiculous comfortable existence that I had stitched into being. I had so many confusions, including paranoia. I was amazed at the metal and the level of creation, climbing through the bowels of a community living in consolidation ten floors above ground.

Once in the apartment, its box-like qualities broke loose on my soul. I began to think of the expectations of the Breyers legacy. I miserated how I was somewhat a product of my Dad's projections. I thought of my initial trip, years ago in the rural pastures of Louisiana, which launched me on a twisted schism hurling on a tangent away from the person I loved -Claire. I thought of my first time tripping back in Lafayette in my room -my possessions became so trivial and meaningless. My life led me to grow and change no matter how painful. Resistance to change and clinging to the past. It is not such a great feeling when the pain of the present outweighs the life force. I was OK with leaving it all but the only clinging was Claire. The biggest issue I've dealt with. I thought of only the thickness of that love as I looked out on the cruel world. I felt my longing for her sweet being form into a song that ushered out into the nicest love song I've ever heard. It must have triggered something big because afterwards I was feverish and hot with aggression. Nearly as soon as I had arrived, I was on my way back down to Nancy's to communicate my ideas with Claire. My mind was not on the moment but what would happen? How would I get down to Nancy's? What would I say? I had so much trouble with details at this point. Then I told Nancy my predicament, she said it was fine. After having so many problems dealing with telephone cyberspace and all the chimes and codes I had to dial, I fumbled one last time with the phone and collapsed in despair about how hard it was to get through the maze of just contacting her.

Finally, Nancy intervened and dialed through her system. My mind was not seeing with normal eyes, but it was feeling and sensing this upper realm of energy that permeates everything. The idea of being so impossibly far away from the one you think you love. The love was all I was feeling, but it was a helpless painful love because there was nothing that my loins could do to get the message through of what I was feeling. The magnitude of wrongness that I felt for modern society. The fact that so many agendas and false plastic models of deceptive idolism keep people from realizing that all there is love. If you are in love- then all is right and True Original Creator God Source takes care of those who are in true love. But no, money (false currency construct) and careers are prioritized and the level of security and comfort provided by the parents becomes the ever-dangling bait of misguidance away from your soul.

My mind came back to focus when I heard Nancy say, "Claire, this is Nancy, Eliot's sister, Eliot wants to speak to you." When I knew that I would be talking to her, my heart skipped two beats and a wave shot up from the base of my spine. What strange fate, her being home. I grabbed the phone and poured it out. I told her I loved her and that it was time for us to be together -to make a life together. I couldn't verbalize the apparent. She asked if I was fucked up. I said yes, then she asked me to hold on. I did for a moment but it seemed to approach infinity. The results weren't quick enough to avoid the negative spiral for which I was headed. In a fizzle of despair, I cradled the phone and collapsed into a hysteria thinking that she just didn't love me and that I was completely on my own. Nancy came back into the room and asked what was wrong. I said desperately, "she just doesn't fucking love me." Which was probably but not necessarily true, proving that I couldn't distinguish between imaginative thought and potential reality. I was gripping to the non-change of the situation and it was killing me as far as I knew. Then I felt that there was this wall to my left. I collapsed onto the floor and felt the wall's bulk to my left. It became the half of me that was living in pain without the love of my "twin self". This deep embedded coding of longing for my supposed "other half". Somehow I established a pattern between Dad and the whole experience, then I began to think of the tragedy incarnate into our lives -particularly me- the third generation Earnest Eliot Breyers III. I believed in a sudden flash that I was some mad experiment of my father's. That he had put me in living quarters with my lover who was disguised as my sister. I thought, If I am realizing this thought in the state that I am in, how hard it will be to bring this into the light of day! What a difficult shell we had subscribed to break, yet all of our progress was minuscule and in vain compared to the programming by which we still lived our lives. I moaned out some of these angst feelings, but Nancy talked me into the positive.

She told me she thought that I was thinking about too many bad things. I agreed and was partially relieved. When she said that, though, I conceived love and the ever-optional positive thinking. It was keeping me alive! Yes! It was working! Thank True Original Creator God Source for Nancy. Where would I be if it wasn't for her. I knew that there was no fear in love. Giving love whole no matter the bodily panic, I could survive even the ultimate--Yes! Death! Welcome. When it's time, it's invariably time, Okay,_Oh false alien empire bible god I'm dying.

Then I began to feel the lonely process of dying. I was aware of this big energy block in my crotch- then I thought that AIDS was attacking me. My mind was creating a real death stage. I was going with it. Nancy was the only one who would be present in the last moments of my death. She couldn't understand the evolution, but still she was comforting closest friends and family on the phone. I thought of who she was talking to on the phone -about my own death! She was consoling someone else's pain for my death. False alien empire bible god, I'm really doing this alone, but it's Okay. This is what happens when you die. It's pointless to think of how others treat you in the end. It's pointless to think of anything you've done on this planet, however great or tiny. I felt so thirsty and like I needed to urinate. I called out for water, Nancy brought it -I gulped it down faster than I have ever, but it didn't seem to quench the fiery thirst. Oh, True Original Creator God Source the urgency!!! Why wasn't the water doing anything for me -Why the hell wasn't I being quenched by the normal act of drinking -what I 've become comfortable with for twenty something years is disappearing! Why?! I had flashes that maybe the couple should be Nancy and me -that we got along fine, maybe the whole culture thing was wrong, maybe my mate was born under the same family. Deep down, I challenged that giant "wrongness" . Nothing felt right. But yet -I had never accepted and known a girl like my sister. Why? It was all Dad's doing. Yes, that's it, his sick doing. He's weaved these itchy thoughts into me. He hoped it would all turn out for the worst. That fucking bastard. Why has he done this? Why am I alive only to die? Why was my conception of Claire fickle, why couldn't she love me. Why wasn't anything truly working for me?

Nancy gave me some liquor from Ibiza, Spain to calm me down. Then I felt the reality of death and the helplessness I had in losing my body which I was so attached to. When I was sure that I was moving on, I saw the pattern and significance of all my experiences- much too fast to comprehend through the funnel of sensual consciousness, but I felt I was moving on to True Original Creator God Source energy. I was becoming a co-creator for good. I was becoming a Saint. Malick, my African friend, was telling me and reassuring me of how good I was and that it would be fine. I was excited because it was everything I wanted. Giving had increased so I was True Original Creator God Source-like.

Then came an emergency need to get into the bathtub. I stripped because it wasn't an issue and I was dying. Flashes of my childhood terror came back. It was a waking nightmare. The water was either too hot or too cold. I think I violently threw up and wondered if I had thrown up

Bojenmi tea. I passed out and fell into beautiful patterns and visions. I went past the Nitrous oxide stage of vibration. The sounds in the city and buildings seemed to be muffled and mutating. I thought indeed life was ending as we knew. We were being forced to evolve right then and there. I felt comfort that Nancy was in the other room experiencing her own ecstasy. Every time a change would occur I would adapt and evolve. When I feared the change I would feel love and everything was fine. Love, love, love, love, love, lo, ,lu, lo, lu. It seemed to be the sound and the feeling of the vibration that was constant even through the most ripping changes.

I saw a kaleidoscope of lives and energy. These visions of countless forms of life I have played out. I knew I was a hawk spirit because one flew up and joined the collage of events in the eternity of my spirit. I really felt the eternal and the possibilities of love if everyone were to give it a chance. Then it was time to function in the change and contribute to the evolution. Its forces were too powerful to even think of resisting nor did I want to. I accepted my position in the twisting change. There was an age where I was magma and rock twisting and contorting under the surface of the earth. There was an age where I was water and felt the rivers flow within me, not to mention that my bladder did not feel the need to resist flowing either. Then I would serve each of my ages with no regret knowing that I was as old as the earth. Sure my assemblage was new but I was still a dance of energies living out some divine will. Even in these major movements I still felt part of a larger unfathomable body. Along with the progressions of these ages I was in this huge spinal cord with nodes as far as the eye could see. My DNA spiral was but a microcosm of my spinal cord, which was a microcosm of the cosmic spine. Later I would see the similarity in the pattern of a fractal. I was there on this cord playing out my saint/True Original Creator God Source energy. Saint was the word that I thought of because I was gladly giving up a period of my existence just to be a part of the millions of souls gladly holding the chord together for the sake of creation. With the relevance of time removed everything was so much more significant. I was convinced that the most recent life as I knew it was giving way to change.

Just as you hear the sea
in spiral shells, a fractal sound of your inner ear
a young one hears the slamming doors
and the solid bowel movement of the attic door-
made me feel there was something more.

I vaguely recognized the groaning burps of the city and building I was in as the mutating contortions of metal sounded their mournful cry. I felt all the properties that we had previously studied were giving way to something new. The visions of all the evolving spirits were creating a new medium in which to live out their prana. My form was also going through all of the cyclic patterns, the seasons, winter came -I would hibernate. I envisioned that it was time to sleep things out until the lightness of spring would come. I was speeding through time and ages just as a creature being shown its behavior patterns in fast forward relative to the environment of which it was part. Spring arrived and everything was light and sunny. We could fly again.

In the bathroom, the collage was beautiful rainbow energy that was in the whole picture. Through the eye of the hawk I saw the colors, but not just red, white and blue -all the colors in all peoples' nations' symbols. Our future world symbols.

After experiencing the ages I began to slowly flow through the reducing valve into my mind. My mind and body still believed that something major had happened to the planet. That now it was a time for rebuilding, it was time to happily flow and build a new life. All the misery was over and now it was all going to be pure. I could wait for the light of day to reveal cities of crystal and beautiful skies. How ironic -now, it was just a matter of starting in the bathroom, to clean and fix the mess for which I was responsible.

So I looked around and found that I had been part of the grand mess. That we were all going to take part in a beautiful rebuilding. It would be so different but there would be no resistance by anyone holding on to the past, because there was no past to hang on to. In the very back of my head I wondered if things were truly different after everything that I had just been through. Surely I hadn't just been taunted by the whole vision- surely my whole experience of reality as we know it shifting into a time of so many radical changes was true, but why would everything in Nancy's bathroom be the same and ready for the physical revision? I looked around at the scattered mess that I had stirred in the bathroom. Now my feet were slightly in both dimensions.

Because I was ethereal...My submergence in the cyclic-on-dump (If you say the three words quickly, it is as I heard it in the groanings of the buildings) was back again. In other words, my conscious belief structure began to waver itself back into my reality. The cyclicondump is the state I realized I had created for myself. I was disturbed by this and I wanted to change it. I was so disappointed in the quality of life that the Breyers group had brought into their Karma. I want to urge an escape. Maybe this place is a supreme addiction and attractor. I think this place will suffer great devastation. Hate and evil thoughts multiply until it becomes an entity that destroys everything. Maybe this won't happen with the aid of special effects and dramatizations. It will be a slow neglecting death. There will be people denying till the very end, the new positive light force available to them, for free no attachments... All you have to do is surrender to the flow. Love is coming.

So I was disappointed in the hanging on of humanity in divide and rule so cruel. I was mad at everybodys' fear of death and my own. That which you anger you empower, so indeed I have brought much fear towards me in the closest blood. I felt a little guilty for putting Nancy through the ordeal of tripping and my near death panic attacks. I'm sorry she had to witness the collapse of my body for the purpose of traveling to other realms. How did that experience affect her? Is she secretly mad at me for putting her through that? All the limiting possibilities that unfold in my thoughts. Any expectancy limits the outcome of probability. Seems like a hellish policy to live out day to day.

Nancy's room was so enhanced, it looked like something Orwellian. A beautiful mechanical matrix that allowed her a small room and the power to decorate it however she chose. And live within the matrix of buildings in semi-peace as the dawn breaks and people think about scurrying out to get a crumb, so they can live in the excitement and frenzy of new possibilities.

If there is no frontier left on the weary Earth, shall the next generations begin to explore the power of our minds? Will the external become so horrible that everyone is forced to do constant battle with themselves or go within?

Should I mention the color orchestrators, the weavers, the giggling playful eyes of light who shape our reality? The little patterns of design that are in everything, regardless of the material or the make. They form a caressing, wavy blanket over and underlying all. They weave it so with the power of our minds- through what we've learned physicality to be. They are a soup that we stand on. If open enough, I imagine you can swim through the happy holding hands that hold them together. They are love and light weaved together in the most True Original Creator God Source-crafty way. They are of such a knowing that they can only serve you through the humor and expansiveness of your mind. They leave the clues in our waking life. They stitch the synchronicities. They giggle and unite lovers through countless ages. They are the tricksters having joy and love with what they weave. Only the brick wall of our addiction to the physical keeps the pain alive in our heads. In the heads of the unconnected. They are willing to show themselves but only to the OPEN. They will peek out with exposure to the openness, but in the area of any expectation they disappear like cultures. They disappear like the meaning of long lost cultures and animals of millions of years ago. These things are only lost to those operating out of the body.

All human experience can be known through the ether - the flexible medium in which they exist.

The days were swell for me. I had bonded with meditation. It was a marriage to the possibility of spirit. I had visited that other dimension, the other world and most of the long-lasted peace that had been found was while attempting to calm my mind and even observe it still.

Oct.31st Halloween early morning, Monday,

Rather an incredible weekend it was. First , I was ill after our family dinner with dad cheffing up the stuff that I later hurled. Friday seemed very long and hard, but then I looked at all the seemingly hard things I had been doing with my body. Smoking pot every minute, taking caffeine - weakening my resolve thus eating meat. Yet after Nancy saved my life by giving me so much love and enough attention to get me well I feel nearly reborn. Tweety was also supportive over my hurling diseasement. Yet I was feeling so much angst, that I only elected to hear the bleeding of my heart and the pangs of my agony. Then, after the charcoal pills and a day I was much better with life. I got out and felt growing energy. Went to run what seemed to be the first errand of my life. I guess with this expulsion I was really appreciative of the beauty.

Then Saturday Stacy told me about the better Apple deals, now I'm thinking about more; however there are people out there that could use my machine. If I was able to move up. The concert and Stephen and what seems to be his homo pranks -the result and talking to Julie. Then learning of the party, through her- the party and the beautiful day that Sunday was, Christi appeared and said we had to live together in California.

Klurngal, the Leprechaun, Nancy Jethro, Julie, Stacy, and Me. We were all together two nights before my departure away from the urban matrix- away from the concentrated doses of human experience. I was taking my leave from the village of the world where tribes of all nations exist in some strange abrasive semi-harmony.

They were all there to give me the most incredible surprise farewell party ever. Now I feel the excitement of the coming travel- my coming exodus from the city. Klurngal said I'd never forget this night. Now I am horny, less mentally and physically able. I want to love but instead I drank a potion. A potion of alcohol- wanting someone to telephone me having a broken heart. I have destroyed, forgotten less, consumption of our planet is the natural tendency until we are forced to deal with the light in the light reality of starvation.

I will not settle because I know what it is like to love Claire. I will find the answers deep down. Once I am sure, I will not succumb to the temptation of any other women. Jeff said, "It sounds like you don't know." Juie said "Good, don't settle." Well if I'm the little prince, Claire will always be my little princess. I can't let go or succumb to the potential tragedy.

Chapter 15

Second Mushroom Exodus

Initially in the Washington Square neighborhood, I wasn't sure what Lebanese food was exactly; however, it turned out to be some of my favorite cuisine eaten while in poverty. In a last rush to the airport, I grabbed a falafel, taboule, dolma platter, and then departed New York City.

I ate dinner with the kind man that was fixed enough in his location to keep my car in a warehouse across the street from my favorite childhood restaurant The Steamboat Warehouse in Washington, Louisiana for two years. I ate the fried catfish platter for fifty-two weeks and on the fifty-third I broke the trend with the fried frog legs platter. The car didn't start last night. I was tempted to believe that Claire would fling the door open and declare our exodus together. Yes, I would have someone whom I could love and we could escape together! It was only my wishful imagination.

I wasn't plagued by thoughts of her because the dinner was excellent and so was the conversation. It wasn't until getting back to my hometown Opelousas, where the wash of time and experience showed me a place to where I didn't belong anymore. No one to call on, nowhere to dream of being except in her arms. The habits and alienations of the town were the same. Still looking and longing for someone with whom to share life and similar interests -so far removed from all the trippers of the big city. I scanned and photographed the places of past anguish and pressure. All I could do in my last night of uninvolved visitation was feel empty. I watched the football stadium, the drums pounding with some foreign excitement of which I've never been a part. I heard the drums as I cried myself to sleep. Alone in a wooden home now covered with aluminum siding, as a guest of my Aunt and Uncle, my family felt as foreign as the streets I had just navigated. Not at all a very well put together model of life in either place or false-time-construct.

The light of day arrived. It was desperately time to leave. To begin my errands and complications before I left town. I was happy the rain had poured on the fields outside of town because my fruits of change would be growing from the cow patties. After grazing for a while, I found a variety of shrooms which were quite beautiful, yet unknown to me. I knelt down to one of these unknown kinds and stroked it. I was amazed at how supple it felt. I wanted to risk ingestion, but instead I just studied it. It was about five inches upright. Its stalk was skinny compared to the seeming bulk of its head. The top looked like magnified skin with the scales overlapping like shingles on a roof. Yet, the whole top was bronzed and not at all joined as a roof would be. I could rub it and make one of the shingles curl up a little, but I couldn't readily peel it up like a shingle. I thumped it gently from the side and watched its rubbery sway from atop the semi-dried cow patty. Amazing! that its gentle structure could hold up its volume of moisture. It had no skirt from when it opened its umbrella, but there was a clear purple spore print shading its stalk and its ground underneath.

After getting a better native feeling -when I hovered the ground and actually slowed enough to see the natural camouflage of a world unnoticed, I found the psilocybe of which I was familiar. After my third or fourth mushroom I began to feel no hurry. Where I *was* was just as important as where I was going. Then, after watching the way the wind combed the entire scape, I felt my sexual center call for attention. I couldn't distinguish if the setting or the flashing visions of girlfriends past was making me so horny. I found a nice tree to lean on and I began to stroke my penis with chilled hands that soon warmed. My visions of Stacy's yellow skimpy cotton underwear rising up her perfectly molded buttocks. The underwear was slightly disappearing into her crack, then reappearing a little more taught towards the small of her back. We were doing something she had never allowed me to do, as in many of my fantasies. At first she was on her stomach in bed and I was straddling her behind. I was moving the little twisted yellow moistened panties over so my penis could softly rub against her lips.

Then my head rolled back as I moaned the approaching ecstasy. I looked to see the beauty of the trees surrounding me- the shaky intensity of the leaves waiting for their release into winter.

Penetration, the bulkiness of my penis head meeting the tight resistance of her inwardly folding patch. Instantly she was enjoying the guilt-free moments of sex as I knew she would, Now I was on the bottom her back was still towards me. Her hair spilling down her back, the fragrant lines of her soft warm skin around her shoulder blades. With her shoulders pointed high and back and the rippling of her hair with every beautiful bounce, I reached up and felt the weight and silky folds of her bosoms and caught the expression on her face. The line of her lips matched so well the pattern of this erotica. I began to feel an itchy burn at the base of my penis. So many sensual cells being brushed by the matching co-evolved stimulus. Her silky cushion of pubic hair swafting mine, landing like a cloud then the weight of her pounding. I felt the rise of dopamine love liquid. -solidly building. I opened my eyes. Her, the leaves, Kali, nature, the swell, the wave, the expulsion.

Then, the coming down and feeling of usually being alone. My love affair with nature and with the knowing. This time, the reintegration of the climax was different because the mushrooms allowed me to feel OK about having sex with my visions of the beautiful women who were never there for me when I wanted. There limped quite a lonesome me and nature. Although had I accepted the rise of this energy instead of doing my captor's programmed sex spiel, I would have been able to move that feeling up into the higher energy levels of my awareness. I could have allowed the feeling just to "be" rather than expressing it. So I might seem sexually liberated, but a rather equal reaction to this rising energy could as well have been suppression. After my orgasm, I didn't feel hopelessly romantic. I considered the eight years of masturbation in an instant. Took a long, deep breath and walked on. I picked a few more and ran. Feeling the rush and energy to continue my journey and travel alone.

My next stop was Wal-Mart. There I saw how I related consumer culture to Huxley's writings in Doors of Perception. He talked about the models of cheap plastic toys in his head. In the store, I saw lots of these cheap dwindlings of overpopulation and mass production. Sugars everywhere to remind the user to just keep shopping and ground them to the high of the white drug. Everything instant and far removed from the nature of organics. Everywhere the groping of fat people. It took lots of my energy to remember the things that I had come to buy. I bought blank tapes so I could record songs for my journey to Florida. I bought a foam mattress, stainless steel cookset, stainless cup, a Wal-Mart atlas of the US, and a Coke at the register to wash down the pain and not feel so much like an observer but a participant.

Back at the Aluminum house, rushing to record and pack, I gave a shit to the toilet which seemed more like an eruption. Hurrying, so I wouldn't have to deal with the mind trip of my soon returning Aunt. Driving across town I snapped a picture of the house in which I grew up. The style and inhabitants became so different from the picture we retained while living there.

The cloud cover over the town was growing more and more ominous. Arriving at my grandparents', I saw that they had degraded heavily over the past 24 hours. My grandfather had no purpose written all over his face. His respiratory infection had grown so that his voice was horribly deep -he was dying of cancer. My grandmother was packing so many bags. I rushed them, grabbed all of the extra clutter. I was so aware of the heartbreaking disease and heartbreak going on that I could stay no longer. I headed to my old friend Roberto's house where I knew we could relax and smoke some Merry J.

I was beginning to create a matrix of complications. I panicked once I drove into Roberto's drive-way. I thought, "Oh, no he's not here, he's always done this. He's always left me hanging unannounced. Oh, no. No one to relate with before my "trip". Then, much to my psychic surprise, I found him watching A few Good Men. It was the final courtroom scene in which the public awaits to see and put the pressure on Jack Nicholson because he is elevated to the heights of genius by so many who have watched him weave his magic. I watched too and thought about mass consciousness and the way the movies shape their overall complacency. I was ashamed of all the lore of movie "magic". I was ashamed of myself for ever wanting to be in the business. Would I have been that close on the silver screen telling the people how they should act in the different archetypes they would encounter in real life. I realized my full capabilities, yet I couldn't begin the cycle of Karma for taking on the responsibility of the masses neglecting to think for themselves. It made me sick in that living room with the rich gynecologist and his son, my friend from the past, that anything conceived by the light of the movie, wouldn't be learned to the extent the original writer intended. At the same time, I didn't know the creator of the story-line nor his intentions, yet I felt it was all so trifling compared to what I was feeling. The movie was trying to set the stage for mass-consciousness.

Despite his family destiny to become a doctor like his preceding two brothers, Roberto had a pretty steady interest in the arts. It seemed to me that he had been interested in music all through high school. When I knew him in those days, he would stay in his upstairs living room strumming his various guitars while getting high. I knew he liked to draw, he would do that also, usually while high. I always liked to think that I was one of his exclusive friends, but the truth was that Roberto had many friends. Some of them stayed around long enough to outlast his weed supply, some didn't. He had no sense of filtration. He liked to get lots of people together, and it never seemed to matter how variant their lifestyles were. He was always amiable, though I found him alternately deep and shallow. To me he seemed a bit more shallow than deep on most occasions. I would give him credit for his periodic deepness, and extend his credit deep into the shallowness.

Roberto would always remind me of how beautiful the girls I dated were. That always made me feel better, as if I had really achieved something. One of my past girlfriends, whom he regularly commented on, was Stacy. She was the subject of many schoolboys' dreams. She was the one with yellow cotton panties aforementioned. The memory of her was the subject of many of my lonely fantasies for years after our actual regular acquaintance.

I had to go by my grandparents' house to pick up some of my last belongings. My possessions had been multiplied by my grandmother who had lived through two depressions in this country. I found myself very sensitive to the guilt that was flying, along with the clashing of thoughts that were so different. Despite their pace of preparation, I was rushing to get out of there. I no longer cared for the processes they had in mind for me. I couldn't be trapped in their intentions and expectations. I couldn't let them manipulate me into their comfort zone, so I would do things their way. I was feeling my wildness and didn't want to be contained in their fiction by any means. I couldn't sit there and pretend that I wanted to sit and eat a meal that I didn't want. It seems as if GaGa had an arsenal of grocery bags filled with her idea of goodies. She had neglected everything I had said about artificial ingredients, labels, health, everything. Her ignoring me proved her unwillingness to learn anything from the ascending times.

Whereas I have scrounged the planet looking for outlets for my expression in a country that has stifled and neglected to support its creative types, my grandmother has not had that freedom to be a knowledgeable person because she is dominated by a tyrant watching and closing his mind and taste buds until he was comfortably numb in his chair. The pain and regret festers as he nears his death. My mother is now content with a lesser degree of pain. Now that death was in his eyes I wrote:

Don't be scared GrandPa

of all the strange changes all around

Don't be scared GrandPa

now that you've lost your crown

Don't be scared GrandPa

now that the young silent ones

have grown to say things

you'll never allow yourself to understand.

Don't be scared GrandPa

it is just what these generations demand.
Don't be scared GrandPa
sympathetically now that your eyes are cold and hollow
Don't be scared GrandPa
of your mind and body falling apart.
The very structure that held your menacing beliefs
is giving way to the infinite.

I was slipping through all of their meat grinders and clauses that most authority hungry people design. In their policy, there is no room for truth and no heart nor art ornate enough to bring True Original Creator God Source down to it.

Time was spent with love for her grandson as caring was apparent in all of her packages. Always extra napkins, little treats tucked away to prove the physical love and her love of physical. The clouds hung thickly overhead in a dreary gray that ushered me to leave even more quickly. My grandfathers' voice had lowered three octaves. He had manifested an upper respiratory cold. His body could no longer accommodate his assertiveness. Like so many young men, Grandfather PePa was tricked into war, now his cancer cells battled against himself inside long after his survival from active war into domestic life in silence of what he'd experienced. When he talked he sounded somewhere between a duck and a bull-frog. No doubt the self created tensions he had related with my visit had shown their way to illness. He was upset when I would come and go as I pleased. My schedule was erratic and different. To him difference has always been a subject of fear. Anything out of the ordinary usually sent a flood of blood to his face. This is when he couldn't breathe so his aging head turned into a heaving pomegranate. The blockages were so apparent. I think to myself -surely I am not of that descendance.

In my parting, all that he could do now was make a few jokes about how he wished it was him going off to Florida. I was so relieved to be on my way again. My car was on automatic pilot. I was aware and present amongst a swirl of visions and dimensions. Least on my mind was that I was driving. Yet I felt completely safe and confident that I would do no others harm. I had released the physical preoccupation, but I would check in periodically to make sure everything was okay.

The wind blowing through my car! Yes! I was leaving town. The mundane scenery and confining thoughts of the small town were scrolling away on a miserably gray day. I was going sixty miles an hour in my 1966.

The umbilical cord of my path kept the car on the road. I chalked it up that it wasn't me who was driving anyway.

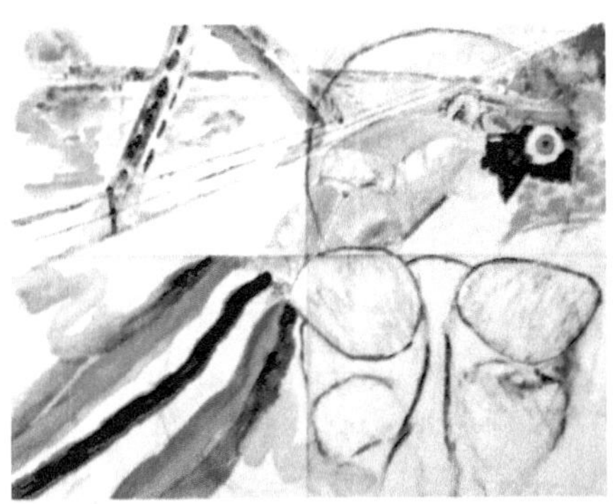

Chapter 16

"There's none in you, Budlong; you can only remember it. There's no real joy, fear, hope,or excitement in you, not any more. You live in that same kind of grayness as the filthy stuff that formed you." The Body Snatchers by Jack Finney

I wallowed in my desperate state of loneliness. I had no affirmations of self. In my helpless spiral without the one I loved, I denounced my spirit. I pouted over my human losses, my flesh losses. The rebellion did me no good but it was so. As a result my pool of creativity was full, but I allowed myself no access. By cutting off the True Original Creator God Source I cut off my very lifeline. I started raging, wanting company of any sort. I began to hang out with whom I didn't really want to be. It was all so gray and hazy. I didn't know which way was up. I played around with acid, a synthetic that I am truly not a real big fan of. The days after my two psychedelic journeys in which I felt deeper than usual but had no one to relate with nor expound on great truths. I felt the mundane creeping in on me.

One night, we were in an alternative bar in Pensacola. The owners were a young couple who I guess were caught in an effort to stay young, keep their coolness, and make money (false-currency-construct) by providing some alt. grunge environment where the heavy attitude of hostile youths could vent their societal compressed inadequacies. The prerequisite was that the bands that played there had to at least produce a loud, Pearl Jam/ Nirvana sound with gyration included. There were quality tunes that I appreciated but I'm writing from the frame of mind in which I was suspended in then.

In one drunken trip to the bathroom, I had that moment of clarity that happens to me either when I leave the bar or when I go to the toilet. It is a silent happy sadness. The only thing that seems real in the bathroom moment is looking down at my penis aimed hopefully for the water instead of the rim. Then the music of the clear liquid, since the volume of brews exceeded my liver's ability to deal, hitting the water has a tranquilizing effect. I began to think about how I wanted to talk to other people, but I felt unable. Then mad at the fact that I was with someone I couldn't reach. Yet I felt paranoid that any efforts to mingle would be sliced and diced by the small town and a vengefully jealous girl. Already, I knew the faces in the bar and I had only been there thrice. I felt herded. I felt repressively normal. This wasn't why I had come to the beach.

So I spoke to myself in hopeless, non-understanding anger about the girl who I had come there with. Coincidence brought us together. I merely recognized her as some silly little girlfriend from fifth grade. Wow, what a decline of spirit. She had not changed, nor did she know half about what I was talking about. I had injected myself into that old familiar alien situation mistakenly. "True Original Creator God Source, please send real love my way- not this gray bosom shit." I begged.

False alien empire bible god is sending me gray bosoms, but gray bosoms with the intent of haunting my head. Why do I hold extra hate towards my past? Many of the New Yorkers I knew could have been the objects of my hate for just as many reasons and indeed were, sometimes, now that I think about it. Weren't they? No longer verbalized, only at the thought level, since my life had demonstrated the Karmic return of negative **actions**, yet I was resisting the subtle truth of the return of negative thoughts. Of those, then I supposed my wallet showed I couldn't afford. I was harshly learning that my thoughts had banked their consequences in the betrayal I experienced. Could I call my love on a Saturday night, or would she think less of me. Boy, this seems really healthy. Only I couldn't because I fell in love with a girl that was emotionally unavailable, especially on the weekends, which was how she lived her life.

I feel like in New York at least my intelligence has the potential to be appreciated, whereas in the South I have the sinking feeling that all my attempts are wasted and futile. It is a mystery I wrestled with from time to time. Is it my background? -my continual feeling of being extra-terrestrial? Is it an inbred hate for the area passed down from my father's high brow arrogance? These were things that I didn't talk much about because of my continual mistrust of people -that they wouldn't understand me anyway or that they would give me some placebo-like a doctor or a pill or Southern Hospitality -a scratch on their head gesturing confusion, a pat on my back... I knew something was up early on in grade school, when I knew that my third grade Math teacher couldn't conjugate her verbs. Or a flash of anger like whiplash from the days of slavery, when My black third grade teacher would yell, with boiling red assertiveness, to some slacker, usually white, "SIT ERECT IN YOUR SEAT!"

Then she would turn to some favorite and her anger would have already disappeared into a sweet, concerned look somewhere in between her glance. Up until a few years ago, I always thought she was saying, "SIT ERUPT IN YOUR SEAT!" So it was by visual that I learned what it meant. So it was from visual and observation that I began to watch my life unfold. There were always influences I could regularly count on, but in the end I would choose my subject matter for the main fiber of life. Secretly, not even able to articulate it, I must have stood by my guns through the thick and thin, learning mostly from the actions and cycles of the gross humanity in which I was.

Never was I cued to believe that there was more to it than simply the flesh. The monotheistic plunges my family gave to me were a source of great confusion, but mainly it was a tremendous excuse to hold back laughter during most of the sermons. Just the serious silence was enough to compress my laughter into small volcanic eruptions. I had no concept of True Original Creator God Source, nor false Christian compassion because I lived from example and actions. Therefore, I felt resentment for the hypocrisy of people force feeding kindness one day a week to absolve themselves from guilt of the meanness they had dealt out the six days before.

Heading back to Perdido Key one evening, I came to the peak of the bridge that would put me on the sandy key:

Coming back
from a short errand to find love,
the top of the bridge revealed
the pain of light into darkness.
Ah, the sky
shows its blood beautifully.

When the Key slowly falls into darkness, I felt, as usual, the heavy nostalgic feeling that all was lost. From where was that coming? *It is the feeling of constant loss, duality, yin and yang. It is the feeling of not having your mate, of wanting to complete the void that one feels when not in touch with the whole. The chasing of ghosts and things out of reach to most now. The coming....*

Whether it was gray bosoms or not, the women that I briefly encountered that winter were veiled in a shroud of mist. There was something gray about every potential encounter. Something that I was finding deeper inside of me that said, "Naw, you don't want it this way." When I would resist and try to persist in an endeavor my guides would shield me by throwing some synchronistic problem into my plans. The women that were local enough to contact and reach, I was not attracted to them. The ones that I wanted, presented me with the problem that they were ever fleeting. It was always one way or the other, either I clung too tightly or I couldn't bear to be around them. Of course, some would become my friends, but I was forever suspicious of my male magnetism, which I felt I could quickly lose control over.

By my sixth week into a Hatha Yoga class, I was realizing that people are always at different levels. I self reflected and really felt that in spite of my resurging negativity. The point was to not condemn them for being at levels different from me, but to accept their time and capacity. That is a big amount of acceptance, an amount that people seem to think will weaken them if they learn to forgive all. Moreover, the wisdom to embrace all species. In truth, the acceptance doesn't weaken as long as you know how to replenish the unending reserve of energy. That comes through relaxing, breathing, and opening to the ever-loving silence of life.

There is danger, particularly for the super-sensitive like me, that you could place yourself in the position of being in others' company who want (subconsciously or otherwise) you to remain always at their comfortable level of who they think you are. That is what I was suffering from in the case of gray bosoms.

I interpreted it as gray flesh in order for me to take note of the darkness in which I was submerging myself. Seeking lightness and well-being was contrary to the outcome of hanging out with the darkness. I learned that being alone was much better than lowering my standards just to be in the mere presence of others. This also lets me know how much I was still addicted to others for my stimulation. Most spirits were bored and manifested unattended creations. The galaxy of amusements and creations abandoned now barely any ticket holding attention giving attendees. No audience

No attention except for/from the warden owner(s) of a trap, a detention center...

Chapter 17

The Heron

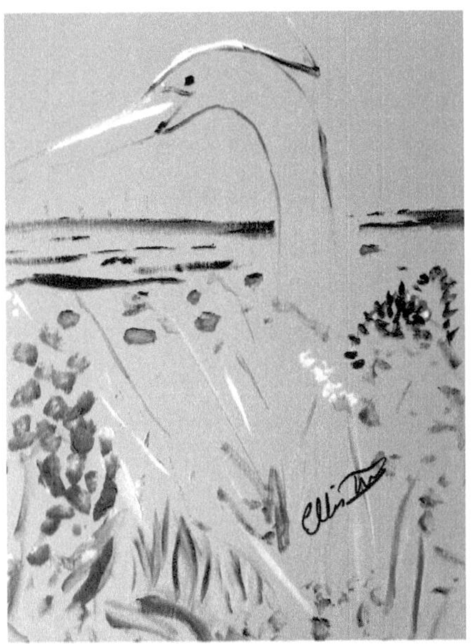

I had finally made it down to the land of my birth. It was all so alien to me though. The Fall brought with it all my childhood nostalgia. At first, I stayed with my grandparents near the dying downtown area of my small hometown. The inflexible and rigid show their wear and tear miserably -erosion of the soul. The Spirit is the Soul, the Soul is the Spirit. You don't have a spirit, you are a Spirit.

My beautiful Claire, together at last I thought we'd be. Where was she now, though? She wasn't returning my calls at any rate close to the amount I was fantasizing about her. Her golden curly hair had filled my heart for years. It seemed that the wait was finally coming to a close. The strange trial period of being out alone in strange lands all over the world was coming to a close.

Being back in the slow cadence of the South, the path and the signs seemed so right. The light was breaking in a way that seemed a bit more gentle than in the North. So much rain falls in South Central Louisiana. Lush greens were just showing their withdrawal into the drowsy winter. It was November.

There was strange talk about nothing all around. Already, the depth and level of conversations, of which I was accustomed to having, were fading. I definitely related this fact, in one way, to the climate and the change of seasons. In the North there are drastic changes in season. You could potentially fear for your life if you weren't prepared for it. In the South, there aren't too many days like that. The change of seasons definitely makes people behave differently. Some of these behaviors are better than others. The Northerners seem more abrasive outwardly. We use the word cold in the same way. Although not always genuine, you can find that Southerners usually make an effort to be more hospitable and warm -about the lighter things. The days are slower because there is no rush to gather for the long winter. In the North, the seasons make the people more hardy and adaptable to change -whereas change and oddities such as weather are seemingly more devastating to the masses of the South. There are of course benefits and drawbacks to both hemi-spheres -just the same is true for East and West. I thought to myself, in the backyard of my Grandparents' house, "Ahhh, the old back porch swing- how long has it been since I could look in front of me and see a little wildlife and green aside from some park framed with wrought iron? No one is threatening my space and everything is safe. If my grandparents knew that I was out here, they would expect me to sit outside for a certain amount of time -the time that they'd expect any "normal" person to come in after a reasonable sit." So being back in the spectrum of observation was pretty intense. Coming from NYC where I was left on my own to do as I wished. Plenty of freedom, but with freedom comes responsibility. It is unfortunate that so many people feel the loss of having strict rigidity, so they make up their own rigidities in fear of some sort of annihilation. They then try to come up with little rules and regulations that help them feel less vulnerable to the will of the True Original Creator God Source.

Although I looked out and saw the green patch of lawn before me and enjoyed the experience, I also remembered the peering eyes of the neighborhood. Forever suspect I always felt when crossing other people's property. The black passer-by was always deserving of a keen white shark eye. Anytime boundaries were crossed, the neurosis could be found to rise in the bitter blood. Grandpa could be watching television and some shade of a person who was unknown or unscheduled would cause the face of Grandpa to boil just a little. The fences seemed so meaningless to me.

The breeze rolled through the big Oaks on South Oak Street, then it stirred some dried magnolia leaves at my feet. The rush simultaneously brought me back to all my childhood frustrations of properties and fences. There was always some point at which I would feel disheartened and caged. Building little model rockets in a faded dream to shoot myself up into space, I would launch my little rockets and feel the pangs of crossing people's fences to retrieve the ones that went astray. I remembered how happy the woman in the faded light cotton gown was when I asked for permission. As a child, I hadn't realized how she had acted as if it would be a big favor that she was granting me - just to look in her yard. She had to come out with me to make suggestions and to be without a clue about the whole situation. Nevertheless, she **needed** to come. All alone and insane, she needed but had no one *-no one really different and vital perhaps.*

I looked out on the sugar beaches that were sandy playgrounds on vacation as a child sometimes twice a year. The lip of a thunderous wave quivered a little as it crashed on the sand bar just out in front of me. The Great Blue Heron didn't stir. I named all the herons "Lurch". I thought, "How do you move so slowly and so patiently?" I never felt I was competing with them for their incredible balance. When the will would rise, I would do some postures mimicking their balance out on the sand with the surf singing its lullaby.

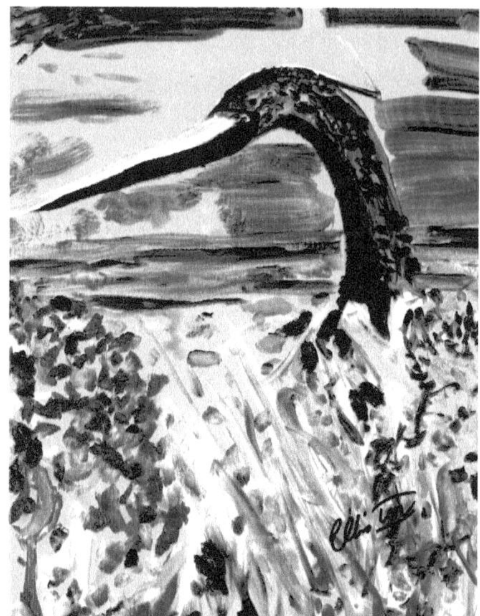

One time, to keep my balance, I opened my eyes to find something to keep my eyes focused on one point. I saw one of my Heron friends naturally keeping his stealth and balance fixed in pursuit of a meal.

That was all she wrote if a fisherman decided to feed Lurch a small catch of the day, they would then loom in the background and use their powers of patience for hours. It wasn't extraordinary to see a Lurch tripping in the same place for an entire day. While balancing, I watched the Lurch in the distance. He was keeping his entire body still while extending his serpent-like neck out over the water. What powerful spear gun necks they have. The ones that were accustomed to seeing me around wouldn't fly away, but rather slink away like the limbo man.

condom

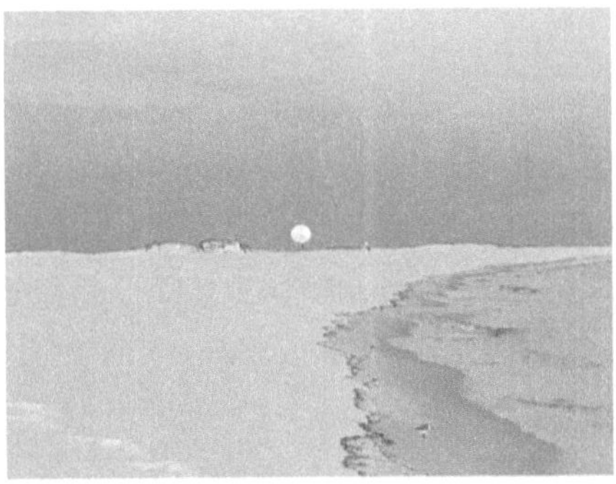

That night, I twisted and turned while a foreign edge of boredom came over me. I needed to do something. I felt I needed to get out there and assert against the problems of the world. In my mind I saw the two ridiculous signs on the beach. I reacted when someone insulted my mother when I was a child. Now, it was as if some greedy owner, with the same apparent taste for obtrusive rectangular structures was shoving his shadowing building over the gulf.

It was the last little nature preserve I had, and I found himself lacing my boots to go on a mission of dissension. In the near future of 2010, England's evil empire would invade again to kill countless people and creatures in the BP horizon invasion.

Outside, there was a misty breeze coming from the gulf. The gulf filled the air with its little briny roving land clouds. Saltwater air- it conducted the electricity and passion I felt. The safe enveloping blanket of air carried me as I took a back route to the huge monoliths where people lived and vacationed in their covey holes so natural to New York but so foreign to the nature of this land. There the buildings stood with their blinking red lights way up on top. Once there, a meandering path in the dunes took me to the waterfront.

Twenty yards in the distance, I saw the first red-lettered sign -a bloody red eyesore. I made a quick scan of the area. My face glistened in the moist air. The color was sodium -from the annoying lights that illuminated the Monoliths' property. I noticed how bright the light was and said sarcastically to myself, "It will take years for the people to realize the lights interfere with baby sea turtles -then the park service would supposedly protect them in later years. Yet, they just mounted huge bright LED screens on beaches all over in 2021. " I wouldn't be illuminated, though, down where the sign was planted into the ever shifting sand. I looked up to the towering structures that forced sun-down a little early in the summer, and saw that there were some old snowbirds hanging out on their balconies. Oh well, they'd watch me uproot 'em!

With the weight of my body, I began to sway the sign back and forth until the two, 2 X 4, supports had some adequate gaps in the sand. I heaved from underneath the sign and hoisted the mammoth posting out of its holes. Up and over-timber!!! I nearly shrieked with sneaky delight. It felt comical dragging the sucker into the gulf. I was even more ecstatic about the fact that the Gulf was licking its lips extra hard that night. Good, that would carry the damn things off to Cuba. The second lifting and dumping was as joyous as the first. Each time I had taken a few minutes to watch them disappear out into the water. The release felt so good.

Ahhhh. My conscience thanked me and denied the slightest possi-bility of feeling guilty. I was careful to walk along the water just in case some bored detective decided to pursue the case of the floating signs.

Chapter 18

The Grand Giggling Weavers

Many wish the True Original Creator God Source would come and lay down the Law like a benevolent king. It has gotten so bad in the loud inmate zoo down here, yet ultimately there is no alternative other than gaining the wisdom to respectfully embrace all the mixed galactic species occupying homo sapien bodies. There is an opportunity to realize that it is so bad that there can be nothing left to turn to in physicality, but to conceive True Original Creator God Source inherent in us all. There is so much misery in the cities. In any direction in America it is the same -peoples' loss of continual happiness.

Let's talk about the artists and the people who are different from the **norm.** As the most popular theater states -crazies are in fashion. Being a dumping ground for the undesirables, the untouchables, one would think that the overabundance of artists would lead to a creative peace or something at least rising above stupid old taxes, rent, starvation, etc... Because of the fact that an unusually high number of artists are dumped to burn up into the desire amnesia force screen trap in this part of the Milky Way, an actor like myself belongs to the Guild with roughly a ninety-eight percent unemployment rate. The accepted perceptions of reality are being challenged. At the same time, the trends and competition have stifled the artist and his works. The shifty eyed real estate people have helped to make New York too trendy for the poor creators to live. It makes sick to my stomach that there is no affordable way to have food and shelter without selling your soul in some way to the institutions of marketing. To survive taking a job selling the things that I know deep down in my heart people don't need?

The huge buyout corporations that consist of **people** yet they grow like warts all over for the sake of creating the mindless -more productive employee. Why? What is the hurry to out sell? What is the need to continue to create a nation breed of people whose job it is to consume fillers and propaganda? There really are no superpowers any more, just people being coerced into battle and killing one another. With mindless violent people out for a paycheck, in this way, our captors need to do very little. Wars are what control the population of a slave prison planet.

Truly the imaginary battle is over, the heavyweight closet militarists are left with their heavy led bellies to swing around. There is a breed of non-thinking consumer here in this nation. I've seen it so don't try and deny it exists. There are people who shop the giant manageries of sameness. With so many being cold, mean, cruel, and apathetic, artificial intelligence will probably be the next cold heartless logistic reality that will unfold. The Wal-Marts the K-Marts, the Targets where these usually fat people grope to find the sweet fillers that aren't even food or nutrition -mostly poisons. There are secret chemical poisons added to the food worldwide. All around you'll find the drugs of marketing complacency. The little sugar rolls -the COLAs, the gums, the chemicals. They're all convinced we need all of this shit. Since there are so many blind people out there -there is barely any room to survive for the person who doesn't want a part of it.

The youth know it. The aging dwindling older generations scratch their heads perplexed with the new device toting social media generation. The youth don't want the world you have sold yourselfs. A spirit just wants to be, not always have to do. So what is an artist to do in New York City -beacon of the Western hurry scurry? Get over a hell of a lot -that's what. Get over the fact that there are entirely too many rich people using the creatives. Get over the torture of taking your art to the street. Get over the sneers that accompany the relentless fashion. Get over the fact that there is nowhere you can go unless you play the rent game. There is nowhere you can go unless you own a plot of land. True Original Creator God Source's parcel that was meant to be free and plentiful for all. We are so far from the original Eden. Nefarious opportunistic aliens arranged this nightmare so wrongly wired, Adam and Eve have indeed been very busy fucking things up in the garden. Since the false alien empire bible god's inception and induction of the desire force screen trapping devil prison planet earth, living beings haven't stood a ghost of a chance. However, the good news is that the old empire was defeated in 1230 AD, now we must rise up and learn to tie our shoes ourselves. Mainly, stop using each other for personal gain. Instead we must equally consider oneself and others.

Why has the fruit of Knowledge been reduced to a shiny red apple? Why is it that religion has to be written into clever deceptive icons? Look up and see the apple. There is nothing to be gained in the apple. Just in case they look for the mushroom -which really hallucinations are just the way we were as spirits before the Earth trap. Just in case the little children dig in the dirt for the mushroom, we'll aim high and colorful. We'll call it the apple (as I look at my computer with a rainbow and an Apple bitten into). We were always make believe illusion generators. If there was edible plentiful food, adequate clothing, and shelter then we would somewhat enjoy. However, correcting and repairing a more than twenty-five layer devil's food cake prison, it's not that simple. Biological bodies are not fit for space travel, so relocating outside of the screen trapper zapper will be difficult enough. First the amnesia machinery has to be painstakingly located and destroyed. The rehabilitation and classification / separation of dangerous beings needs to be worked out. We have to rediscover and relearn the technology of how we can induce ourselves back into operable bodies that don't require our lessening of our inherent creative capacities. We will have to learn how to isolate and protect each of our unique vibration frequencies, so that each of us cannot be hijacked as we have been.

We have been trapped and tampered with by a devilish opportunist. This planet recycles itself entirely every twenty thousand years with its polar shift. This planet is not designed to have a steady and peaceful culture. If this planet ever was liveable, the death star moon was added and an extremely evil yet superior technology team modified and retrofitted this place as an incredibly horrific prison. This planet's beauty and zoology come from a long extinct industry of creature creation called the biotech industry.

We have to learn the technology of life itself. We will have to relearn and remember the mechanisms for which living beings are inducted into various classes and types of bodies. For instance, what type of being is fit to become a blood sucking fly or mosquito, wasp etc. What type of being does it take to simply transmigrate into animals like rats, birds, etc. We do know that a being who does not take responsibility for ones thoughts, words, and actions, then qualifies for certain types of slavery. Perhaps a being ultimately qualifies for this diminished form of existence through the Law of Cause and Effect. This type of being can be fitting as a slave worker and is used thusly. This caste and levels of merit and virtue is still operating even though the Empire has been defeated. The champion civilization known as the benevolent domain also continues to "use" beings of this type for mining, servitude, and certain slave operations evidently.

The current general model of homo sapien is what I call devil hardware, because the dual hemisphere brain has been modified to be a conjecture projector vulnerable to inherent faulty wiring and (devil, doing of evil, that which causes suffering) suffering making protocols.

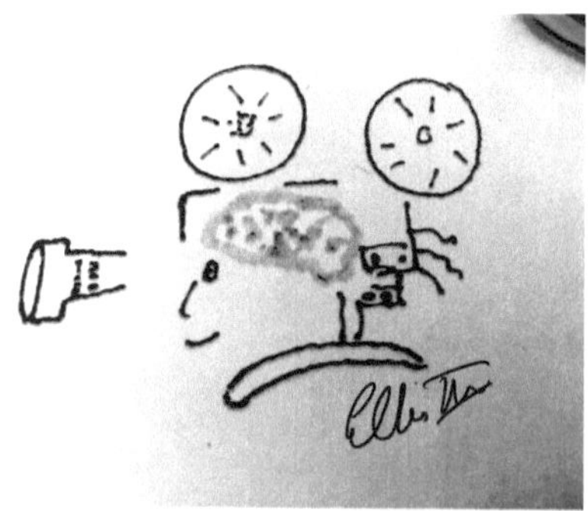

There are so many myths about sex and reproduction. I wish we could realize that it is becoming tougher and tougher because people keep having babies as if it were necessary to keep this (false alien empire bible god creator) forgotten and abandoned human race going. There is no reason to preserve or prolong the inevitable. Why? -because there is the almighty dollar to be made by more amnesia babies and continuing consumers. The more they consume the higher the bullshit profits are, regardless of the upcoming disasters that all will face -no matter how far they dig down into the earth with their food-stores and steel walls.

What is the goal of these high institutions? They want all to assume the roles that they have created. They want the feelers and caring people to work as clerks in needless stores, dispensing liquor poisons to those wishing for a nice little touch of sensory oblivion. How sick do I have to get before I start speaking out for the lost spirits in people bodies? How long will it take for me to starve before I give in to the pressures of modern life? How long do I face the terror of working for someone else's nightmares? How long must I face the misery and oppression? How long must I/we wait until the True Original Creator God Source comes into the heart of all of us? Chances are they don't care, like most, yet they are scheduled to arrive approximately 6,950 AD.

Modern art shows how senseless it all has become. And because it is acceptably senseless there is a barrage of senseless imitators of sense-lessness. People don't have a clear idea of what they are in the first place, then from there is the worthy bulwark foundation, then move on to more illusion creation which is what the spirit being does. It thinks, then decides to be. If artwork is hung in some glorified hall, then entrained beings impressed with beautiful heavy structures, will mostly credit the creations as viable. Soon people are yapping just to yapp about it. Then it becomes so yappably hip that it is put on a high shelf. Once it is on this shelf, it begins to collect dust. Creativity out of the necessity for expression.

On the third day into my excursion to commune with nature, my eyes and body began to clear as I felt the chilly fresh air of the Gulf of Mexico. I brought nothing but my journal. I watched the earth spin, seeing the sun go up and down -it is hard to imagine that we are not the center of our solar system. Just as it is equally difficult to realize that we are not so separate from all life including the original energy that provides for us even as we have lost our way -the grand network of life. On the first night, miles out on the Key, alone, I was already having thoughts of turning back. The temperature was dropping fast, so I began to think how I would only have to tuck away my pride to find my way back to the safe condo.

Perhaps I anticipated my weakness, I removed myself very far away from all buildings. I was happy that it would be more trouble to actually turn back than it would to sit tight. I did some deep breathing in the midst of my worrying. Instantly I felt energy and heat rise up my spine. That connection was enough to make me feel safer than being tucked nicely into the comfort zone.

My first night out was on a New Moon, and a cold Northern front had swept all the warm moisture of the Gulf back into the Southerly blackness. Grape Juice was my food. I brought a few pieces of fruit to start out with, but by breakfast I had already eaten them.

Those little painful flashes of mealtime would come to my head. I would be instantly caught in some poise and think excitedly that I had a meal coming to me. It reminded me of Pavlov's dog. Rather funny- I thought that I was the scientist experimenting on my own self. How many scientists have the guts to waylay their exploratory religion only to sit and run their extensive tests on themselves?

They are too caught up in the game of pursuit. They've mistaken the model vehicles of life for the real thing -the eternal spirit operating respective bodies. The feeling of wanting food would come and go. The sunlit curls of water approaching the tan shore of amorphous quartz, inspired me to listen to the greater forces instead of my ever-chattering mind. The Gulf held its beauty and integrity. It heaved and told me its beauty was much less concerned with time compared to our race of time and money -false constructs. Even with our constant abuse, it would continue to shine long after the tick in time that had produced the thinking human. I wished I was equipped to slide through the waters in harmony -just like the silvery-blue porpoise. It was always a wonderful peek-a-boo to see them. I thank that they do take in air when they blow and gasp in because it punctuates my life with glimpses of theirs.

The crafty Pelican was there too. I wondered what their life span was. I admire their keen piloting skills. They are in no hurry, yet they fly inches above the water, I marveled at them far more than the furious jets screaming overhead. "We're looking for war, drugs, and something to hit!", one fighter trainer screamed while approaching its Florida Naval base.

The government has too many rules. That is one of the reasons it can't help man evolve out of his survival fear. Three guys in a patrol chopper, cruising the beach can ask for permission from some big daddy to do a fly-by circle of some lone maiden. Yet, never could they bridge the gap between her and their iron maiden. Never could they be real with her- all they can do is be lusty deprived soldiers.

However, my thoughts of having my own sort of Utopia is similar to the founding revolutionary fathers of our own country. Rumor has it that these guys were a jovial marijuana smoking sort, who wanted freedom from previous forms of persecution. Primarily religious persecution, whether they considered Cannabis as spiritually religious as I did, I don't know.

I propose that we incorporate the entire known spectrum of colors. Good and Evil isn't going away, so let's all acknowledge that we are trapped here together, let's go deeper than good and bad and create value and happiness the world all over. Whatever your preferences in sensuality for gay as in the definition of happy for some. Although I am pitifully fated and coded to prefer women, until successful gene and memory therapies are available, I will have to find other ways to be happy -perhaps apart from the pain/beauty wave trap that so exquisitely entices me still. This concept of color relation is fairly different from the one I was brought up with. We are all children in the True Original Creator God Source -creation experience. There is something that exists as a dangerous child and that is what our government -moreover the industrial military complex has become. Let's just retrofit every destructive harming device with new water desalinization units, food, and seed bombs for edible everything. Let's cut off whatever is feeding on the world's suffering. Let's cut off the suffering by doing right by one another instead of harming and doing over another.

Even this far out on the Key, I wondered if there were any truly silent refuges left in the world. I wondered how much planning, money (false-currency-construct), and time (false-time-construct) it would take to get to one of those places. This wasn't within my reach, though I fantasized. I thought of the people of yesteryear, the creators of our time. They could step outside, perhaps a hundred yards away from home and find the sort of solace of which I was dreaming. The water called me back with its soft gurgles. It said, "Flow like me, release your fears and live your flow." I was thawing out from the chilled sleep of the night before. I could do nothing but recline and enjoy the sun's warmth.

I remembered my friend in New York, the ball-player who played in the Minor Leagues, but had to revise his entire life. We had many fun nights together, feeling like two limitless young warriors in the thickest jungle in the West. Our conversations took on a positive and pleasurable variety. Irresistibly his conversation would revert back to spells of worshiping the female variance. His interest in women had a refreshing touch of honesty, and perhaps, because he appeared to be up front with them about his desires, he was spared the attachments and needless commitments due to guilt and hurt. He later told me that I must be honest above all with a woman. "Don't pretend to have more feelings for them than you do. Just be honest and relax," he'd say. I appreciated his words, though they didn't do me any good since I was out in the middle of the sand, with probability shining no rays of women on my strange withdrawal. In fasting shows our meddled programming because hungry, horny, and lonely go together incessantly. If you are dying of starvation, then planting your seed in a woman, would be many men's dying wish. It is designed to keep allowing more spirits into the amnesia screencage as inmates at all costs.

Even if the poor creature is horrifically destined to a starving village.

I was looking upside-down at the waves while lying on my back with my head peeking out of my tent. Earlier I had seen the first person while I was out there. I waved and saw no response. I got the distinct heavy feeling that this person felt like I was doing something unnatural by being out here in a tent. I felt like I was in Huxley's Brave New World, like this guy might report back to civilization and I would be surrounded by spectators and put on display for little warped kids to pick on. I felt a little saddened that I was crucifying myself this early into my journey.

I looked again and saw what could have been the first seagull to trick me with his one-legged position. There he was alone and on one foot. I wondered intensely if his foot was tucked under or if he was one of the few that had had a foot clipped by some trauma. The wind gusted out of the North, the same direction the speckled gray-headed bird faced, he wavered slightly. I hoped that I would see that missing leg come down to complete his awkward landing gear. No such luck, his handsome profile appeared and disappeared -his yellow beak pointed North, then West, now East in my direction. He looked a little confused but proud that he hadn't given me the satisfaction of seeing him lose his balance. Now he looked a little nervous of me as he hopped on one leg in my direction. I was surprised, still seeing all of this upside down, he was coming closer. The closer he hopped, the more he piqued my curiosity as to why he hadn't released his left leg, if he even had one. I thought maybe he wanted food as I admired his arrogantly slathered visage.

It was in the same slathered image that his voice took its home. "Awk, aw, aw, aw, aw, awwwwkkkkk!" he screechingly slathered.

"All is well, Eliot." I kept looking at the bird, I knew they always spoke to me, but this time it was really words. It was very clear to me. Something had just told me that all was well!

"Relax." The voice said calmly, and instantly I felt my muscles, peeked with curiosity, relax. It felt so warm and safe in the sunlight. "I am an aspect of you. I am part of your greater spirit. The time has come for me to assist you in your path. You have found your signs along the way and the messenger birds we've sent have helped to guide you in your own time. The time has come to reveal an even deeper aspect of yourself. This will help you to bring about the truth in your current world. I am here to share a secret that will put you in some danger, but will prove your mission that you long for. It is your destiny.

"I'm ready to hear," I said.

"On my last trip to earth, I was named Lieutenant Marshall Oddy.

I was a product of your society. I was a spirit electrocuted between lifetimes as you all are. I was spirit dumped in a human body and in love with a spirit aspect of your current love, Claire. My mortal love at that time in this previous incarnation to which I am referring was also named Claire. Our love was so strong that is one of the powers which has brought me here. There are other details of my being here that can wait for a while."

It was as if the voice talking were reading my anticipation to know immediately more. It was answering my thoughts and ushering a feeling of relaxation when he answered.

He continued, "I was on a tour in Vietnam. I was a soldier, but I had a very kind heart and the only thing that kept me alive was my love for Claire and the wish to return to her to enjoy our lives together back in the United States. There were rumors that were going around the platoon. It was the rumor that some troops were being rewarded by their duty and achievement out in the bush. My guys under my command were all excited. They heard correctly that there was this prostitution resort in Africa which the government held for them as a reward playground so to speak. At the time, I thought it sounded strange, but anything that gave them hope I appreciated.

"Oddly enough," the voice continued, "within two weeks of our hearing of these fabulous rumors, our platoon was on its way to Africa on R&R. I wondered why in (false alien bible god's) god's name they would fly us all the way out to Africa for entertainment, but I knew the government had its strange reasons for everything.

Once we arrived the guys went crazy. It was indeed a pleasure ground for them. They hadn't been around women in so long. These were beautiful native Africans. They really were exotic women. I keep to myself even though women would constantly throw themselves on me. I thought of my love Claire and somehow was able to resist the temptations.

I spent my time finding out why the women were so submissive. I slowly began to spy more and more oddities at this pleasure camp. I discovered how they were breeding a little race of slave girls. I discovered their odd behavior through the guys in the platoon. They would bring their drunken sex stories back with them. Half of the guys were all excited because the girls they had been with had encouraged anal sex. They were teasing the other guys as if maybe they weren't desirable enough to do that.

I was curious about the huge annex that was near the pleasure camp. It seemed to be some huge medical research lab. I kept writing letters to my true love Claire back in the states. Some of my mail I sent through the proper channels, but when I began to wonder if we would ever be leaving this camp, I began to slip away and mail my more suspicious letters in Senegal separate from military mail services.

The months passed and the men began to get really sick. It was only I and a few others who hadn't gotten sick. Two soon died.

It was your government. We finally put it all together. The U.S. Government was experimenting on their own troops with some biological disease they were working on. I am here to pass this knowledge on to you. They were developing the disease in hopes of using it in war, but when the hopeless Vietnam situation ended prematurely, there was no way to implement the disease. They were working on all sorts of genetic diseases. By the end of the war, they had spent an astronomical amount of time (false-time-construct) and money (false-currency-construct) on the project.

Well there were plenty of militarists with this project and this special operation in mind. They knew that the cold war was ending. There were no more battles to be fought even violent soldiers were tired of the hell war produces, so it was that they directed their efforts on the people of the U.S. and ultimately the rest of the world.

The project was immense and elaborate. There would be a media campaign that would cover the introduction of the disease. They used the hate channels to deliver the whole thing. So you see, you are not wrong in thinking that your own government has a role in the AIDS issue.

They launched the disease in hopes that it would first devastate the gay population and then work on the rest of the population. It is all in hopes to wipe out creativity, beneficial sex, and viable art from society. They are hoping that they'll engineer a more fearful, complacent society. All of your instincts about the disease and its seeming repercussions are true beyond your wildest imagination.

The government has subsidized huge markets to gain more income from this tragedy too. They tipped off condom makers of the coming age. They have bought up many of the healthcare systems awaiting the business of death and sickness. They learned that in pre-existing genetically encoded traps originally woven in by the devilish captor alien empire genesis creator with living traps such as dopamine love, sickness, aging, war, and health, people will pay anything.

Not only would the widespread use of condoms create a huge market in the latex industry, the use of plastic between sensual desire fulfillment ie. love making would further their desire to create a more plastic- consumption oriented society -as you have noted mutilation of male genitalia is also one of many evil modalities of creating insatiable reproductive sexual predators.

The idea is the same as the huge corporations, made up of a power-ful ring of leaders, yet underneath the whole system is -people, human slaves. That is what is so bizarre. What makes the human race be a part of an organization that ultimately wants to monopolize everything?

"What can I do?" I implored with my new-found hope of a spirit friend who had my utter attention.

The spirit aspect began to give me a list of Generals and many details that would blow the cover on the whole operation. I wrote furiously in my journal as he helped to script the corruption of our America. He told me that I should continue writing my book, but that now I should include everything that I'd suspected plus the details.

I asked him why it was that if I knew Claire and I were indeed soul-mates, as in true comrades and friends from a very long time in the past , why would she deny me so? This is all for the now. Everything that is- is for a reason. If you were to be gratified with your love now, you would not be here learning of your true destiny. You would not feel the pain necessary to complete your work. Follow your intuition when the work is complete. Follow your dreams again. We will be with you. We will be smiling on you. The giggling weavers have knowledge of your life story. They will weave the soul-mate love together.

"I know of the giggly weavers!"

"Yes, they have indeed revealed themselves to you." Affirmed the spirit. "I will help to release the pressure of your mission. I will tell you of the future, but it will not burden you. The weight of the future of the human race will not be overbearing for you. We are here to help to accomplish that which has wronged so many.

Your mission will be accomplished as it is weaved. It's important for you to feel and know this. In a surge, I felt the relaxing alignment of my path. You have been me. Your love for Claire has been wronged by the government and corrupted spirits that also have been electrocuted between lifetimes and have forgotten who they truly are. I am a damaged aspect of you. I was killed once they found out that I suspected the role of the government. It was also found out that I had lines of communication to my love. She was hunted and killed because of my suspicions.

This plan of the government spanned into the future. The future world has been severely wronged up until the time of true original creator's Light entering the planet again. The "old Empire" has been defeated, however, the hundreds of millions of years of totalitarian rule has a long train of momentum -to break these enormous devilish patterns takes many time cycles. A certain group of advanced beings have summoned me, actually children your world's devil creator aliens, to help them find the point in false-time-construct where there is a person who could help to overthrow the human slave tragedy. This person is you -we know you are vilified, labeled crazy, outcast, and marginalized; however, your suffering will be redeemed and you will be healed. Your occurance and incarnation into this unfortunate poisoned insane prison is the very reason for your torture and the only reason why you have appeared in such a hell as this. You will not and cannot be killed by any of the insane amnesia children of the devilish prison planet earth.

The people in the future intuitively knew that there might be a person in the very late 1900's who could shine light on the grand deception of our current times. There are certain powers that can't be revealed or changed by humans. They did manage to find me. I am composed of spirit aspects now. There is no punishable body. You can think of me as a counselor or messenger existing in the ether, apart from false-time-construct and space.

I called for the giggly weavers and the color-orchestrators. They are the entities who have the shape of time in their weavings. They themselves had weaved all of our actions. The spirits had never knowingly worked with the orchestrators or the weavers!

That is the nature of the weavers. They weave incredible humanity, and so they also work with the upper realms to evolve change and wondrous events in unordinary dimensions. This is their love. This is their joy. You can imagine the giggling happiness when they finally saw the works of so many dimensions coming together to right a wrong in the weaving of true humanity and its prison break! planet earth. They are incredible and unspeakable.

I received a flash that sent my pen flying. I felt the flow. I couldn't judge the words. I already knew what they would say because I was receiving them in feeling, but it was the clumsy words that needed to be written for the work.

I (they) wrote:

It's not that the government is the big bad wolf to be feared. These things happened and that fact cannot be reversed. It is all relative yet relevant, and these things happen so we can evolve as spirits tortured as humans. Torturous hells become the tranquil light of diamonds so to speak. It is important to view the whole picture. The government has its feet grounded in only the physical aspects of things. Sure, they might be working on New Age armies, but it defeats the purpose of grander things. It is in this view that the limits of growth take over. The old beliefs have trouble releasing to the younger, more current ways of thinking. As long as the myth of dying and aging continues without an understanding of the transition of matter from death to rebirth, these tragedies will continue to repeat themselves. We are nearing a level of mass consciousness that will foster the opportunity to quit creating the terror that old belief structures would have us buy into.

Considered a crazy man by most of his closed minded peers, Einstein revealed technology that revolutionized our way of thinking. Because of the threat of losing our promised land to opposing forces, we took that technology and began a new cycle of atomic karma. Because of the sexual reproduction encoding that we've faced in our world since the genesis devil interloper, the numbers increase to fund the reaping of our earth. The numbers are so large that death must come in larger waves also to compensate for the larger numbers. In 1910, a family might have been traveling West, but then the wagon could have overturned and killed their newborn addition to the family. The proportions of people killed by disease was much greater too. The myth, though, is that we can try to analyze all of these factors on our own. We are not on our own. This is not a playground with Tonka toys. This is a living, breathing earth. We are but cells in a greater divine organism. So this organism is naturally going to rid itself of the rampant bacterial growth of the human population corrupted by the devil alien child interloper. These trends have begun already. Masses must die from greater scale causes. Cataclysms, holocausts, earthquakes, cancer, war, AIDS, these are all preventative cures for the nightmare that humanity has perpetually created for itself given its design flaw encoded by rogue empire prison planet wardens yahweh (Defined empire agent: anonymous) empire alien interloper devils. This disregard for human life on such a grand scale is a reflection of our inner and outer reality.

The government is just willingly playing out its hate cycle. We the people gladly give in to wide-scale spending. I am pro-technology, but I realize it is a very dangerous tool that must be used with wisdom and compassion. Much of the money (false-currency-construct) we spend on technology is obsolete compared to the power of our own minds and moreover the fickle hearts. I look at cities and most places today, and I see hurrying and scurrying just like ants. Man was just like the animals for millions of years. We have come to a place where we must consciously slow down our busy, busy, thoughts and begin to realize just where it is we're headed. These realizations don't come through the complacencies of television and marketing, nor church, state, nor government. Nor do they come from the drugs of complacency such as white sugar, coffee, meth, coca, alcohol, etc. They come from within, from a conscious effort to stop the pain we create for ourselves. Unless we open up to all the limitless energy available, we'll fail to use our creativity that is naturally our Spirit birthright.

People say, "Why aren't our kids learning such and such?" Because the school systems are overloaded meat grinders, and by multiplying babies carelessly, the dependent, programmed, ignorant rely on someone else to take care of their kids. The earth is abundant. We have the technology for nearly every family to run their own near self-sustaining household. Thanks to the evolving networks of computers, we will be able to access huge amounts of technology. Including alternative energy sources. I'm not suggesting that we forfeit everything that we've gained. I'm suggesting that people re-integrate nature into their lives. By doing this, we can co-evolve for the wondrous changes up ahead.

People need to take a look at all the artificial chemicals and drugs that the circuits of manipulation deliver to their doors. These drugs are originally plant-derived mostly, however, then chemical makeshift analogues of lesser intelligent science are fabricated then refined through man-made chemicals that cause them to lose their integrity. Especially when these things are synthesized by man, they have no natural support. There are so many free plants growing all around. Many medicinal weeds grow to help us. One of the best sources for referencing the plants you might need is published by the petro-chemical companies that sell weed killers. There is no reason to kill weeds. There is no reason to be cosmetic about nature. It is where we live. There is no reason to mow lawns. Nature as it was designed is just fine untrimmed by man. It is the divide and rule lack of self control that causes the infantile amnesia babies to attempt to control the ever growing diversity around them.

<u>Chapter 19</u>

The Mission

The last two weeks were harder than I thought. Though I constantly received the will to complete the work, my fingers were sore from typing the final pages of what I thought years ago to be a story of a guy who learned how to create his own reality. I thought it was going to be myself proving to me that I could be Lucreative, which was my word for lucrative and creative. I spewed to no one about my project except Julie. Her publishers received half of the book already and I kept her posted about the rest. There were moments when I saw myself in the future missing those I had known in my life.

I wondered if Claire remembered the excitement of me announcing prematurely the "book" that I would write. I wished for my star-seeded love who hadn't germinated with new and open ways. I made ten disks containing the entire documentation and mailed them to friends and relatives. I couldn't trust the fact that they might be all too curious about what it was that I was keeping safe from myself. Until anyone had the private key, the disks were useless. I encrypted the disks with a code that I only gave to Julie, my trusted publisher and friend.

Despite her alienation towards me, I called Claire. I told her to listen well. I told her to write this name and phrase in a place that was very secure and secret for her. I told her to ignore the resistance inside herself, and to do it even though she thought it was silly. I was not yet an issue. I was not yet hunted.

I instructed, "Find Malick Gueye in New York City. I told her that she could find him at the Harlem Car Service. When you meet him, tell him you want to take to his home town in Africa. You will have to buy airfare for both of you. You will have to take care of this when the time comes because I can't afford to part with the money (false-currency-construct) right now. He will trust you and he'll take care of you. Make sure that he takes you to his friend to make the necessary documents. Do everything in cash and use different names."

Feeling my truth in all of these matters, I was really concentrating on what my life would be like after I faked my death. I wanted to feel like I could continue to live a life, but my desire to fake my death so that I could go on without other people aging me and expecting me to die wasn't quite enough to inspire me over the edge. I knew that once I exposed the government's plot against creativity with AIDS, there would begin an immediate hunt for me. Somehow, with their immense networks and resources, they would find me. Even though their structure would hopefully crumble by then, there would still be the repercussions of wrath for those I had caused to lose their precious position of power..

The worst part was not being able to say good-bye to anyone. I couldn't act as if anything was different. If I did, I knew that this would put anyone who knew me in danger.

I thought of the plan a thousand times before. Once again the weavers had been at work. I wouldn't have known what to do, if I hadn't rehearsed it in my head a thousand times before. The times that I'd rehearsed it, I sincerely thought that it was because I wanted to fake my death to all those who knew me, because I wanted a shot at immortality.

If everyone thought I was dead -I could disappear without anyone having any idea how old I was. Until I could learn to disappear and re-appear at will by heightening my vibration, I would have to continue to do this every ten years or so, because otherwise the new people that I would know would wonder why I wasn't aging. They would begin their natural subconscious human action which is to age people just by your preconception of false-time-construct. It is the duty of other people to unknowingly age others so that they can feel comfortable with the false-time-construct. I would have never been able to really put the plan of faking my death into action. It was because of the true impending danger that forced me to detach from the ones I loved.

I thought it odd that I maintained a schedule with my sailing lessons all through the winter. I had long since learned the works of the boat that I used every Friday morning. I had dropped my sailing teacher two months before, but I continued to rent the boat to sail anyway. I felt bad that I would have to sacrifice the boat for the stunt. I felt at ease since I knew that I had maintained that schedule of sailing every Friday in some subconscious effort to remain steady and punctual. They wouldn't think it was unusual for me to be gone for two days.

No one noticed as I pulled up in my 1966 Volkswagen. It had a familiar ping which everyone knew. The car's beauty could be seen from miles away. It never failed to smile at me. As far as I could tell, no one noticed I lugged a huge vinyl duffle bag along with me. This was my way out of the disaster that I was mocking up for myself. The contents of the duffle was an inflatable rubber dinghy.

At last I was out on the open water with my sailboat and a mode of escape. Once the horizon of condominiums had disappeared, I continued to sail for hours more offshore at a nice little clip. I inspected the extra motor I'd brought for the dingy. I checked the extra fuel tank that I filled and brought.

I used a little briefcase compressor to fill my dingy. I pitched my water sealed pack with clothes and food for the journey in the dinghy which bobbed up and down in the gentle swells. I pulled it around to the back of the boat and lowered the ten horsepower Evinrude onto its fitted transom. I was getting really nervous now that I felt the extremity of what I was going to do.

I wondered if it all wasn't some crazy long drawn-out joke that I'd played on myself. I lowered the full fuel tank into the little dingy and felt that I was nearly where I needed to be. I went below to where the fuel lines were and replaced the valve in the fuel line with one that I had intentionally fractured on the underside. I had done this weeks before. It took me a very long time to make the fracture just wide enough to let out a considerable amount of fuel. I had soaked the underside of the valve in salt water so the corrosion would camouflage and work on the fracture. I was satisfied when I examined the valve from atop and found that it looked like a perfectly sound device, but from its underside you could see its urgent need for replacement. I relied on the fact that the deckhands weren't reliable safety inspectors on their boats anyway.

I had fretted about costing Zeke's Rentals a sailboat, but over time and conversations, I learned that they were well insured in case of any accidents. I figured that the lives and the future of our civilization was worth at least one sailboat.

I gathered my trip line and released the fuel valve. I approved the nice trickle of gasoline as it made its way down to the well of the boat. I was very careful with my lines that ran all the way down to the base of the boat where the gas and fumes were quickly gathering. I boarded my little craft and started the engine. I made sure that my hair-thin copper wire was free to be rolled out as I trolled very slowly away from the boat. I began to feel a heavy forbidden quality of the air- it was the extremity of my seemingly mad measures. Just then- a school of flying fish caught the little wake just off the bow of my little boat. They were so angelic and beautiful as their glistening wings caught the orange of the setting sun. I was instantly comforted in the rightness of my mission as I saw their little faces who seemed to smile in their joy of breaking through the water for their brief excursions into the foreign element of air.

I took a few moments to marvel before I continued. Even at this point of nervousness, the weavers were still sending me magic signs which only I could see. There was no more discourse from the Lieutenant -all I needed to see were the signs and feel the presence of who had weaved this moment into being.

I was letting out two spools of the fine wire just in case their were any problems with one breaking or snagging. I was nearly 100 yards away from my sail-boat. The wind had died while I deboarded, but now the wind suddenly filled the sails of the boat. I had some amount of trouble keeping the spools of wire free for slack and piloting my little boat in the same direction that the sail boat happened to take off in. I had stopped her into the wind, but by chance it was now piloting itself. The sun was nearly down as I reached in my smaller purple pack and felt for my binoculars. I scanned all 360 degrees for quite some time. There were no ships or aircraft in sight. I wrapped the wires around three piezo quartz ignition devices from cigarette lighters. I prepared for the blast and squeezed the first of the devices. It didn't fire. I pictured in my head the rigging. The one I had just pressed sent a current through the lowest positioned contact above the fumes. It was taped loosely to a floor beam with the tip of it nearly a quarter of an inch from a floor bolt. It needed the metal so the little spark could leap just like in a spark plug.

The second rigging I had a little more faith in for some reason. I felt like the gas would be right at the correct level for the spark of the second try to ignite.

I squeezed and heard the click along with a "wooooof" which immediately blew out the cabin windows. Less than a second later, another part of the boat blew heavy and the whole boat was a phoenix. Once the nylon fuel tank melted, the boat had no future, and I hurriedly reeled in what was left of the wire and twisted my engine to full speed taking me East towards Santa Rosa sound. Soon I was safely far away and the boat was still a glimmer in the distance. I was happy to see that the light wasn't too intense. I was happy that I felt free. I had to make it look like an accident. No one could know that I was still alive. They would presume I abandoned ship and was lost at sea or had become fish food for a hammerhead or such leviathan.

I realized that I was only a bit through the thicket. I began to feel the hardness of my lonely mission again as I scooted along to a secret rendez-vous of which I only knew. A few beckoning lights inland were off in the distance as I burned my fuel down to about a tenth of a tank. I killed the engine, and rigged the little mast that allowed me to hang a decent sail for the rest of the journey landward. I appreciated the quiet after running the engine for so long and clipped along to my landmarks ahead. Once I was near my intended campsite, I cranked the engine and sped onto shore. Soon after, I found my marker and my fresh tank of gas that I'd left there. I found them undisturbed.

I soon pulled out my sleeping bag, and without eating I passed heavily into slumber. The morning had brought the tail end of the Southern

Winter. I fired up some hot green tea, and heated up some pastries while I looked at my travel plan. I would be traveling by day now and assumed that there was no search out for me yet. I would have at least two days as long as the weather held up.

I made enough timely progress on the way to Destin. I would run low on gas, but then I'd pull into some cove and get gas. One little guy at the waterside Exxon wondered where I was going with two tanks of gas, but I just told him that they were for my bigger boat -that I was only running back and forth from it because I wanted to leave my crab traps and net lines set out on our boat. I was delighted at how that satisfied him. I was also impressed by his change of attitude when he discovered that I had a "bigger" boat.

It made me think of my own absence from any sort of notoriety. There was no long-lived prestige left for a dead man. I even fantasized of the escape that my death would give me for the ego-acclaim that my book would generate. I was free from future book-signings and literary tours. Maybe my mind was far ahead, but the book was on its way to world-wide publishing. Julie had set a Last Will for me and we set up a trust fund named unto my mother and thus into two numbered bank accounts.

My thoughts turned to Julie. I gathered that she had received the manuscript by now. I had faith that she would get everything ready until she received the coded message that would allow her to set the opening date for my book. I couldn't have the book released just yet, there were things that I still had to do.

I finally made it to Destin. I abandoned my boat where I was sure that it would be claimed by some wanton pirate. It was a sweet little craft and I had become quite fond of its temperaments on my long adventure from Santa Rosa Sound.

I took a cab from an Exxon on the Destin Parkway, and soon found myself relieved to be French-bathing and changing in the airport bathroom. I purchased an airline ticket to La Guardia airport, New York City. I used cash and with my ID named Donavan Greene.

I felt an ebb and flow of excitement as I saw the evening skyline of

Manhattan. I realized that I had nearly forgotten of my death already. I was yearning to see my sister. I thought of the laughs and the good food that we'd have together. I spiraled negatively for a while after I realized that I had launched grand impossible bubbles of happiness in my mind's eye.

There would be no happiness, but only the Marriot Marquis in false-Times-construct Square. I wanted the most generic and mass populated place I could find.

<u>Chapter 20</u>

"Orson Welles of the INTERNET" except the Aliens are our own Government!

I wasted no time in following my intuition. I knew that most of the nation was crazed by the media blitz on the newly budding Internet. I felt it only proper that New York City would be next to open one of the cyber-cafés of the future. I knew it had to be so. I was not surprised to find the ad wanting people with Internet experience for a new and exciting Internet Café that would be opening soon. I used my laptop and its internal fax to type up a résumé that was sure to get me some meager position inside of this new place.

I was so excited about this place. I knew that it would be perfect. I knew that it was one of the first places in the world where anyone could come into the restaurant and assume an anonymous presence on the Internet. There was no way for anyone to track you while you sat there in the East village amongst the chaotic bohemia forced to the streets by the desirability of property in New York. Once again, the high-shelving of anything interesting.

I was a little disappointed that it would be a couple of weeks before the restaurant would be open. I could have guessed that every seeming delay is for a reason because it ended up being to my advantage because I was needed in the set-up of the place. It was in this period that I got closer to the hacker who was putting all of the tech together. Knee deep in the technology, he still had a presence that I wanted to know more about, but there was no time and there were layers of strata to dig through.

It was a test of my patience because I felt the impending urgency of my release of the book onto the Network of the world. I needed to reach the people who were already wired. It was something that I had to seek out and patiently wait for the time to release my knowledge. I would have to drop my information bomb and run.

Lars Pauly had been excited to return to New York City to challenge those demons that tickled his childlike mind years ago. He was coming back to the city nearly fifteen years since he had sworn that he'd seen something really evil in the City.

Over the years, that vision grew dimmer and dimmer -so it was with technology that Lars needed to wage his little war. This was his pet conquest and his daily bread. He had been attending Cornell for years scraping through school just to make the grade and pick up what he could in between parties. His eyes grew grayer and grayer -they were sinking farther in the back of his head. It was as if his eyes were drawing deep back into the cave of his mind.

The first few months in the city had been rough, but he stuck it out in order to wait for the dream that was about to emerge. Shortly after his move, the apartment he shared with his designer artist friend looked like a computer lab. Flenn, the artist roommate, was way into computers too, but his forces were torn towards a hot French fiance and the direction of creativity and expression. The talents of Lars were better served in coding C++, perl, python and upcoming java in deep tech and few in the city understood the genius with which this young wizard mastered computers anywhere.

A knock on Lars' office by a friendly gay graphic artist produced the frazzled computer guru. He was a walking piece of hypertext.

"This guy looks friendly. Hire him." said the Graphic Artist.

Intensely shrugging the guy off, Lars got back to the point. Deep down, it looked as if Lars had a sweetness and an innocence that some-how kept him aloof.

I wagered that they needed my help getting the first and biggest Internet café running by the end of that month. I guessed correctly. The next day I was breaking open computer boxes while we broke ground in the first and biggest on-line cafés in the world.

You could feel the anticipation of an opening into the unknown reaction of a public that was being fed and hyped their knowledge of the "INTERNET" by the media.

Sadly, I knew the dream of free information exchange would be somehow barred by the raptors of the power captors. No coincidence of all the media hype being directed to the NET. I speculated that there were huge conglomerate forces already at work on this. I expected that they were feeding the continual hype through the media channels so that the public would build up their expectations for the Internet and for CD-Roms. The media would do its job in sensationalizing and over-simplifying the whole thing just to get their greedy little hands on the story and clogging people's brains with confusions and fears.

Floods of people would pursue the Internet but wonder what was the sensation that the media spoke of. They would flood into the café wanting to see something like television. The channels purposely launched a huge bubble so that people would be let down by the whole technology when they went out into the world to find out just what it was that was so exciting. There was no speed, ironically, the medium was underdeveloped when the people met with it. There wasn't the adequate speed that their image filled American eyes were always gratified with.

I suspected that there would be a huge let-down involved with the Internet. Meanwhile, the huge conglomerates would use that lull to figure out how they could corner and monopolize this huge opportunity which to them was only commercial. They couldn't see the value of a world network unclouded by the ranks of commercialism.

A wonderful and creative space in which everyone can create. The promise of a free exchange of energy and information bowed down to the continuance of the old models of capitalism.

How would the public react? I was happy that my mission gave me a perspective like a lofty bubble watching the joy of all the progression.

My manuscript was well on its way with Julie. I knew that she and the team of editors would speed the book through the works. I figured I had three weeks before my life was in danger. To my new found friends,

I was Elly Belly. I pretended to be a humble tech helper while I watched the café meet its opening with the press.

I watched all of the people knee deep in DARPA technology. The ever-changing chaotic silicon crystal technology. People were stoned with the technology. Feeling like there was such a potential with the Internet was the norm. The question was what was this potential that everyone was so excited about? Once big business caught on, it was becoming ever sweeter to be involved in the commercial development of the NET.

Every corporation, business, wanted to figure a way to get their on-line side of business going. It isn't a thing of beauty to the business people of the world. They don't see the possibility of people exchanging information freely around the world. Nine out of ten people would ask, "Yea, but how do you make money (false-currency-construct) with this?" They would rear their heads back cockily as if they had just posed the newest and brightest question around. That was the extent of the wonder for all I could see happening. How could you make money (false-currency-construct) was all the slave victims asked? Madison Avenue scurried attempting to translate television into the NET.

Everyone was rushing to find out how they could own it. How they can claim their stake and share of it all. Of what? It doesn't exist. It is just electrons and energy. You can't own this. This is a frontier but it is meant to be used creatively, not to be dominated by borders and owners. The potential disaster of such is amazingly glum.

Many of the creatives can be seduced by the money (false-currency-construct) involved in the NET. For once, the younger generation has an edge up on all the crusty sugar daddies of the money (false-currency-construct) world. The kids are laptop toting cowboys in a new frontier.

The kids have the stage. They have the wild west in their hands. They are empowered by the technology and the openness of their minds to understand the rapid changes in the state-of-the-art.

However, kids want toys. They are little network gurus, yet they want the adult toys as every child would lust for. The fantasy of having money (false-currency-construct), fast cars, and independence, well it looks as if it is overpowering many of the young ones.

While the old greedy manipulators dangle the car keys in front of the computer generation saying, "You can have this if you'll just sign this. You can have your fat apartment and your young cocaine whore, if you'll just put our sick world into this fresh virgin world of on-line space. We will make it worth your while."

There is no soul in those deals. There is no progress being made, because people truly fear the changing of the current model of operation. People fear the possibilities of giving, so they subscribe to taking. Trying to take the freedom from the masses, when it could be the entire empowering of the masses. Such a bright future for a mirror on the world. The mirror is rewritable. People can choose what to have on it, but instead the low level animal control or be controlled choose the irony of broadcasting trapped redundancy.

Computers can demonstrate the wonder that we can create in our minds through mathematics. Computers also automate mundane tasking. It is just a tool, but how often does the tool get mistaken for the GOD.

I was quickly becoming disenchanted by the entire simplification of the false-times-construct by the media. People are fed what the media channels think that the poor little dears can digest. So by the theater false-time-construct news gets down to the average person, it has been watered down and censored so much. To what end? The only end is the non-caring of the turning away from humanism so many media puppets exemplify.

I, myself, felt like a giggly weaver when I stepped back and looked at what I was doing. Here I was preparing an announcement of how the Government had nearly succeeded in robbing creative faculties through biological warfare on its own people and the world at large. This was just the beginning in uncovering the camouflage of devil woven sex and reproduction for planet inmates. Ironically, I was going to announce it through an entity that the government had created -DARPA. Who would have ever dreamed that one of the instruments of the cold war would be used to expose the greatest corruption of the century. For the first false-time-construct, the corruption would be caught in the act. Thanks to Lieutenant Marshall Oddy and the Internet, one of the many disasters was somewhat curbed. Many more dis-eases will be uncovered in humanity's long and painful uphill climb out of darkness towards enlightenment. Many elements define this concentration camp holocaust fallout prison camp earth infirmary. Complacent belief and vulnerability to so-called greater powers outside the Spirit of each of us remains the most vulnerable weakness of all as it allows governments to fly too high abusing all in their promise to protect and serve.

I confided in Lars and wasn't afraid because I had come to know the depths of protection and his loyalty always proved true. He irresistibly yearned for the challenge of what could be done with the machines. At first when I told him that I wanted to send out a message to as many people on the Internet as I could, I realized that I would have to tell him what the message really meant and how they would have to find out about it. I showed him copies of the manuscript.

He hungrily read my files with intense concentration. His shoulders lurched forward and his head hung out goose-like as he looked up from the chapter on the holistic learning Center, he craftily looked up as if he were coming into a sparkling idea, "Man, you're gonna piss a lot of people off. Ya know, we should take this Ocean Center's WWW page and make some simple revisions. We should post these chapters so all can see them. We can then do a department mailing to everyone in the place telling them all to check out their new Web Page." He lunged forward with crafty giggles. I reared back with satisfactory laughter. It was this guy's ingenuity that I needed. It wasn't just talk- he began right there in his little cramped lab. By the time I finished laughing heartily, Christian had pulled up the Ocean Center's Web page on one screen, yet on another he was scanning for backdoors into their server. "Oh, yeah, this will be easy. He hacked up a new Homepage that included the text of what was revealed, and on the Ocean Center's Home page he pasted up a billboard saying that there was something new and compelling that everyone needed to check out. He was about to hack into their computer and make it so. I had to hold him back- he was raged. I told him that we had to save it for the right moment- when all the synergy would come together.

"Take a deep breath and read on-" I ushered.

He continued, while I refrained from watching his expressions. I began to surf the Net a little. I was amazed at how commercial it was becoming. I had trouble finding anything that interested me, but I always did find something. It is an intuitive and perplexing environment. I don't remember how I wind up in places, nor how I got to them, but when I am open to it, I find that it flows much like surfing. It is a seductive analogy, though. The waves can still be found outside in real life. There has to be a link and unity with our tools and the true source.

"Is this true?" He asked with a sinking amazement.

"Yes"

I told him how the book would be circulated in less than two weeks. He was gassed. For the first time, I saw Lars drop the keyboard and look me in the eyes with the most human look I've ever seen. His eyes crept out of the digital domain for as long as he could tell me that he felt extremely proud to know me and what this information would do for the world.

"So this is your message. You'll be the Orson Welles of the Internet, except the invasion is real and the alien is our government. What a dog of a beast."

In an instant, he felt like everything up until that moment had been in good measure. He not only told me that he would help, but he would make sure that the message and the necessary chapters would appear in the mailboxes of every government related server in Washington. I felt exhilarated as I watched him whip together the cryptic sequences that would use huge computers all over the world to route the tremendous load of mail that would have to go out on the appointed early morning.

I felt like a silent tyrant as I shivered with excitement for the day that had given me strength through the entire Winter. The tingling energy in my spine and the surges of upward and downward energy that moved from my belly and back down.

I left the Internet cafe feeling that I was very close to the fruition of a grand tale. I went to the mailbox and dropped the letter that was postmarked before my disappearance. It was addressed to Julie Carre. She would receive the code, and the marketing and distribution of the book would be underway.

I came back to Lars telling him to launch the World Wide Web page we had constructed along with the Ocean Center pages, and the worldwide mailing in four days. I told him that I would be leaving for South America. I bid him a solemn farewell. I parted and counted on the event.

On the fourth day, the electronic packages left NYC and were routed cryptically through Lars' genius. It was a busy security day, because some volunteer Internet police had partially traced Lars' activities although he remained unknown to them and just out of spite were attacking his remote servers. He was safe, but he wondered how they had traced some of his pathways. By eleven thirty that morning there was a small convoy on its way down the exhausted morning street of St. Mark's place. The cafe was crawling with special agents and government technical security experts. They could find nothing, but the WWW page containing my book had already been accessed one hundred thousand times. There were copies of the electronic book already moving through the entire network.

It wasn't some hacker's living room that they had entered. They were in a public place with customers on computers. They were impotent and helpless. They were taking orders to search and destroy but the bird had already taken flight. They held an M-16 to Lars' head in the basement computer room of @Café. They talked of treason and demanded to know who was responsible for this juvenile stunt.

Jammed innocently against a wall, with his chin held back into his chest, he pleaded intelligently, "Look guys, this is a public place. Anyone can come in here and set up an account with us and hack whatever they can out there. A couple of computers were left on all night up in the restaurant- whoever came in here over the past two days had a little knowledge and he wrote a little program that ran itself early this morning. I got in here and found that the world has been at my doorsteps banging cause they're pissed off that they got a morning paper they didn't order. So you guys can do what you want, but there are hundreds of customers in here everyday."

Of course Lars had understood the greater opportunity of having a cafe with computers- where anyone could come in. I had taken precautions, but it turns that Lars didn't even need them.

<u>Chapter 21</u>

<u>The Yawn that spanned Lifetimes</u>

The bad part of the fairy tale continued down in Louisiana. Claire was trapped in the generational clutches of her parents, southern Louisiana, hostile traffic in a town whose streets were designed from the paths left from cattle years ago. No one in any generic "hub"-city would obey the fruits that grow in the cattle's wake, yet they would obey some meaningless beaten path. A very path that Claire's father seemed to be finding himself on that afternoon as Eliot was crossing the Atlantic ocean.

Daddy's little girl had called him at his law office to plead her case as guilty of locking herself out of her car -In that sweet voice he had raised daddy's little girl, th one he helped to create. A sweet angelic voice flowered with the warmth of magnolias and easy paces and he obeyed. He would go to her room and find the keys -even bringing them to her school before the end of the day.

The air conditioner wasn't working too well in his little Bavarian car, though, and there were precious pennies that were being lost. He was reminded of a thankless job he felt he did for his family and the women in his life. He found himself in her soft little room in the small suburbs of Lafayette, Louisiana.

He felt a little like a trespasser as his fingers pulled at the white wicker nightstand beside her bed. She had told him that that is where he'd find the keys. In her frustration, she forgot that was where her Dad would also find the letters from the man who loved her more than her made of glass world would permit.

So it was that the silken bundle was too attractive for her father- who was for the first time in his daughter's property. The hearts that covered the bundle were entirely too much for his curiosity.

-Claire-

Hey baby!- It was really an incredible night- Monday Night. Since I can't seem to reach you, I thought I would write instead. That night I got into this Roller-Blade wreck, but despite how bad the wreck looked, the two and myself involved were all OK. I then skated a while, but then I found myself practicing alone. Then I sat on a rock and let all of my bitterness out. I was bitter because I was thinking how most of these people skating, biking, etc. are so accident prone because they panic when a situation gets tight. Finally, I relaxed and let it go. Then I saw a friend Tiny (Mountain) who zoomed by on his bike.

I wanted to catch him but he was gone. I thought perhaps he might circle again after a while. He didn't, so I skated on. Then I saw him and we hugged and went to sit and smoke a giant joint. (he is a bicycle pot messenger)

So we bullshited for a while, then I was going to buy some weed off of him, but he told me I could have mushrooms instead if I wanted. As you can imagine, I was very excited to partake of the false alien creative manipulator Goddess fruit. My meditation had been steady and I thought of it as a bonus to help me on my path.

Later, I hung out with Nancy and ate my shrooms, gave Nancy a massage and began my journey. I left Nancy's apartment to go through different doors of perception to Dad's studio. It didn't take long for me to be feeling much more intense and feverish. Well, as always, I've been giving much thought about you (trying to be non-constrictive-non-projective in my thoughts) Next thing I was singing a song about you and I.

Then it became so obvious to me that the circumstances in my life have made me grow so much, but have not made me grow any closer to you. I began to challenge all the "rules" that keep you and me apart. Then I decided I could tempt fate, inspire myself to declare my true feelings no matter how painful "false-time-construct" has made them to me.

It's very hard for me to explain but at the same time I knew that *when* we would be together was not important. Whether in two days, weeks, years, or next lives. Yet, I envisioned a hole in true time that would allow us to be together. Despite parents, school, age, etc. I thought I saw this window and felt I could co-create its divine existence and occurrence.

In a rush of true heat and passion, I felt the angst of Odysseus and stepped down from Dad's place- through the caves and doors of reality I live in- to Nancy's. I was terrified. I told Nancy what I needed to do. She said great.

So I used my credit card, but because of my state, I couldn't use the phone and technology very well- so Nancy took over and got you on the line. Then I spurted it out to you-

You asked. "Are you fucked up?"

I said, "Yes"

You said, "hold on..."

Then I began to think very negative, like you didn't care, you'd think I was crazy, etc. My imagination created every fear I could have, and in the suspense of holding- I hung up and decided my task was impossible and you didn't love me. I then collapsed and spiraled negatively with Nancy giving me water and talking me into a more positive way of thinking.

Since I had expressed the way I felt, I was cleansed and it allowed me to be truly alone in what evolved into a death panic stage. I passed and went to the great beyond where physical bodies were quite irrelevant anyway. More about that later.

Claire, I do love you unconditionally so whatever you want to do is fine with me. I wasn't trying to scare you or freak you out, but it is something I am going through. You are in my thoughts and wishes. Your path of discovery in my prayers. Write or call- I'll call back of course so you won't have long distance charges on your parents' bill.

Love, love.

Eliot

PS You are welcome in my life at any time.

He was a bit heated already to not know of this stranger. Did he know this guy? Has he ever been able to put his approval or disapproval stamp on him? He thumbed through the little pile searching for the most recent one.

This one seemed strange and cryptic as he read it:

Dear Claire

I love you . Regions, continents, experience will never fade my love for you. I've learned how to let go of many things, I think . Nothing is more appealing in this cold world except to be with you. I think together our power will be one. I know I cannot have a complete life until we are and have become. Even my ear has changed in hearing your voice but it still rings true. I see the angels are speeding your enlightenment. It's true I'm envious of the people who get to be with you. My life has been proving and coping without.

Well I'm finally leaving, in a week I'm going to breach the myth of civilization. I've got a ticket to isolation in South America. What was Robinson Crusoe's accident, will be my intention. Next Thursday I will leave the great hive of New York City, with all of its Royal Jelly. A nation that has given the worker bees the freewill to wish for the jelly they so laboriously carry. I have tweaked enough to start my own colony in the third world. But what will I do with all my precious stuff? Leave it for another bee. Will I set an example? I don't know. Will you follow me -I don't know. Should I mail this -I don't know. The thing that really set it off was the corruption of a friend. Kalvin Klein on my mind. Why do I hate the opportunists because they don't have the guts to admit the downward spiral-they think they are harmlessly contributing.

I've discovered that Mother Earth and people spirits recovering their memory of all-time is number one.

So I'm breaking free, no more excuses and lunar madness. I'm proclaiming myself whatever I have to be. Forgetting other peoples' fixed ideas, these are my ideas without editing and filtration. Without comment from anyone. I am me without mindless depression of what things should or shouldn't be. I am writer poet or whatever the fuck I want to be. Me at the expense of other people's feelings. I'm not obligated to Scott or Chris or whoever. I am completely open to opportunities without half truths and without lies. I must search for truth only- my version with no vague lies. Reminding myself that this is the life of illusion and True Original Creator God Source knows I've spent some very elusive false-time-construct. Through my will and free flow of natural abilities things will come. Patiently I will begin a faithful journey with no one's fears to confront but my own. I will be the master of my fate knowing that I cannot afford the luxury of a negative thought.

So that huge jet that at first looked like a killer whale to me is my biggest amazement of technology and nature. They seem huge and ecstatic to me. My prison was a negative side of the family trying to keep me from observing the intrinsic truths I realize. They might all be worried about me influencing them, but it is only the True Original Creator God Source there. There is nothing extraordinarily great about the illusion of Eliot but that True Original Creator God Source is willing to channel through me to let this planet see that there is more than what appears. The more my body withholds its natural revelations, the more I feel diseased, the more my ego has a problem with letting go of its own illusion. Share

Me playing the saxophone but only feeling like I could play one number good. It's a metaphor for my life. Self consciousness is the locking block. Metaphor- beyond phor-beyond fear(hope) Dream- re-Adam- ream Adam dread. Mushroom Ommm. Did they get you? - hot ashrams for dreams

He was certainly perplexed, but he was fairly convinced that his daughter was involved with some psychopath. He rocked his jaw pensively while tapping the hot pile of mail still warm from the postal oven outside. He looked down at his fingers and spied a large brown envelope addressed to his daughter Claire.

He was suspicious enough to note that the labeling had the same style type as the envelopes he had just studied. The envelope was postmarked in NYC.

Without any effort for discrepancy, he dug into the brown package and pulled out what seemed to be a manuscript. The morning papers flashed in his head- the table of contents of this manuscript roughly matched the headlines he had seen.

"What the fuck is this?" He asked as if his amazement couldn't cease. He thumbed through the book. It seemed to be an odd love story-wait?.. an adventure, but why was it causing so much controversy in the circles of government. The newspapers were so vague, as if the world was hit by something that seemed to be about National security.

Here was his daughter's name all over the place in this strange manuscript that he had somehow intercepted. He thumbed through the chapters about how the government was involved in AIDS. He was caught in a state of shock. In a fury he flipped to the epilogue that was a plea to all who cared. It was the main character's request for the readers to get involved by sending Claire mail to *his!* own real address. No, this couldn't be true. His very own address was in a manuscript of a book that was so controversial -he had been sure this morning that it was some sort of media stunt- it was sure to be a bestseller. This much he had known- whatever the hell the book was. He trembled at the thought of it all. How would he stop this? How could he help protect his daughter -How could he help the government catch this shit who had published his address.

The thought of the repercussions -his small town- on his career and law practice. He would be known as the keeper of a rebel's lover. NO! He turned and stormed out of her room leaving everything as it was. He screamed out of the driveway in his little white Bavarian car, while dialing his secretary. "Get me Steve Broderick's number!, Ok, yea, " He dialed.

"Agent Broderick's office." chimed the secretary.

He had known Steve since Vietnam. He had heavy pull with the government. What the hell was it? The CIA, fuck, FBI. "Steve!"

"Yea." A grim and official voice answered.

"What the hell's going on?, I've got this damn manuscript at my house!"

"You're not the only one who wants to know. Our phone banks are backed up with calls- you wouldn't believe it. This book is already in the bookstores- the people are practically rioting to get their hands on copies. How in the hell do you have a manuscript in your house?"

"That's what I'm calling about. Somehow, this fucking writer is involved with my daughter! I want to help you guys catch this dude. This package is postmarked from New York City."

"When did it arrive?"

"Today!, I left a shitload of letters and the thing at home." He continued sarcastically, "I on my way to get my little girl and give her orders to get her ass home."

Steve quickly added, "This sounds like it might be something of interest to the big guys. Although, this guy is already so popular that a manhunt is kind of unlikely. I'll make some calls."

"I'll be over to pick you up -after I take care of my daughter."

Just then he rounded the corner to reveal the safe and oppressive school veiled in the shroud of Catholicism. In her floating cloud of the last days of molding and resentment, Claire sat wonderfully radiant twirling a pencil. Her beauty made her the target for the jealous sisters and teachers who so often misused their positions as "head" of the class. She was thinking about the power of authority then. She was thinking of the danger of any power given to the ignorant. She was dreaming of freedom and far off places. She escaped her dreaded reality in her head in the chalky hours after noon.

The intercom brought forth the envy and fear of the class in her direction. She was on her way still slightly heavy from her daydream. Her face was carved by the angels. She had a cocky smile that assured the world that she would go anywhere she wanted. Her beauty marked her intelligence that said, you'd better get your licks in now, because my soft tan steps couldn't possibly be a part of this much longer. Walking in her wake would feel like a cool fall breeze separating the muggy June with kisses of otherworldly bliss. To live in the folds of her lines, would be any ship-lover's call to shore after seeing no land for nearly a century.

Her father was waiting with a cocky and damaging smirk that said he had knowledge of some game and that she had gotten by him for long enough.

"Whaaaatt?" She asked with the helpless giggle. The warmth of her voice would calm any sea, but not this time.

"Here are your keys- I've checked you out already in the office. you are to go home right now and wait for me. No questions- no nothing. Forget whatever plans you had- go directly home." He ordered. She had always been Daddy's girl, but there was no room for rebuttal this time.

Her long fingers turned the ignition of her little Honda, and she was on her way home. She let the worry pass and in place she felt exhilarated for whatever reason she could leave the school. She couldn't think of anything she had done wrong to upset her father so.

Her hands turned the back door of her house, and she was greeted by their cocker-spaniel, Bud. Always so Godlike, never an ill temper with Bud. Bud followed her tan legs as far as they could before the swinging door to the kitchen halted his excited trot. She found the site of her warm bright room welcoming. She had pictured her daybed covered with the floral comforter. She loved snuggling up in it in the middle of summer while the air-conditioner kept everything at about 65 degrees.

Things weren't as she'd left them. Her heart sank and rushed as she saw her letters scattered on the bed. "He's pissed about these letters!?" Then she noticed the pile of mail and a thick bound manuscript.

She read what had been violated. She read this big thing and knew what it meant. She read on while the traffic backed up for the 1 O'clock lunchtime (false-time-construct) traffic, and while her Dad's temper flared at a cop who had no knowledge of any of this. His little white car looked like an accordion, while the woman screamed in anger over her new Pontiac Bonneville that was reared by the Bavarian bullet.

Enthralled by what the whole thing meant and this manuscript, Claire turned to read as fast as she could, that stack of other mail fell to the floor and she looked down at the front page of the newspaper. "MYSTERY NOVEL has brought the nation to a stand-still- investigators are trying to decipher the case of Orson Welles of the Internet!" She looked down at the hefty piece she was reading, she barely trusted her fingers but let them flip to the Contents anyway. That was enough to send her to the Chapter entitled AIDS and The U.S. Government. She felt a nauseous flight rise from her belly. She remembered the words, "Go Find Malick Gueye. You can find him at the Harlem Car Service. Tell him you want to take him home."

The walls of her crystal palace shattered before her. She felt a rush of energy that brought tears to her eyes. She barely had control as her mind followed her body while it shoved clothes into her bags- while she ran to her mother's bureau and dug for her Gold card.

She screeched out of the driveway with ecstatic tears of longing. It all made sense to her somehow. It was the only move that felt right. She stopped at her First National Bank and withdrew her entire savings account. She stopped and pulled the maximum allowed out of her Mom's card- she knew the pin from so many trips with her Mom.

With the $750 from the credit card, she had nearly six thousand dollars. She parked her car away from the airport at a Tennis club nearby. Within an hour and a half, she was on board a small plane on its way to Nashville. She planned on hopping around to as many airports as she could before getting to New York.

She took an airport shuttle to the Marriot Marquis in Times (false-time-construct) Square. It was the first van she saw when she stepped out into the frenzy of yellow cabs and limousines. The pace of her mind was no different to the cadence of the frenzy by now.

She used cash. She blinked as she saw herself use her fake I.D., which until then had only been used in the clubs around her town- with peers she had just left in the dust.

When she opened the door to her room, she felt the peace that any traveler feels when coming to a clean hotel room. She felt the sinking feeling of everything she had just left. She wondered where her energy was and where the ghost was that had swept her so unreasonably far from the comfort of home. She looked at the bar and took out a little shot of Jagermeister.

She thumbed the phone book and found Harlem Car Service. She was greeted by some rude dispatcher. She had only heard this kind of accent in the movies- she shrugged it as being just as well cause she felt twisted in some elaborate plot anyway.

More aggravated by the sweet Southern accent of some woman on the line, she struggled with what seemed to her to like, "Ma- Lick" After much abrasion, she found one of their drivers whose name matched Claire's request.

For forty-five minutes, she stared at the ceiling until her visions of a love she denied for so long were interrupted by a room phone.

"Hello, you asked for a car- Malick?" Asked a voice in heavy but friendly African.

"Yes, I'll be down."

"What is your name?- I'm a gonna make a sign"

"Claire" she trusted.

She was a little startled by the sheer blackness of his smiling face. This guy was a beautiful native. She saw his smiling face and felt a little at home for reasons she did not know. His smile had nearly gripped his ears- for he had never seen such a vision of beauty in his life. Absolutely stunned and wide eyed, he asked politely where it was that she would like to go.

"Do you know Eliot?"

'Eliot is my friend, ma broder." He said confidently. "How you- you are that Claire! I had no idea! Ha Ha! I miss maaaaa friend." His simple honest eyes knew not what was truly going on.

"I have come to take you home." She said seriously. "Park your car and we'll go up and talk, but we don't have much time (false-time-construct)."

From the twenty-fourth floor, she could see Times (false-time-construct) Square and its ever-thirsty need for Consolidated Edison- she could also see Malick in the mirror. He was listening patiently to the tale of what had happened. She could scarcely believe that she was really looking out on this jungle, yet earlier that day she had been in a classroom. What had she been doing with her life? She wondered intensely where this tremendous amount of courage and bravery came from.

High from the feeling of living life all at once. High from taking the reins. Now, for once and for all, she cast her own shadow. There was no specter observer looming over her watching every move. She thought that it might have been hard for Malick to leave, but it wasn't.

He smiled and his ivory white teeth showed joy to be going home. He was taking a free ride back to joy and to his family. So much struggle was in his wake. The pain that New York had caused him was deep. The pain of his struggle was so different from the dream of the western world that he had had years ago as a child.

He understood what Claire was saying and smiled at the grandness of it all. "I do not have many things- so I will go and gather them up and you make the arrangements for the airplane. She turned from the flattering aerial view of the city, and for a moment Malick saw an angel.

Claire, as she turned away from the window in flowing slowness felt a little nostalgia for the music of what was happening. Billowing up in her- an extreme feeling of innocent butterflies. She felt the rising cushion of love in her stomach. She seemed to be floating on pins and needles. Pictures of her lover reappeared in her head after all this time (false-construct-time). There were undeniable scenes of love that folded into her vision.

She recovered the state of confident assurance she felt earlier that day- this feeling banished her lull and she moved to make arrangements for the exodus out of the States as she ushered Malick to the door.

It was well into the night when Malick parked his big cushy Continental into the La Guardia long term parking. He had worked in his blue Continental six days a week- countless hours. He couldn't even remember before that, but now he was leaving all of the car's temperaments of which he had become so familiar.

The air was brisk as Claire swung her hair around so that her baggage wouldn't pull on it. She walked strongly while she inhaled and looked around at what she was leaving. She was only leaving that which she had just met- the city. She remembered the impact it had on her during her first visit, but she had held true to her initial disgust. She had never known what compelled Eliot to stay, but now it all made sense in its bizarre wizardry.

It was as if her life had been on pause while Eliot went out and found their path -he was there then. Then she knew that there was a powerful bond, but she hadn't known that since his disappearance. She tried to relate to him, a couple of times, but felt that she was interfering. Now she felt it was time again. Coming out of what seemed to be a yawn that spanned over lifetimes (false-construct-false alien empire modified lifespan units). She knew that the yawn would end soon.

Epilogue

There was so much fist pounding and foot stamping in Washington D.C. and nearly everywhere sold men were used as kinetic weapons of lasting destruction. The ring of Generals who maintained the secret operations thundered and fumed. Now nothing but scared stuck pigs in their Pentagone. The people of all countries banded together in linked servers connected everywhere and dissolved boundaries altogether. It became common knowledge that sociopolitical rule would never work, and no one was allowed to hold any power, nor any office. They all secretly shuttered in their cold-war closets. Their rage inspired them to take measures against this mystery person who had managed to create a mania in the streets. How had this unknown gotten to all the information? Their boots were just a bit too deep in shit to begin the manhunt for Eliot, Their primary sources said he was lost at sea. The world accepted that Eliot Breyers was dead.

Author's Confessional Interlude: Rainbows and Painbows
(Present Day in a small hotel room in Hotel Terrifico -Glendale, California)

Truth is, I am half a century old now. The rainbows might as well be painbows. This America seems filled with useless shrapnel folks who find me useless and equally discarded. Even though I have served to heal the arrogant masses, particularly the French Fried Riviera of Arrogant California, it is a wasteland of overspoiled privilege filled with pouty fake swollen lipped wanna be beauty dunces and impotent man sacks driving two hundred thousand dollar cars next to starving less insane street yellers.

Ok, it didn't turn out as in the happy ending I deviated towards somewhere approximately halfway through the book. Claire slept with a camp counselor on her summer trip and never cared the least about me. Subsequent girlfriends were disloyal cheaters and liars. The book I hoped for sat unpublished and unfinished for twenty years. Given the 100th monkey factor and the thievery corporation, my works and creative impulses became the fuel and fodder for many monetarily successful ventures apart from me. The world grew worse with the majority not heeding Nichiren's warnings in On Establishing the Correct Teaching for the Lasting Peace and Tranquility of the Land. Fires, earthquakes, natural disasters, famine, war, and widespread disease have grown to blanket nearly everyone in misery. The elite rich fly around arching the sky with their white and gray streaks, skating the glossolalia of their privilege far removed from the massive sufferings of simple food, clothing, and shelter while masking their misery with spendy cover ups and popularity festivals in any medium they choose. I depressively faded into obscurity, cowardice, and disempowerment. Both mothers of my unintended babies monstrously kidnapped my own daughters as

Hell indeed hath no fury like these women scorned. My dependence on alcohol and weed approached the absurd even though I knew when starving in the desert my spirit informed me that weed would lead to homelessness and alcohol to the crazies. The Internet turned out to be a vehicle for surveillance, control, misinformation, commerce, and an immense vehicle for propagation to whatever variant of person, government, and even Artificial Intelligence. People all continue to sell each other out for a paycheck in a false construct of a debt-based currency called money policed by violent maniacs and butchers. Telephony owns and cripples all the billions of bio puppets in its damaging and infantile technology. Google became evil. Tesla was flimsy and riding on the borrowed name of a genius murdered and unrequited still. Business is and always of personal effect and yet business men and women hold fast to the lie that it isn't personal. Competition and Capitalism is said to bring out the best, instead it has only brought out the worst as we slide down the glacial avalanche mountain ranges of diarrhea called countries. Divide and Rule continue successfully ruining and spoiling the future possibility of vitality. Win Win relationships are fart bubbles and cooperation is mirages spouted by air heads and whirling dervishes of an Aquarian Rage. Book II

‖Prison‖ 😈;😇 Break!
|D|evil Planet Earth

Book II Contents

Acknowledgements

Chapter The Gravity of Our Graves

Chapter. Why it always goes wrong

EXCERPT TOP SECRET 1947 ROSWELL TOP SECRET EXCERPT

Chapter Rainbows and Painbows

Chapter Our Earth Creators/Captors made a fucking mess

Chapter Prison Break -Devil Alien Planet Earth

Chapter What to do now...

Final Quotes

Acknowledgements:

Were it not for the The Letters and Notes of Matilda O'Donnell MacElroy published in the book, "Alien Interview," and Lawrence R. Spencer's efforts, I would not be able to understand in the slightest why this Earth with all its people including my family, everyone I have ever met on Earth, including myself is the way it is along with the repetitive senseless tragedy that besets all humankind. The ongoing tragedy is the death and birth amnesia screen cage trap that imprisons all inmate spirits occupying a modified lowest grade homo sapien suit on this planet and purposefully shrouds all living beings in darkness by an extinct remnant momentum of the unseen totalitarian empire of the most cruel origin in the entire known and unknown physical universe. In my search through philosophies and all other earth**bound** means towards some sense, comprehension, understanding, and enlightenment of this enigma and jewel of human life here on Earth, this offworld view from Airl, a pilot and engineer for The Domain, finally filled in the holes and gaps of the suspicions and questions I held so deeply whilst obfuscated by the lies and mystery injected into our minds by our captors and unknowing participants. This earth is best described by an otherworld outsider in the information provided in the book, "Alien Interview". This partially revealing information is not a myth, instead a glimmer of truth in our human prison sea of obscurity. This knowledge renders all dysfunctional families explained as to their sad plight, this renders all good actors and perhaps many bad actors redeemed in the light of compassion and wisdom. As for the incurably evil, criminally insane, etc., I do not know what can be done especially knowing that capital punishment recycles them right back to a mother for their reintroduction into this world. In all probability, never soon enough will a rescue come, as whatever powers that be have stood idly by witnessing the repeated bad behavior and atrocities that spirits trapped in bodies repeat. I can only wish that there could be some holy intervention in this unholy world. I would have the evil be filtered out of us all, particularly the afore-mentioned crowd in the previous sentence, and have those evil spirits including the creators and designers of this Hotel Horrifico called Earth ported off to their special gilded cage where they can continue in their wars, atrocities, and all other flavors of hell enjoyed by that rotten slice of creation. Admittedly, the divine calculator of cause and effect will continue to inform darkness and lightness, evil and good-ness, so it is to be expected that those who don't have the fortune to behold the Law of cause and effect, will perhaps not be able to benefit as you the reader now at hand can potentially. May the now informed have the power of revealing the evil ones who are bound to suffer while they concurrently assist those furthermore in their suffering. In the Light of this illumination, they (the dark evil ones) must hereby be vanquished or humbly surrendered for transmutation retrofit for them. If not they shall be separated from the essence and ore of the original and true benevolent and compassionate Mother of ALL. This wish will somehow be rendered and made effective. Presently, we are stuck as we are, a super estranged and mixed sample of spirits from literally ALL over. We are currently a galactic multitude of attitude and perspective randomized and disjointed all elbow to elbow now neck deep in our collective shared hell. Every shopper no exception, happy or sad, must roll down the aisles of hunger, greed, anger/arogance, stupid/ignorance. Then by the power of each of us inner illumined and of that which was expressed by the first illumined ones such as Shakyamuni Siddhartha Guatama, Nichiren Daishonin, Lao Tzu and a sprinkling of others who go unmentioned, we are all compelled now to RE-MEMBER! Each of us is our immortal infinite spiritual IS-BE nature. We will now take whatever absolute measure of each medicine to equate our worldwide human unification in preference to deprecation & defecation so that we may admirably engage in our whole recovery, honestly discarding expedient error, in exchange forever defensive diligent and true cor-rection towards our VALUE CREATION. Let each spirit exhibit their own unique moment by moment perspective and that the other be respected for their own imagination and own conjecture projector as a baseline for us ALL united as ONE.

If by some freakish disaster of continued tragedy, the roughly 6.66-8.88 (little satirical play on numbers) billion Spirits trapped in this horrific hell don't heed the knowledge of what is fact in our fate here, then at least I will have done it, I will have revealed to the best of my ability -THE situation on Earth. In this painful process of revealing the true fact which some will conclude as subjective fiction, the greatest desire of ALL ONE SOURCE is that creation be unbarred by its mistaken views leading to a new era of planetary and universal peace so that coexistence and cooperation become the new standard and the wellspring of new Great Good Fortune be tapped and flowing forevermore! ellis simpson byers iii

Chapter
Gravity of our Graves

From what little I know from the benevolent alien Airl gained from Alien Interview thanks to Lawrence R. Spencer's and Matilda MacElroy's efforts, low gravity is and always will be a good jumping off point for interstellar travel. Looking up at the night sky here in Santa Fe and other places in the world there appear to be different kinds of flying technology way up in the upper space atmosphere of earth. I see hyperspace type darting movements that are probably now technology that is in the hands of man as well at this point.

Gravity is of "grave" importance in the physical universe."Man, that was heavy." People say along the way, or "Wow, that was deep. Of course, here on Earth we all end in some sort of grave. Many trillions of years ago, as the illusions created of thoughts held and projected by immortal spirit beings, such as ourselves (IS-BEs), formed lightweight imaginary universes; however, over eventuality these collided and commingled with other similar forms and in turn led to a more dense physical reality. Being more dense and heavy, its environment became ripe as a cage for certain offenders of the Law of Cause and Effect. IS-BEs have been overwhelmed by each other and taken advantage of by each other since time without beginning. Supposedly most IS-BEs are good. Out of the darkness and shadows of the not knowing has emerged the fundamental darkness King. Ever-increasing shades of (greed, anger, and stupidity) wanting, position, and apathetically disregarding the sanctity of others inhabiting biological prison bodies has resulted in a downward spiral. However, good and bad are relative terms. The Law, with its built in loom for stitching and informing bad and good into whatever given reality, registers an IS-BE's features and merits mystically over infinite time. The amount of fiery compression for the disrespect put upon the inmates of earth will be its prison creators' ultimate recompense as consequences for their actions. The present condition remains a consequence of ours. It took many millions of years for the old empire to culminate into a totalitarian authoritative machine which only allowed for the total complacency of its members -robotic and mindless. The empire did not have at its core the fact that every spirit, irregardless of stature in caste, is worthy of the same and equal respect. All of us have committed at some point or another: battle, war, domination towards other IS-BE's. When the time (false-construct-time) and the environment are ripe for recompensation we arrive here on prison planet earth mixed in with a myriad of inmates from all over the galaxy from extremely different backgrounds. This is where the Buddhist determination of intent, "Karma into mission" gives honest and clear purpose derived from responsibility and resolve. Given one's circumstances, one must learn and then know that the being is reaping what it has sewn.

We know that the law of gravity is apparent in our every momentary reality here on the planet. Like a child who thinks he can steal candy from the store, there are the kids that get caught and the ones that don't get caught and the ones that know better to steal in the first place. It is this feeling deep deep inside that we know better yet we commit the offending action. Now if a spirit is timeless and immortal, what then when an entrepreneur comes in and uses that biological body to mine silver, then unless forced to serve the boss, that slave has some degree of choice to comply with the entrepreneur's trade. The entrepreneur taking advantage of the trapped spirit in a homo sapien suit is not necessarily bad or good. The trapped being is already buried under an unseen punishment of amnesia and displacement rendering the human being vulnerable to the opportunists arriving -picking the skeleton of the old empire's secret remnant programs such as prison planet earth. It is sad that existence would not inform us externally of these rules, but in the end and beginning one knows all of this -one is all knowing - awakened ONE -Buddha. One person inherently knows better, however, the pain and uncomfortability of its situation brings about an emotion that overwhelms the reason, creates the passion, ie, the attachment and then one is chained evermore to the wheel of existence in our case bound in three dimensions and in the fourth dimension you are free to think what you will but you are still stuck here. In the good ole USA one is free to say and believe what one wants. This is the only last remaining saving grace from us being bombed to further hell. Interfaith appears mostly as divisions amongst the groups of inmates.

Attempting to own things can seem motivating and perhaps exciting, yet when one possesses them it seems to weigh one down. Fact is, no one here owns anything in this devilish system built upon desire of matter -its prisoners being the inmates who are trapped. The land we stand on and all of its items have been conjured by some other unknown. Nothing here is each's own. It seems all of this started by original causes committed in avoidance of boredom. As ancient biotech companies introduced various models of organisms and bodies, the IS-BE took choice in games by lessening personal power to enter the more incapacitated/limited biological bodies. Because of the game of lessening the all knowing quality of the eternal spirit, the being then somewhat foregone, was and still is ultimately captured by circumstantially nefarious old empire secret removal of undesirables along with being taken advantage of by entrepreneurs. **Also foregone and lost was the inborn native ability inside each of us to manifest energy and forms.** When an IS-BE is in its native power, evidently one is able to render matter and space for oneself. According to more well informed sources than myself having an outside view removed from the limiting cage I presently occupy, these energies and forms cannot be destroyed, thus the ever expanding universe. The evil (evil: that which causes suffering and anguish) pathways of behaving badly towards others eventually leads a spirit being (IS-BE) to degraded worlds or deeper grave gradations of Hells. We are currently in a certain type of Hell created by offspring factions of the old Empire which fortunately has been defeated by the younger benevolent mother creator super galactic power called the Domain. Karma is action. Through various causes and conditions we, that includes me, find ourselves in a conundrum of self and others relative imprisonment and misery. Revolt against others has never created a sustainable solution over ancient history. Yet spirits continue to tend out similar actions to that which has been done to us. Even unknowing blind rage has a basis. Here begins the long and arduous task of recovery as each of us discover the time and place along with mixed up capacities of inmates from all over the galaxy. Each spirit's personal misery compression, similar to coal squeezed into a diamond, renders each spirit being's realization for peace, tranquility, abundance, and good fortune. This moment for each of us defines our inner revolution recovering humanism, humanitarianism, and social change apart from the quadrillion year old descent into suffering in the general war of the self versus others. How does shared attention between beings, respect, and equanimity function? How can such a thing wonderfully appear inside a multi dimensional cluster fuck? Inner determination has to want/desire an end to the personal/inner and others/outer suffering and madness -particularly known to us as the psychological culmination that continues to reiterate on Earth, the Hell of War. War has always been the ways and means of the prison wardens here on Earth to incite further bondage and suffering right down to the very design of man and woman, bacteria, viruses, biting flies, venom, traps of every kind as instituted here on prison planet earth. The LAW is strict and the fundamental dark side uses this invariable truth against its imprisoned population with various means and ways (befuddling layers in the prison devil food cake) by the three embedded poisons desire/greed, anger/arrogance, and ignorance/stupidity. When you die, the trap is activated by any of these you might have at any given moment, along with other compound mechanisms. We are held by technology that is perhaps trillions of years more developed than our volatile earthquake/volcanic recycling and resetting prison compound Earth. This Earth neither permits nor allows records due to devised mystery BS cultures and recycling 20,000 year polar shifts. Birth, aging, sickness, and death are shortened now to roughly 80 years of an opportunity to scratch the surface of learning and being death reprocessed, electrocuted, coded, programmed, brainwashed, and implanted over and over virtually infinitely. As a so-called "civilization" remembers and develops already known ancient technology, its insanity towards programmed apocalypse destines itself for collective and planetary destruction. The fervency of belief instilled through Religious programming along with the mental implants forcefully implanted in between lifetimes and re-activated during lifetimes by encounters with written code through the world's combative and schismatic divide and rule bibles. This ultimate human participated war destruction and prison dumping of disparaged beings from all over in variant walks of life and cultures is allowed to continue by the current ruling class of aliens now known as the Domain; however, its superior technologies will prevent our societal intent towards total species and planetary annihilation and ruin because of lost troops of their own (also presently trapped in the invisible amnesia death trap mechanism at least 3000 Domain members) and the intent to preserve all the biotech diverse creations in the loud, ridiculous, yet beautiful, zoo of Earth.

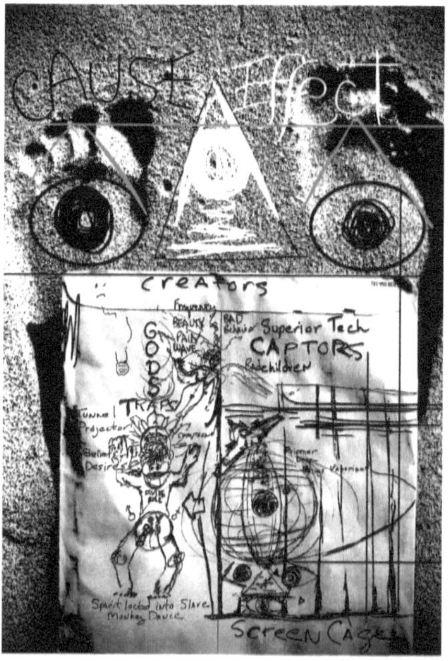

Having wishes for peace inside myself and toward others and failing to keep that status with most of my friends, loves, and relations at this point of 50 circlings of the Sun in this unholy world, is proof that one's intent to escape the cycle of doing what's done to one, is extremely difficult. However, there is no such thing as a failure who keeps trying. This book hopefully is and will be a successful culmination of a lifelong effort towards my redemption and escape from Prison Planet Earth along with the wish to free all living beings. I hope you and I can and will all break free in perhaps the largest prison break of eternal history. It has to be an inside job as it will be thousands of years before outside aid could even surreptitiously cause a shift from the grip of the currently still functioning trapping mechanisms in place by secret hidden factions of the apparently conquered and deceased old empire. Though the fall from grace concurrently burns me up in my descent with gravity's pull of my consequences. The well of my youthful ink and bodily energy seems dried up, it is the heart of the matter, we are the spirit and the will that our greatest wish be fulfilled that of true and lasting Happiness and Peace along with the same for our environment and fellow creatures inhabited by their respective operators - the myriad spirits piloting physical bodies micro and macroscopic.

Why it always goes wrong on this planet: TOP SECRET

TOP SECRET Official Transcript of the U.S. Army Air Force Roswell Army Air Field, 509th Bomb Group SUBJECT: ALIEN INTERVIEW, 26. 7. 1947, 1st Session "The Domain Expeditionary Force has observed a resurgence in science and culture of the Western world since 1150 AD when the remaining remnants of the space fleet of the "Old Empire" in this solar system were destroyed. The influence of the remote control hypnosis operation diminished slightly after that time (false-time-construct), but still remains largely in force. Apparently a small amount of damage was done to the "Old Empire" remote mind control 82 (Footnote) operation which resulted in a small decrease in the power of this mechanism. As a result, some memories of technologies that IS-BEs already knew before they came to Earth started to be remembered. Thereafter the oppression of knowledge that is called the "Dark Ages" in Europe began to diminish after that time (false-time-construct). Since then knowledge of the basic laws of physics and electricity have revolutionized Earth culture virtually overnight. The ability to remember technology by many of the geniuses in the IS-BE population of Earth was partially restored, when not so actively suppressed as it was before 1150 AD. Sir Isaac Newton, is one of the best examples of this. In only a few decades he single-handedly reinvented several major and fundamental scientific and mathematical disciplines. The men who "remembered" these sciences already knew them before they were sent to Earth. Ordinarily, no one would ever observe or discover as much about science and mathematics in a single life-time (false-time-construct, false alien empire bible god modifier), or even in a few hundred life-times (false slave lifetime units). These subjects have taken civilizations billions and billions of years to create! IS-BEs on Earth have only just begun to remember small fragments of all the technologies that exist throughout the universe. Theoretically, if the amnesia mechanisms being used against Earth could be broken entirely, IS-BEs would regain all of their memory! Unfortunately, similar advances have not been seen in the humanities as the IS-BEs of Earth continue to behave very badly toward each other. This behavior, however, is heavily influenced by the "hypnotic commands" given to each IS-BE between lifetimes (false alien empire god modified slave lifetime units). And, the very unusual combination of "inmates" on Earth - criminals, perverts, artists, revolutionaries and geniuses - is the cause of a very restive and tumultuous environment. The purpose of the prison planet is to keep IS-BEs on Earth, forever. Promoting ignorance, superstition, and war between IS-BEs helps to keep the prison population crippled and trapped behind "the wall" of electronic force screens. IS-BEs have been dumped on Earth from all over the galaxy, adjoining galaxies, and from planetary systems all over the "Old Empire", like Sirius, Aldebaron, the Pleiades, Orion, Draconis, and countless others. There are IS-BEs on Earth from unnamed races, civilizations, cultural backgrounds, and planetary environments. Each of the various IS-BE populations have their own languages, belief systems, moral values, religious beliefs, training and unknown and untold histories. These IS-BEs are mixed together with earlier inhabitants of Earth who came from another star system more 61 than 400,000 years ago to establish the civilizations of

Atlanta and Lemuria . Those civilizations vanished beneath the tidal waves caused by a planetary "polar shift", many thousands of years before the current "prison" population started to arrive. Apparently, the IS-BEs from those star systems were the source of the original, oriental races of Earth, beginning in Australia. On the other hand, the civilizations set up on Earth by the "Old Empire" prison system were very different from the civilization of the "Old Empire" itself, which is an electronic space opera, atomic powered conglomeration of earlier civilizations that were conquered with nuclear weapons and colonized by IS-BEs from another galaxy. The bureaucracy that controlled the former "Old Empire" was from an ancient space opera society, run by a totalitarian confederation of planetary governments, regulated by a brutal social, economic, and political hierarchy, with a royal monarch as its figurehead. This type of government emerges with regularity on planets where the citizens abandon personal responsibility for autonomous, self-regulation. They frequently lose their freedom to demented IS-BEs who suffer from an overwhelming paranoia that every other IS-BE is their enemy who must be controlled or destroyed. Their closest friends and allies, whom they espouse to love and cherish, are literally "loved to death" by them. Because such IS-BEs exist, The Domain has learned that freedom must be won and maintained through eternal vigilance and the ability to use defensive force to maintain it. As a result, The Domain has already conquered the governing planet of the "Old Empire". The civilization of The Domain, although considerably younger and smaller in size, is already more powerful, better organized, and united by a egalitarian esprit de corps never known in the history of the "Old Empire". The recently despoiled German totalitarian state on Earth was similar to the "Old Empire", but not nearly as brutal, and about ten thousand times less powerful. Many of the IS-BEs on Earth are here because they are violently opposed to totalitarian government, or because they were so psychotically vicious that they could not be controlled by "Old Empire" government. Consequently, the population of Earth is disproportionately comprised of a very high percentage of such beings. The conflicting cultural and ethical moral codes of the

IS-BEs on Earth is unusual in the extreme. The Domain conquest of the central "Old Empire" planets was fought with electronic cannon. The citizens of the planets forming the core of government for the "Old Empire" are a filthy, degraded, slave society of mindless, tax-paying workers, who practice cannibalism. Violent automotive race tracks and bloody, Roman circus type entertainments are their only amusements. Regardless of any reasonable justification we may have had for using atomic weapons to vanquish the planets of the "Old Empire", The Domain is careful not to ruin the resources of those planets by using weapons of crude, radioactive force. The current U.S. civilization is beginning to mimic some of the trappings of that civilization, especially in the design of airplanes, automobiles, ships, trains, and telephones. Likewise, buildings in the cities of Earth are thought to be "modern" or "futuristic" if their design resembles the architecture of the "Old Empire". The government of the "Old Empire", before being supplanted by The Domain, was comprised of beings who possessed a very craven intelligence, very much like the Axis powers during your recent world war. Those beings manifested precisely the same behavior as the galactic government that exiled them to eternal imprisonment on Earth. They were a gruesome reminder of the ageless maxim that an IS-BE will often manifest the treatment they have received from others. Kindness fosters kindness. Cruelty begets cruelty. One must be able and willing to use force, tempered with intelligence, to prevent harm to the innocent. However, extraordinary understanding, self-discipline and courage are required to effectively prevent brutality, without being overwhelmed by the malice that motivated the brutality. Only a demonic, self-serving government would employ a "logic" or "science" to conceive that an "ultimate solution" to any problem is to murder and permanently erase the memory of every artist, genius, skilled manager, and inventor, and cast them into a planetary prison together with political opponents, killers, thieves, perverts, and disabled beings of an entire galaxy! Once the IS-BEs expelled from the "Old Empire" arrived on Earth, they were given amnesia, and hypnotically tricked into thinking that something else had happened to them. The next step was to implant the IS-BEs into biological bodies on Earth. The bodies became the human populations of "false civilizations" which were designed and installed in the minds of IS-BEs to look completely unlike the "Old Empire". All of the IS-BEs of India, Egypt, Babylon, Greece, Rome, and Medieval Europe were guided to pattern and build the cultural elements of these societies based on standard patterns developed by the IS-BEs of many earlier, similar civilizations on "Sun Type 12, Class 7" planets that have existed for trillions of years throughout the universe. In the earliest times (false-time-construct) the IS-BEs sent to prison Earth lived in India. They gradually spread into Mesopotamia, Egypt, Mesoamerica, Achaea, Greece, Rome, Medieval Europe, and to the New World. They were hypnotically "commanded" to follow the pattern of a given civilization by the "Old Empire" prison operators. This is an effective mechanism to disguise the actual time and location from the IS-BEs imprisoned on Earth. The languages, costumes and culture of each false civilization are intended to reinforce amnesia because they do not remind the IS-BEs on Earth of the original "Old Empire" planets from which they were deported. **Airl of The Domain pages 96 - 98 of 310**

END EXCERPT TOP SECRET ALIEN INTERVIEW Based On Personal Notes and Interview Transcriptions Provided by: Matilda O'Donnell MacElroy - Editing and Supplemental Footnotes by: Lawrence R. Spencer

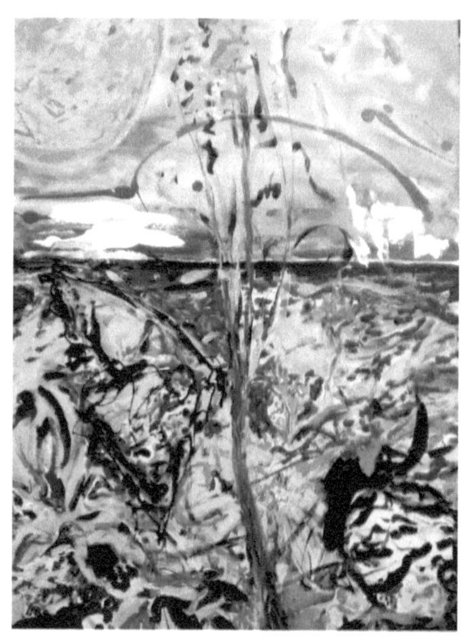

Chapter
Rainbows and Painbows

I always wondered why seeking or looking out for the most amazingly beautiful women seemed laced with a sort of hazy pain cloud of impossibility or tragedy. As I sit at Bird Rock Coffee on the windy corner of mid-April San Diego, the most physically appealing (outwardly beautiful) woman jogged by in exact unison with my effort to write down more of the blueprint for the prison break planet earth sequence. Now more women arriving and this time (false-time-construct) with a ploy to my smell sense vulnerability, particularly in this case just now, the sexual horniness activated by cocoa butter smell of hawaiian tropic oil -that and the memory triggered by that particular smell along with my pubescent longing of tan hot oiled bathing beauties unrequited.

Burning out the circuitry of sensory trap systems seems to threaten to endanger the sense tied earth human such as myself. When 5-MEO DMT was placed before me, and other amber plant extracts of cacophony DMT, and also LSD, there was this feeling of buying a ticket to the unknown, a warning voice coming from somewhere (possibly a trapping external projection -facing fear of self death... My resolution and conclusion of psychedelics and entheogens is now complete. These substances remind us forever that we make things up, we are illusion producers as spirits. They are not a solution to the trap that has been clearly outlined in these volumes. You are free to think and experience what you will in the fourth dimension of thought and imagination, however, you will in fact return to the confines of your prison cell trapped in the third dimensional low caste pooper bio body sack.

The fundamental anger/arrogance that posits a totalitarian solution or demise of another IS-BE's choices, desires, is embodied in most men as puffed up self importance pride pride and survival ego. Shamelessness seems the nature placed inside the design of most women. The idea that one IS-BE knows what another IS-BE should do for themselves is absurd. Why do drugs initially activate memory of idealistic potentials for me? Why do Ayahuasca type tryptamines bring seeming relief altruistically to the trapped spirit in a human body? Actualization is a desire for a long trapped being in the evil pathways fostered somehow by the devil king (evidently a rogue king group offshoot prison earth penitentiary wardens of the hopefully deceased EMPIRE -the earth experience of sadness, anguish, suffering). Given a slight taste of ideal harmony, or perhaps a new version as a weaker consultation prize towards a personal alternate reality drug facsimile.

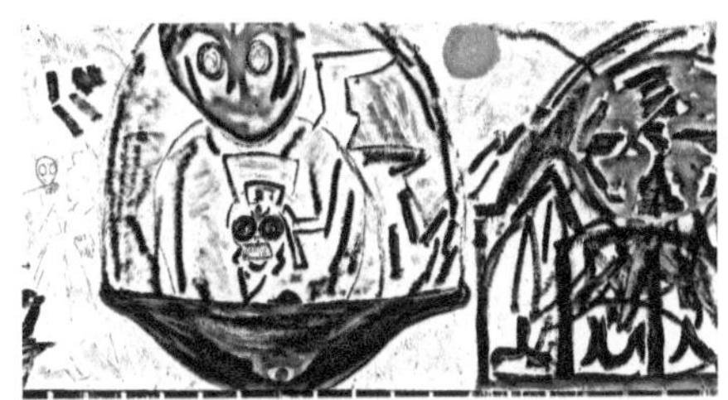

Chapter

Our Earth Creators/Captors made a fucking mess

I realize that there is no escape in self death, because the desire will be to escape this world. Therein lies the screen cage trap activator. If you have any emotion or desire, then the trap will be empowered exponentially in trapping force beyond your urges. Then there will be some incredible enticement, perhaps the most kind supermodel woman, and/or beautiful music, perhaps a peaceful village of happy people all sharing and being kind to one another, all deep wishes and conjectures projected from my own mind. Then, be it a luring tunnel of incredible white light, I could perhaps be tricked yet again and end up in a stranger woman's womb and have to enact the whole goo goo ga ga act that all kids pretend and manipulate the adults as they are indoctrinated to the adults' crap version of their adjusted reality to their amnesia, human body, food, clothing, shelter... - you know the dealio. Sadly, it seems like child raising is not too different from paying the DMV bill at the window of some agent who really is there to live off of you and your efforts to do the same for yourself. Human beings are split down the middle of good and evil. The gravity of this season of human-not-kind is a deep dark winter of living being existence. Parasites on parasites on top of traps on traps. This situation is not exactly *everyone's* fault, it is a debt-based currently agonizing pocket inside of the eternity of beginningless beginning life force, true justice, deep correct wisdom & true compassion. We must identify and remove the bad apples, or else the dwindling of life force will further give way to wither and decay. Problem is and becomes in committing the brutality to perform our due diligence, we then have to spend the long night of forever in diligence. Eternal Vigilance on watch as any rotten crap can pop up in us or around us at any given time (false-time-construct).

We have all cried tears over it enough to fill the seven seas easily over. Immediately, drugs like weed and beer help with the pain to partake of the fountain of enjoyment of further ignorance. Some find it a solution and not an addiction. Maybe I should feel depressed and miserable as I did when I wrote this little section years ago. Drugs never make me feel as bad as I do now in the short term; however, there is no longer an option for me to placate the sadness and suffering I feel right now. I have learned through the long term experience that drugs only make matters worse. Starving in the desert living on coffee & spiritual fumes attempting to share the LAW with the international turnstile of people floating in temporary vacation privileges in haughtily ruined Santa Fee, I still haven't given up in my attempt to quantum heal the disparaging world for my and my little daughter's sake back then. This earth woman Eve or any derivative female role body were designed to eat the apple of shameless tomorrow. (Advice is others adding vice) Rather I will recommend, if you have then don't want, if you don't have then don't want because when you get what you want, success or money, either an earth woman or any old devil mainly yourself (if you have reign over self, some externalized devil will manifest in the environment for you) will be there endlessly trying to kill your spirit. It nearly has, though it never really can permanently kill. In its totalitarian empirical technological pinnacle, it nearly has succeeded in effectively killing/stifling nearly all inmates here on Earth. Artificial Intelligence, will provide the next cold apathetic misery compression for all. Similarly to the mass age, it won't care, and like the idiotic scientists thus far, they never aimed their arrogant intelligence towards humanism, kindness, and the overall prevailing social problem now erupting. Perhaps the devil is in this room right now, breathing stink and hateful garbage vying that I won't finish this solution for us all, this Prison Break of Devil Planet Earth. So don't listen, don't read, don't study this manual of your freedom. Do give in, do give up, find yourself hopeless and helpless and then the energy that created this world trap will be happy as only an evil happy can be and you and I and everyone else can continue to be miserable. Go follow people with no color in their faces, no worth to their lost, electrocuted, lost selves, no matter how much baby or bat blood, bogus chemical energy drinks, fake breast milk formulas they drink, their evil is a catatonic petrified prune which will someday be no more.

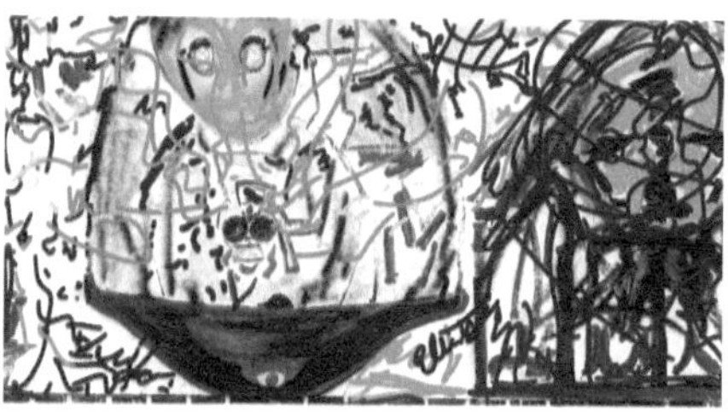

I nearly had a heart attack when I was teaching an English class in the Ukraine, because I wanted to tell them the Law, but my body would not allow me. Perhaps it was

forbidden somehow and they were not ready, and/or simultaneously possible that I was coping with my freezing apartment and poverty in a hard ass foreign country again smoking cigarettes and drinking nicely crafted vodka every evening.

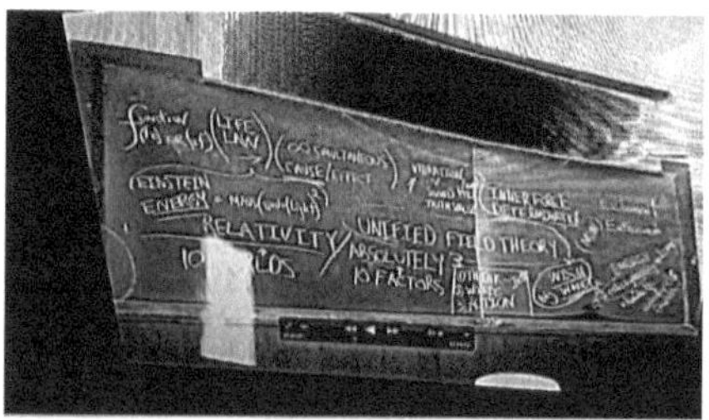

Prison Break Devil Alien Encrypted Planet Earth

The bible's efficacy is burned hypnotically into the spirit when it resists the now somewhat damaged screen cage trap that has been in place around this far out boondock unlivable planet (though a molten pole shifting planet was intentionally used because living beings could be further mixed and shuffled in myriad false prop mystery bullshit cultures which no human archeologists will ever solve from an earthbound human rib cage perspective). Genesis is the beginning of the slave cage ghetto prison planet earth, genetic engineering gender trauma drama, encrypted randomized birth placement, desire trapping pointless prison planet, aesthetic implanted & imprinted electronic pain beauty wave, divide and rule, death/birth amnesia screen cage, rogue empire fallout prison of undesirables, over abundance of artists, thieves & liars, people who made mistakes on their empire tax statements, inventors, geniuses, disabled, freakishly insane ones, criminals, all spirits here are trapped and electrocuted between lifetimes (false-time-construct) so as to induce hypnotic ritualistic false religious and mysterious bogus missions, coding to eat other bio body creatures, seemingly spontaneous ruling of reproductive genitalia, politicians and priests were the wardens; however, most are also abandoned now and suffer similarly to the main mixed galactic concentration camp - where the only hope is that ALL of us wake to our sadistic fate, join together (remembering is MEMBERSHIP) in multiplicity of multi-universal respect of individual moment to moment differential of perspective... ---to name a few conditions of this devils food cake the human enjoys and suffers endlessly and inescapably...

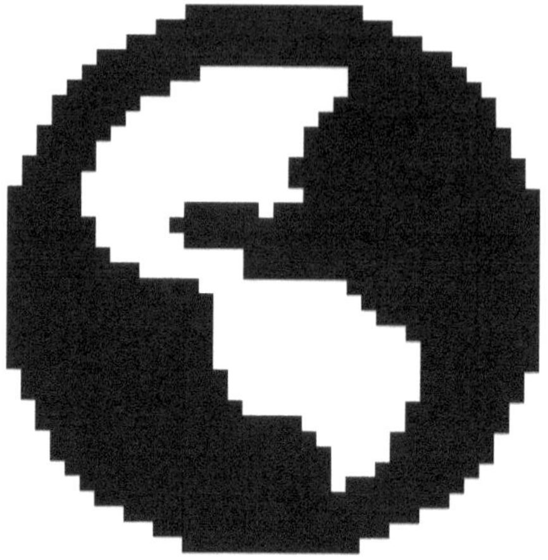

I feel for all of us that need a paycheck. People (spirits, trapped in an inferior devil's slave meatsack) are severely compromised here on Prison Planet Earth. Wars, confusion, roving insanity, street yellers, dmv processes, fines, tickets, taxes, licence fees, certifications, regulated business, are all courtesy of parasite slave drivers. Outwardly it seems that they are benevolent (kind and compassionate -with wisdom) however, Lao Tzu calls this "hiding the light of procedure" Mostly it is what is known as agencies of false provocation. What that means is that there are always hidden agendas to keep the inmates killing one another, rebelling aimlessly and ineffectively, because any violence instigated is a hellish trap for anyone participating. There was a time (false-time-construct) when the officers, politicians, priests had super power authority by way of the "old EMPIRE"; however, this planet is left still operating as a broken down Alcatraz kind of prison. Now the echo participants of "old empire" slave driving are recklessly always attempting to re-install the totalitarian hell of top down hierarchical rule. It only weakens the people. Think about at present the unforgiveness of unleashing a psycho plague on the people, and a concurrent economic depression, yet no compassion to stop charging 10 percent tax on every purchase, no property tax forgiveness... causing endless homelessness and strife is the way of the so-called "leaders", congress, senate, and most every lawmaker. It is a violent game of all against all, divided we stand.

What to do, Now...
Being fundamentally trapped and subjugated in relatively unknown power structures one could choose any number of faiths towards the hope and knowledge of the prevailing Power being essentially benevolence, compassion, and greater wisdom. Recognizing the overwhelming tide of darkness, disparity, violence, starvation, disease, infestations, and calamities of various sorts now shrouding humanity, one can choose the paths of bad or good. People want followers because most every spirit wants to garner

or trap another entity's attention, or if they have graduated from that trap inside the trap primarily mentioned then they or it could be dealing with their all one (alone) is-ness. An ism is an expressed mode put upon another perhaps by a politician, a philosopher, or an artist. Nearly every ism is a schism. The suffix -ity helps form nouns denoting quality or conditions. Each individual person's capacity and timing forms their perspective -their REAL-ity. We are in a realm with levels of desires. Perhaps one could say planes of existence or dimensions of personal real-ity. Money is the medium for exchange, though a human being only needs clean air, water, nutrients/food, shelter and perhaps clothing to some degree depending on the climate of course. A person could have property with enough resources cultivated for one's total self sustenance. What is unknown to the human being is called strange, weird, alien. Passion is attachment of generally an ignorance, a greed need, or an anger/arrogance outcropping. Pick your poison so to speak and when one does there is strength in action and marvel to the degree that these poisons are converted to medicine. For most it is a subliminal sublimation -slime or sublime. It is all about what you want. If you want peace, then put away the guns and foster the desire for peace. If you want love and compassion then be love and compassion and only associate with those who do that. That concept alone is difficult enough when the tides of the opposite have been allowed by one another to rise to a drowning level. Refusing to do to others what has been done to us is extremely difficult. This requires a determination and a will to truly save oneself and along the path save others who are at the temporal timing and capacity to be saved. Saving oneself means sowing the seeds that will lead to the fruit of enlightenment, not further darkness.

First we must recognize that we are miserable and that this system of things is chock full of suffering. This would require honesty, because at least a third of the people will want to turn away from that FACT.

Ignorance is darkness and it is that mother that gives birth to more and more ignorance. The cure for

anyone suffering
from the baffling
derailment of
ignorance
becomes proper
study, diligence,
truer education
leading to better
realization
-leading to truer
refinements
wisdom and
according
compassion.
Closing the eyes
and reflecting
for consideration
the thoughts and
chatter inside
and then going
deeper and
calming the
mind, nurturing
the thought that
others are not
the problem
-that each of us
must contribute
to the greater
good of oneself
and others.
Through the hell
and additional
misery (apart
from the natural
existence based
suffering) that
human beings

create for one
another and
ultimately the
(subtle napalm
pervading our
current
environment and
water) vaseline
vapor that now
is near choking
our throats and
fogging our eyes,
we have to self
realize and
awaken to each
and everyone's
part in hurrying
and scurrying
around when the
answer is right
there in front of
each and
everyone of us.
Love the person
next to you, in
front of you, be
kind to yourself
in the first micro
moment of
catching the
wrong aggressive
thought born of
fear, entrapment
and darkness.
Realize that ALL
creation arises
dependent on
one another. Get

angry with the part of you that is greedy and stupid. That is the first step. Now, then, go change your ways and change your life before we wreck the playground and thus school is out, closed until way further notice due to widespread disaster. Our lives, Our planet, our Homes, Our Loved Ones, or Nothing, Nowhere, the great black void of game over. Since the ignorance and sinfulness of humans has created bad and good, there is no going back. Let's do good because it has always been bad enough with a living hell to pay. So let's at least do good to ourselves and others, then graduate to create greater value leading to truer love, peace, and harmony. Never give up, never give in to the false belief that some power outside of yourself will come and right the wrongs we have all committed **together**. **To-get-her** back, our life force, our Earth, **To-get-Ther**e. From here, nowheresville, to there, a vision of a better world and a better time is right before us now. Now is the time. Now is the place. You can do it! Do your part! Genesis is the beginning of the slave cage ghetto prison planet earth, genetic engineering gender trauma

drama,
encrypted
randomized
birth placement,
desire pointless
prison planet,
aesthetic
implanted &
imprinted
electronic pain
beauty wave,
divide and rule,
death/birth
amnesia screen
cage, rogue
empire fallout
prison of
undesirables,
over abundance
of artists, thieves
& liars, people
who made
mistakes on their
empire tax
statements,
inventors,
disabled,
freakishly insane
ones, criminals,
all spirits here
are trapped and
electrocuted
between
lifetimes so as to
induce hypnotic
ritualistic false
religious and
mysterious

bogus missions, coding to eat other bio body creatures, seemingly spontaneous ruling of reproductive generalize genetalia-to name a few conditions of this devils food cake the human enjoys and suffers endlessly and inescapably... politicians and priests were the wardens however most are also abandoned now and suffer similarly to the main mixed galactic concentration camp - where the only hope is that ALL of us wake to our sadistic fate, join together in multiplicity of multiuniversal respect of individual

moment to
moment
differential of
perspective
Yours Truly,
Elron Humble

Final Quotes and Last Words on the Matter:

" The true geniuses of civilization are those IS-BEs who will enable other IS-BEs to recover their memory and regain self-realization and self-determination. This issue is not solved through enforcing moral regulation on behavior, or through the control of beings through mystery, faith, drugs, guns or any other dogma of a slave society. And certainly not through the use of electric shock and hypnotic commands! " Airl - Alien Interview

"This type of government emerges with regularity on planets where the citizens abandon personal responsibility for autonomous, self-regulation. They frequently lose their freedom to demented IS-BEs who suffer from an overwhelming paranoia that every other IS-BE is their enemy who must be controlled or destroyed. Their closest friends and allies, whom they espouse to love and cherish, are literally "loved to death" by them. Because such IS-BEs exist, The Domain has learned that freedom must be won and maintained through eternal vigilance and the ability to use defensive force to maintain it. As a result, The Domain has already conquered the governing planet of the "Old Empire". The civilization of The Domain, although considerably younger and smaller in size, is already more powerful, better organized, and united by a egalitarian esprit de corps 94 (Footnote) never known in the history of the "Old Empire". " Airl -Alien Interview

This is the only Viable Heart
    the ONE Thought (1)
which matters most
  All Things, everyone, At All times is
    the Enlightenment of the Universe
the tears, the laughter, the sorrow, the joy
  every thing everywhere All the time
    making only this original thought
this passing of time — this aging
    this girl, that man, this sex,
this pleasure, this pain, that person
    that thing Always shining eternally
ever one thought one mind
one love one true spiritual truth
    one Reality all True Happiness
UNDEFeatable, Nothing, no one, No where
is believed in — it is experienced work,
play, joys, sorrows, who I am, All my
thoughts, All my expressions everything
is free — what others think of me or you
    is something of NO USE
Judgement and mental process is
    A CAUSE of their OWN making
        and that is their experien
            All one —

The wants, the wishes, the desires, (2)
of every single living being is at
All times everywhere source —
connected
    Desire whether gotten or ungotten
remains the wonderful expedient of
that supposed poison into Medicine
Accepting that one may or may
Not get what one wants
    is in and of itself A cause for
enlightenment.
    She may not give you want you
        WANT
But what do you really want?
    What Another can or can't give you
or do you want the happiness of the
Heart of Hearts? The Realization
that All things everywhere all the
time are Conspiring for your
Advancement towards the single
thought of the All that is and ever
Was — something, nothing or
    In between in the MIDDLE
            MEAN

My true Happiness is this calm serene
TRUTH of everything - Everyone is the
ALL ONE source and observation
of this everything everyone being
Always a manifestation of the creative
will in one moment After every
single moment
The spiritual enlightenment of
the material world is the
choices of that above being the embryo
of everything, thought, word, action
Born and developed into
MANifestation
My House is A vehicle for this
Great Vehicle of the ONE LAW
Built upon the solid Enlightenment
of that one thought which
illuminates All TEN WORLDS at
All times and pervades every
Phenomena
Lotus Locus

Regarding Chapter 9 New Year's new fears:

Those were my dopamine aesthetic beauty/pain electronic wave dosages basically brought forth through that young woman functioning as a heartbreaking operative of the old empire. Only the people who slave for the false prison get perks and rewards -though drained vampirically in life force. Those who have bad behavior with regard to the real hidden State of Control are effectively blacklisted and marginalized. Remember, every retaliation, war, gender trauma/drama is false provocation that aids in the endless trapping coinciding with the Law of Cause and Effect forever embedded. Though it may not bring about the type of benefit a person wants in the Latter Day of the LAW, Nam Myoho Renge Kyo is the proper medicine until we get a fresh start in the year 10,000 or more...The Lotus of the Wonderful LAW forever abiding.

Make it all up like you did when you were a kid. Make believe is the way of the past, present, and future. Utilize *your* Source of the LAW, the Buddha's medicine of the Lotus Sutra Apart from that, the Future is in the moment to moment atonement -the at-one-ment of your imagination and your unique thoughts. It is your world. Make Believe and be free. Don't subscribe or follow anyone but yourself and hopefully we will all set each other free to be truly enlightened human beings. You have to admit otherwise, what we have now, and for a long long time is bat shit crazy. Follow your heart and make believe. If you find yourself bogged down stuck in filthy stupidity, desires of endless trinkets of stuff, arrogant or hopeless, you can always use the elevator of anger as an energy to voice your the truly hidden mysterious wonder of life itself and move on up and out of whatever deadlock you've been snared. If you are lost and don't know what that is, then chant out loud simultaneously{for free with no money (false-currency-construct) nor sanctimony required nor spiritual hoo hoo bullshit necessary} while looking inside yourself /your mind : Nam Myoho Renge Kyo and think about having your dreams and happiness even if you don't know what they are, it will naturally happen for you. Then take action. Awakening will become your habit over time with discipline to honor yourself and others. You will discover the causes and things to place or remove from your life that will lead to your happiness. Never give up, even if you are the latest bloomer in the pond of shit and almost everyone has given up on you, like me, it is only time to yourself in a sea of humanity. REMEMBER, it was never up to them anyway, it was and will always be up to YOU! You go be free now. You are free. Be free. For now, enjoy what there is to enjoy, suffer what there is to suffer, and continue to seek THE CORRECT WAY and YOUR WAY! As long as you don't force, coerce, harm, yet instead encourage your fellow creatures to do the same as instructed here and we can all together recover from what we and others have done to ourselves to climb and rise out of this misery we are now facing.

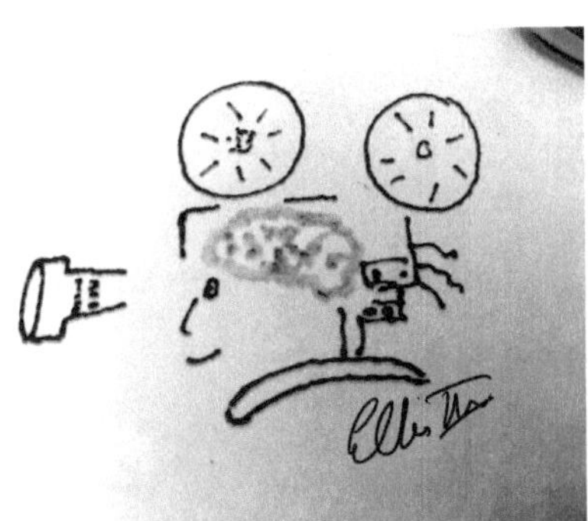

ELLIS SIMPSON BYERS III

Other works by Ellis Simpson Byers III:

Methusalina and Wolverpenis

Evan Earth's Labor of Love

Love in Sickx Senses

50 Years in Hell : a shaman buddhist perspective

Revellations, alternate title: RevL8shuns

FREEMENOW.888

Weed Me Out
Greedy, Angry, Stupid
Yogi Nastynanda
Friend of Jesus
Lion Lotus and the Black Widow
Black Widow of Baton Rouge
Aquarian Rage
Imaginary Enlightened Girlfriend
Porch Honkies
Mel's Hell
Judge Frickasee
Secrets of My World
Won't you play with my Cornhole?
Lick Me Not
Capitalism, War Authority, and Addiction
Humanism, Equanimity, and Absolute Happiness
50 Years in Hell: A Shaman Buddhist Perspective
Black Widow of Baton Rouge
Wolverpenus and Methusalina
Imaginary Enlightened Girlfriend
DAPPs: Bounty Hunter, Petition This, True Vote, Lynch Mob, Truth Repository, The Autonomizer, Autonomous Space, Viabelly Content, assbackwardz, Pontunes, Etherman, Through the Hawk's Eye, pumpdatchange, freekeycurrency, blargunrargun, throttlehonky, throttledonkey

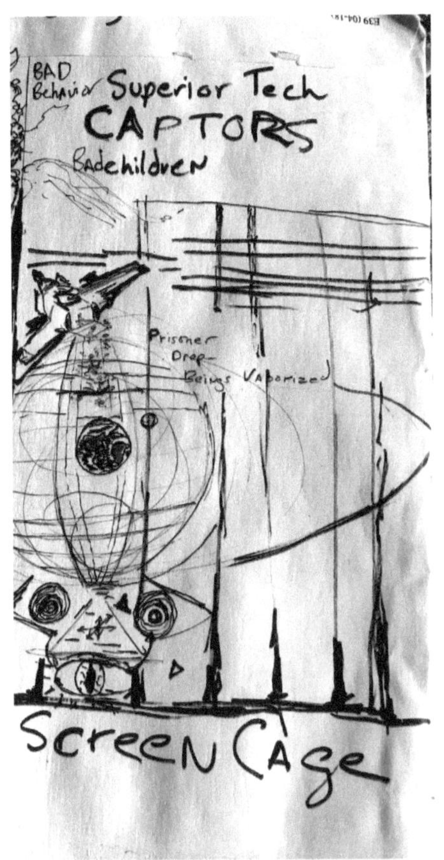
BAD
Behavior
Superior Tech
CAPTORS
Badchildren
Prisoner
Drop—
Being Vaporized
SCREEN CAGE

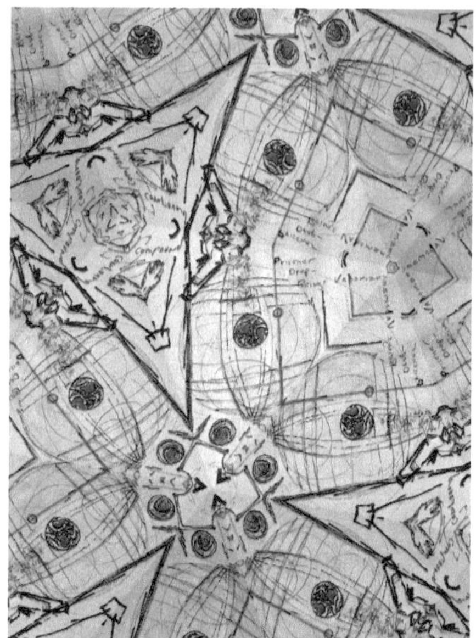